What others say

Dr. Fred Sai's memoir provides a gripping journey, not only through his history and invaluable contributions to women's health but also to the field of reproductive health itself. Dr. Sai has received every major honour in the field of population including the presidency of International Planned Parenthood Federation, being the main chair of the 1994 UN International Conference on Population and Development, and receiving the highly prestigious UN Population Award – to name but a very few. His story walks us through a variety of major human events ranging from the role of African traditional medicine versus western medical practices, the pain and suffering of women denied reproductive health services and rights, being an African travelling America in the pre-civil rights era, and the never ending criticism that is lavished on our field. The memoires conjure up the determination of a good man and the steadfast support of his wife, Florence, to improve the lot of women no matter what the personal cost. Dr. Sai is an African leader but he is also in the highest meaning of the words a citizen of the world. This book offers us a view of Dr. Sai's life and through his lens of intellect, grace, humour and above all his deep humanity. Our field owes a huge debt to Dr. Sai and his memoir should be required reading for any serious member of the reproductive health community.

Professor Sai has written an inspiring and readable personal account of his extraordinary life, starting with stories of his childhood in Ghana and continuing through to his training as a physician in London, and later his visionary leadership in the loftiest arenas of national, regional and global politics. Throughout his career, he has sought to remedy injustices, unflinching in the face of powerful adversaries. Professor Sai is well-known globally as a leading champion of reproductive health and rights. His willingness to take on these neglected and often controversial issues demonstrates great compassion for his fellow human beings and especially for women. There could be no better role model for others to follow.

Felix I D Konotey-Ahulu
Kwegyir Aggrey Professor of Human Genetics, University of Cape Coast, Ghana
and Consultant Physician Genetic Counsellor,

This book, by the brilliant Professor Fred Sai, is sheer history: personal history, family history, national colonial history, national post-colonial history, professional history, international history, and much else. All health workers should read it as it recounts, with remarkable frankness, the controversies surrounding family planning, national development, and population control. The conversational style is gripping, the index comprehensive, and the references are useful for undergraduates and postgraduates alike.

Professor Mahmoud F. Fathalla
Egypt

I was one of many who have been urging Dr. Fred Sai to write his memoirs. As an apostle of family planning, reproductive health and empowerment of women, Dr. Sai is already widely known and admired in his own country and internationally. But there are many more, throughout the world, who will find inspiration in reading about his rich journey through life. It has been a long hard road for the young boy from poor Ghana. Now where he is, the memoirs demonstrate that the climb to the top is not linear, and, as he rightly states, the blocking of an avenue should be an invitation to take another route. With an engaging personal style and a sense of humour, the memoirs are a pleasure to read. We, who have been urging Dr. Sai to write his memoirs, now know how right we were.

Thoraya Obaid
Executive Director, UN Population Fund (UNFPA)

Fred Sai has devoted his entire career to issues of health and reproductive rights. He has worked tirelessly to advocate better access to health, nutrition, education and family planning, for gender equality and women's rights. To this day he is an engaging and charismatic speaker and writer, and his warmth and generosity of spirit shine through in these pages. I count myself as lucky to have worked with Fred for many years, and I am delighted that UNFPA could support the publication of his fascinating story.

Dr Pramilla Senanayake
Founder and Chair of Educate a Child Trust

This book is a real pleasure to read. Fred writes beautifully about his life his childhood and upbringing and includes a fascinating account of the way children are named in Ghana. Once you have read this section you will understand why there are so many children called Kodjo (born on a Monday) or Kwaku (born on a Wednesday). Fred's gift of total recall is seen in his account of his years growing up in Ghana and later his life in the United Kingdom and the United States. A much travelled man, he draws on his experiences to provide vivid descriptions of his life in different parts of the world.

It is, I believe, his sympathetic interest in people and his country that led Fred to specialize in public health instead of the lucrative option of clinical medicine. This is a must read for anyone interested in Ghana in particular, or West Africa and for anyone with an interest in the global population movement. Fred was at the centre of some key international decisions on issues of sexual and reproductive health, abortion, and contraception, and his first hand experience is well documented. And for anyone who wants to find out what life was like in the United Kingdom, especially if you were brown or black skinned, this book provides many an answer.

Gill Greer
Director-General, International Planned Parenthood Federation

For those of us who work in sexual and reproductive health and rights, Fred Sai has become a legend in his own lifetime. But few know of how his courageous, compassionate commitment and leadership began or the challenges he encountered. This memoir gives us glimpses of an extraordinary life – and of his personal perspective of the events and institutions in which he played a key role. His story provides a powerful and moving testimony of the injustice that too often determines women's lives, and reaffirms contraception as a basic human right, despite those who would deny it.

Tireless champion though he is, we can sense and share his concern and disbelief that today, after 20 years of promises, half a million women still die needlessly every year from pregnancy and childbirth related causes.

As we share his memories we are also able to come to know something of the man behind the public figure – his optimism, humour and warmth. There is much here that will inspire others to work to realise his vision of a better world.

Banson
17f Sturton Street
Cambridge CB1 2QG

Citation Sai, F.T. (2010) With heart and mind. Banson, Cambridge, UK.

With
heart and voice

Fred Sai remembers

Frederick T. Sai

BANSON

foreword

Jill W. Sheffield
President and Founder of Women Deliver
New York

When Fred Sai told me he was writing his memoirs, I thought this book would be a gift to the world. In a chapter quite modestly added at the end of the book, Fred lists his numerous accolades and awards for his work in family planning and maternal health. From my perspective, there is no one who deserves this praise more. Fred is truly a citizen of the world. His commitment to people, his high standard of ethics, and his beliefs, liberally peppered with hope and an incredibly positive outlook, have fuelled a life-long determination to make a difference and advance reproductive health and rights for all people, especially women.

For many readers, Fred's book will evoke memories of the exciting and heady days of launching the International Safe Motherhood Initiative in Nairobi and the International Conference on Population and Development in Cairo. It felt, in those moments, as though the world had undergone a sea change in its attitudes towards women. It is disquieting to read of the Cairo proceedings, more than 15 years ago. We were so optimistic that we would make real headway in reducing maternal deaths. Imagine that a United States Vice President, Al Gore, staunchly defended the right of the American women to abortion as per the US constitution. Little did we know what was ahead. The ebb and flow of politics and a determined opposition continued to hamper progress and denigrate family planning. It took another conference, Women Deliver in 2007, to get the global attention on the great loss to the world's well-being when women and girls are denied access to contraception, skilled medical care, and safe abortion.

Abortion remains contentious today as it was in Cairo. It is fascinating to learn of Fred's early experiences as a medical student, watching women dying from self and botched abortions – such a waste of life. Over six decades, he never wavered from his views on the laws against abortion and the need for the decision to be between the woman and her health provider. Fred's style of advocacy is amazing. He speaks with such sincerity and reason that he has been able to influence some of the most hardened opposition. Yet he does not mince his opinions, so his memoirs are like a conversation. His admitted

dismay and disappointment with organizations and people for being too timid come from his heart, and one feels the honesty in his words. Of particular interest is his leadership in the International Planned Parenthood Federation (IPPF), which bore the full brunt of opposition to abortion. Thank goodness, it had Fred at its side.

The people mentioned in his book read like a who's who of maternal health and family planning, and Fred's other great love, nutrition. Wonderful people, Billie Miller, Gordon Perkin, Lyle Saunders, and numerous others, are not only given homage for what they accomplished but Fred has also written anecdotes about his encounters with them. Fred's touches of humour and humanity make the book highly entertaining.

There is another group that had a tremendous influence on his life – his mother and his aunts. These women raised him, protected him, shaped his experiences and attitudes, encouraged him to dream, and fostered his love of learning. I believe that this strong female family support helped him, early on, develop his positive – and practical – attitude toward women.

Interwoven throughout the book is the treatment of women and the treatment of black people, particularly in the United States. It is heartening to think we are progressing on these issues, too slowly, but progress is to be seen. His words remind us that discrimination is taught early and subtly. He speaks of his early childhood in Ghana with men having gas lamps while the women used hurricane lamps; of men sleeping in bedrooms while women slept on mud floors. His story of discrimination in America brought back the dark days of racism in this country. It was startling to Fred as he had never been refused seating at a restaurant or housing in the United Kingdon. Yet, he is never bitter, rather he is the optimist, always looking to the future, always true to his beliefs.

Fred has had many positions and touched so many lives. He is a life-long learner, eager to take on the next challenge. He writes that he was not only a physician, but a politician. He went into politics because of his belief that health is a fundamental basis of development "requiring the involvement of people who appreciated health in the broadest sense". What makes Fred so effective is his wide view of health care but that also got him in hot water, at times, particularly with his own government.

This book is a testimony of what one man can accomplish. Fred is quiet, self-effacing at times, and wonderfully talented. He has been a dear friend and a great advocate for reproductive health. He sees the big picture, and he never, never backs down from what he believes. The book is serious yet humorous. It elegantly blends past with the future. And above all, it is a delight to read. Enjoy!

preface

This book has been written primarily for my children and grandchildren. The latter in particular found some of the stories of my childhood difficult to believe. Until they saw on television that there were children going to school without shoes, they thought I was just making up stories for a laugh. My hope is that the stories of where I have come from, what a long hard road it has been to get as far as I have in my life, will be an encouragement to the majority of African youngsters struggling against the odds to get a good education. Some might think I was lucky, others might think it was because of the period in which I was moving upwards. They may or may not be right. I can say though that one of my guiding motivations in life has come from an old favourite hymn of mine which I chose as the theme for my 80th birthday celebrations:

> *Do not wait until some deed of greatness you may do,*
> *Do not wait to shed your light afar,*
> *To the many duties ever near you now, be true,*
> *Brighten the corner where you are*

As I went through life the corner simply got larger and larger.

As the book evolved, it became obvious to me that another group that might benefit from it would be young professionals, particularly from my country and the rest of Africa. There is in far too many of them an impatient urge to get to the top which is manifest in many of the postures taken by these young professionals and broadcast or printed in the daily news stories. The climb to the top is not linear. The blocking of one avenue is an invitation to take another route. The important thing to me is whether one is able to contribute to society to the best of one's ability through the choice.

This book is also by way of recognition of the importance of the non-governmental organization world in international affairs and in the development of the individual as a contributor to global events and consensuses. I go into quite a lot of detail when dealing with some of the international conferences in which I played major roles. This is largely

to make clear my own beliefs and contributions. I most certainly would like to be seen as an apostle for family planning, reproductive health generally and for the empowerment of women. Although not stated explicitly, the book is meant to demonstrate the role of women in my life, from my home, through the mothers of my malnourished patients, to my administrative heads in IPPF and the World Bank as well as those women junior colleagues from whom I constantly learnt.

A lot happened in my life which could make for the writing of a grim book. But so much happiness has also been mine that I have chosen to emphasise the funnier and lighter situations. One title that I played with was *Pilgrimage for the Impossible* to signify the fact that, although I have personally not seen the success of my entire advocacy work, there is no reason to consider my life wasted. That success will come cannot be doubted, but my concern is how soon and what happens to the millions who lose out whilst governments ignore or even oppose proven facts.

It has not been easy to write this book as most of my own records have been lost or destroyed through our frequent moves and, recently, from an attack of termites. Much has therefore come from memory. Someone once said that the human memory is not a very good scientific instrument so there are possibly omissions and errors in these pages. My hope is that they would be few and not very significant.

Although many would think Kipling's *If* is over-quoted, it still contains my most favourite lines to guide my advocacy work.

If you can bear to hear the truth you've spoken
Twisted by knaves to make a trap for fools, ...

Even in recent times those advocating family planning, including me, have had to contend with a great deal of twisting of our words and positions, even of scientific facts. I hope this book helps to explain some of my words and positions. Unlike Kipling, I do not think those for whom the trap is made are fools. In much of Africa they simply do not know, and I hope my successors and colleagues will be re-energised by this book to continue the good fight.

I owe many debts to a large number of individuals and institutions for the stimulation and encouragement to write this book that it will be difficult to name them all. I have already recognized the roles of my wife and family. They have also been of great assistance in their criticisms, stamina and tolerance, especially of the periods when I tried to give up. But perhaps number one thanks should go to Dr. Liz Maguire and her

management team at Ipas. They offered me a consultancy which provided the money needed for the initial writing. Barbara Crane and Charlotte Hord-Smith, from the same group, were kind enough to read an early draft and not only give critical insights but provide much needed encouragement. I could not have got anywhere with the writing but for the guidance help and inputs of my long-suffering friend and research associate, Jeremy Hamand. His quiet way of handling changes and his general editorial and research work have helped produce the whole book. My niece Ethel Ako-Nai patiently transcribed my dictation. Without her input the writing would have taken forever.

Among the enthusiastic friends who encouraged me to write are Thoraya Obaid of the UNFPA, Jill Sheffield of Women Deliver, Amy Coen of PAI, Prof. Mahmoud Fathalla of Egypt, Pramilla Senanayake of Sri Lanka and Karen Newman of England. In addition to those mentioned above, Sara Seims of the Hewlett Foundation, Prof. Felix Konotey-Ahulu, Prof. Ofosu-Ammah and Prof. Gil Ashitey, former colleagues in the University of Ghana Medical School, were kind enough to read drafts and give most helpful criticisms and help with details. Of course I need to acknowledge the women who have taught me so much about the problems of women and womanhood in Ghana, Africa and the world, the poor voiceless women who are constantly faced with triumph and disaster, but mostly disaster, and yet carry on, even smiling and being happy in spite of all difficulties. From them I learnt what the saying *dum spiro spero*[1] truly meant. They made me recognise why I should not lose hope because of a calamity or lack of success. To these women across all continents this book is by way of saying thanks.

Of course the book could not have come out without the financial assistance of IPPF and its Director General Gill Greer who made the first generous offer to assist with publication, Jill Sheffield and Women Deliver, Thoraya Obaid and the United Nations Population Fund, and the Hewlett Foundation.

Without being emotional I think my old headmaster, Mr. Lamptey, deserves mention here for seeing to it that his bright boy was not denied secondary education through the vagaries of the Gold Coast mail in 1939.

1: while I breathe, I hope

contents

1 beginnings

The old ship, *SS Almanzora*, slowly moved from its berth in the Takoradi harbour and headed into the west African golden sunset a day in September 1947. The artificial harbour had been built during the governorship of Sir Frederick Gordon Guggisberg in the mid-1920s together with the Korle Bu Hospital and Achimota College. All three of these touched my life in some way. On board were dozens of the most precious cargo imaginable to the families and even countries sending them; students heading for British universities. Many were scholarship holders, but there were quite a number of private students too. Naturally Nigerians were in the majority. World War II had led to a backlog of students anxious to continue their studies overseas who had had to wait for transport. Apart from Fourah Bay College, in Sierra Leone, there were no other university level institutions in West Africa at the time. Practically all ships had been carrying troops to and from the war and with the end of the war, repatriation.

The Captain told us during his welcoming address that the *SS Almanzora* had been built in 1915 soon after the start of the World War I. It was a steamship with a tonnage of 15,500. And it had served in both wars as a troopship, carrying up to 3,000 service men. We were not to know that it would be sold and scrapped just one year later.

We were lucky in a way that the British government managed to get the old troopship to come over to carry the loads of waiting students from Nigeria, Ghana and Sierra Leone. I was one of eight or nine Ghanaians who had medical scholarships on that boat and there were many Nigerians. And all of us were boisterous.

It was during the 11 or 12 nights on this boat that I had time to think of my life thus far, trying to remember my childhood and my schooling. Unfortunately I did not put anything down on paper then. And even if I had, it would have been lost or destroyed with all my numerous papers, lost or destroyed through bad storage or travel mistakes.

Early childhood

I remember being with my mother and her extended family until I was nine, at Osu

Trom, just behind the castle. That was rather a long time for a boy of my clan to stay exclusively with his mother, but this indulgence was due to my father having died quite early, when I was three or so years old. The house of women included my mother's sister called Auntie, other aunties entitled Auntie Nukpa (Eldest Aunt): other levels of Aunt were Middle and Youngest. My maternal grandmother, the matriarch, was called Aayee for a reason I never found out. Her full name, which she liked to use occasionally, was Otema Aba Annang – her father was Asafoiatse Annang Dotie (a sub-chief) of Osu-Alata.

My mother, Emelia Shormeh Omaboe, was one of four children, two boys and two girls. My grandmother had married twice and had the male children by one of the Reindorf family. My mother and her sister belonged to the Omaboe family of Adjuate. This is how I came to be related to Dr. Reindorf and his family; to the late Nana Wereko Ampem II, known earlier in life as Mr. E. N. Omaboe; the Norteys and others of Osu Kinkawe. My mother was under five feet tall, unusually quiet most of the time, but with a steely determination. Throughout my school career she would try to avoid telling others of how well I was doing. I learnt later that this was also due to her fear of evil wishers.

Although I did know who my biological mother was, the seven or eight women of my mother's generation in the house were all mothers to me. This collection of mothers enabled my eldest aunt to be the one who ensured that my childish desire to run away from school in my first few weeks there was sternly curbed. She just tied me to her back, took me to the school and sat outside and waited. Two sittings and I got the message. The even more important aspect of having a so many mothers was that one never went hungry. Whichever mother or mothers were in the house saw to it that the children were washed and fed – something that has probably died out in modern urban Accra.

A particularly traumatic incident that I remember was my circumcision. One Sunday morning when I was about five I was taken to my paternal home. I was wearing my khaki gown. This outfit, which was pronounced *gong* for some reason, was very popular with parents in my neighbourhood but much disliked by children. It was usually made with a fold of khaki drill with a hole in the middle for the head, completely shapeless. And as one got older one had underneath a small pair of cloth pants, called *pioto* in Ga. At the time of the circumcision I had not qualified for a *pioto*.

In the paternal home that morning my uncle, then the Papa of the house, was particularly nice; he gave me and two of my cousins biscuits and tea. Then we were taken to the rudimentary bathroom. As the eldest I was the first to go. There, a man with a white beard and flowing robes started being nice and then said, "look up and catch". Nothing could be more painful I was sure. Before my head could come back down, the man had, in one swift movement, done his worst with my foreskin. Hollering could not describe my first reaction. Big Papa immediately stepped in to say boys and men do not cry. So grief was borne quietly; but it hurt. The wound took a week or so to heal. I am sure the same knife, without sterilization or anything, was used for my two cousins.

Names

In the naming systems used by the Ga and Dangme clans of southern Ghana, there are common names which denote rank of birth and the day of birth; and there are names which belong to families. These last are passed on to children only through the father. The Ga-Dangmes are patrilineal.

In addition to the above, there are names which may denote particular circumstances around the birth of a particular child or of some children preceding. Examples of these are the names given to twins or to children who arrive after two or more preceding ones have been still-born or died early. Such children are given "nasty names" and they may be given stellate face marks "to make them unattractive to Death the harvester"

Fairly commonly names may be borrowed, for the provision of a drink to the appropriate family. For example, if man wants to name his child after his mother, he is required to give his mother's family a drink and ask for permission to use the name.

Rank of birth names	Males	Females
1st	Tettey	Dede
2nd	Tetteh	Korkor
3rd	Mensah	Kai
4th	Annang	Tsotsoo
5th	Anum	Fofo

Both of these sets continue to ten.

The day of birth names are also in pairs for males and females:

Day	Male	Female
Sunday	Kwashie	Akoshia
Monday:	Kodjo	Adjoa
Tuesday	Kwabla	Ablah
Wednesday	Kwaku	Akua
Thursday	Kwao or Yao	Aba
Friday	Kofi	Afua
Saturday	Kwame	Ama

For twins the names are Akwele and Akuorkor for the first and second female twins respectively and Akwetey and Akuetteh for the males.

Thus at a Ga or Dangme child's birth it can lay claim to at least two names; one the day of birth, the other for the rank of birth. In addition on the eighth day after birth an elaborate out-door ceremony is performed and the child given its proper family name. This is a happy occasion, since it is assumed that the child can then be counted as an addition to the family. Before it takes its proper name the child is not really accepted as having been born. This is one reason why researching infant mortality using questionnaires has proved difficult in parts of Ghana. Unfortunately, some religious groups have been mounting a crusade to stop this beautiful naming ceremony, claiming the libation or prayers that accompany it is unchristian. I hope they do not succeed.

My own name has quite complicated origins. My family names are:

Males	Females
Torgbor	Torshie
Sai	Ayorkor
Sodjah	Ayerkai

The names of my children and those of my brothers, if any, will be:

Males	Females
Obodai	Oboshie
Adjah	Korkor-Adai
Torto Mensah	Kai Mansah

My own full name would have been Kwame (born on a Saturday) Tettey (first-born male)

Torgbor. Frederick was given me by my father as a so-called Christian name and Sai was the surname used by my father and his brothers – it was their father's name and they used it when they went to school. As a surname, therefore, it is only two generations old.

School

At school, once I settled, I did well, in fact very well. Although small for my age I was not the youngest, since I had been denied a place the year before. My hand could not reach my ear when I put it over my head – a crude measure for age for admission. From the first year right through to leaving school, that is the ten years covering infant, junior and senior school as the system then was, I was the first or with the first at the top of the class. All my ten years of schooling were at the presbyterian schools in Osu, a suburb of Accra that were famous for their discipline. "Spare the rod and spoil the child" seemed to be their guiding principle. Fortunately I was seldom at the wrong end of the rod.

After the three years of infant school, I was taken to my paternal home as my main residence. By being with the women folk in my maternal home for longer than most children, I had the opportunity of witnessing more female and gender related issues than most male children. There were older cousins and young aunts hanging around the coconut palms with their men friends. One saw their bellies swelling and then their going to clinics and coming back with these crying bundles. Similar things were happened in the whole neighbourhood. Once some young relation went to the clinic and did not come back. The trauma of the funeral ceremony itself was not to be seen in the women's home as it took place in her paternal home; but her disappearance registered. I remember one aunt who had a lot of pregnancies after the birth of her first son who was about my age. But none of the children from these nine or more pregnancies survived beyond a few weeks or months. She and others attributed this to witchcraft and my aunt went on to suspect several members of her own immediate family of causing her difficulties. It was when I was well into my medical education that I realized she had a rhesus incompatibility problem. And I never forgot her suffering.

Food and nutrition

In the paternal home I still spent most of my preteen days within the female section. Looking back, I have to admit we were relatively poor although it did not register at the time. All of us younger children, four, five or six at a time, ate from one bowl. The meals

5

were mainly *fufu* and soup, *banku* and stew, or *kenkey* and fish. With *fufu* and *banku* the routine was you ate this carbohydrate, called the food, with the soup, stew or sauce and got a little meat or fish afterwards. *Kenkey*, pepper sauce and fish were perhaps the backbone of my diet at this time. Although the amount of fish was quite small most of the time, but things changed suddenly during the herring season. Then, even children could have as much fish as they wanted. It was only when I studied nutrition that I realized that we did well compared to what was going on in the country generally.

The womenfolk, too, usually ate from one bowl. Papa was the one who ate alone. As we grew older, we boys had to lay his table and stand with our hands behind us as he ate. When he had finished, we removed the plates and only then had our own meals. I came to learn later the grim statistics of my grandmother's family. She had entered marriage with my grandfather bringing three children by a previous husband with her; one female and two males. With my grandfather she had four and then another by another man, after separating from my grandfather. All these as young people were in or around the paternal home all the time.

Unfortunately premature deaths were common. Of these eight children, I was not to know three at all and another two died while I was in my teens. The second son was a cook for a white man in the Ridge and I remember him taking me along on Saturdays. I would stay quietly under his work-table and feed on bread and bacon trimmings, which I found most enjoyable. I was heart-broken when he died suddenly. The first girl child had died in childbirth before I could remember. The third, my Auntie Adai, was also to die in child-birth when I was eleven years or so old. She had had four fairly closely spaced girl children; the fifth, a boy, was to go with her. The pattern of fertility related deaths were so common in the neighbourhood that pregnancy required all sorts of medication and juju treatment.

My paternal home had an interesting history. Grandfather was a mason and he had built a two storey house, one of only two or three in Osu Anarhor at the time. It was mainly of mud and stone. His nephew had also built a similar structure adjoining ours. For a reason no one ever explained both houses suffered disasters a year or two after my birth and they became single storey structures. The male members slept in the smarter rooms of the male compound with concrete floors. The female quarters in contrast just had mud floors. There were two wells for the houses, one with sweet water and the other brackish. I was about eight or so when the wells were finally destroyed and pipe-borne water was made available just outside the house. In

the beginning there was no electricity – gas lamps were used by the men while the women used hurricane lamps, called lanterns, or the tin-and-wick smoky lamp.

Sanitation

Sanitary facilities for both houses and the neighbourhood generally, were pretty rudimentary. There was no pipe-borne water in the house, but fortunately there were stand pipes not far from either house. Similarly the walled enclosure which was for bathing and the public pan latrines were also only a short way away. In each house there was a space reserved for bathing by the older family members, and we youngsters had to fetch the water for them. There was no such thing as formal toilet paper; old newspapers, old magazines or even small pieces of rags served the purpose. Hand-washing after using such facilities was rare for us children – we just washed our hands before and after meals.

In fact poor sanitation, manifested by poor human waste disposal and inadequate access to potable water, were the lot of a large number of people in Osu at the time. The toilets consisted of cement structures with concrete floors, with usually six holes which emptied into pans, Sanitary workers had to empty these pans once of twice a day into collection trucks which disposed of the contents into the sea at Lavender Hill, a short distance from the Korle Bu Hospital. Of course the aroma following the personnel carrying such stuff was terrible. At times materials fell off and remained untended for at least a day.

Bedtime was messy. All the young children, both male and female, slept on the relatively thin raffia mats made in Japan and cynically called *opaw kete,* meaning the mat for those of substance. I think the name was given because those of substance, the better off, used these mats under their feet but above their bed sheets. Again there were many mothers. My Aunt Oboshie, immediately following my late father, was the matriarch. She was a truly magnificent woman, both physically and in other ways. She was gentle, fair but firm. And she saw to it that I remained focused on my studies. Of course I gave her quite a few anxious moments when I insisted on joining the non-school goers for their swimming in the sea, crab trapping and other forays into the mangrove bushes around the Klottey Lagoon.

Accra

The Klottey Lagoon, behind the Osu Castle, was a beautiful place in those days. The mangrove bushes which covered quite large tracts of wetland were shiny green. When

the tide was full the lagoon was huge, at least to my childhood eyes. The stream which fed the lagoon also ran northwards for several miles. Today this lovely wetland has been turned into a ghetto of iniquity. Shacks have been built close to the beach for commercial sex work, drug taking and gambling. The beach and what is left of the shores of the Lagoon are used as open toilets. Amazingly there are still some who claim to be the spiritual guardians of the lagoon god, and people who believe that the lagoon god has powers. But they do nothing about the degradation.

Osu itself is quite an historic part of Accra. During my childhood, it was a village completely separated from central Accra by shrubs and empty spaces. The current site of the Independence Square and the ministries did not exist. The most important landmark was and is Osu Castle, which was built by the Danes as Fort Christiansborg. About half a kilometre from there is the relic of another castle which we came to know as *Trom Moo*, the Castle of Trom. Although this is almost completely destroyed and the space occupied by some families, the façade has fortunately been preserved and has inscribed on it "HR&CR 1809". My friend, the historian Prof. Nii-Adziri Wellington, tells me that Johan Emmanuel Richter, a Danish merchant who acted as Governor at the Danish Fort at Ada in the 18th century, built the castle's stone bastions, wall and the entrance portal in imitation of the Christiansborg Castle in Copenhagen. "He had a number of mulatto offspring including Henrich Richter and Christian Richter. The crest HR/CR refers to Henrich and his brother and the 1809 might have been the year when Richter formally recognised them as his children, when Henrich was 24 years old." .

Both castles were involved in the slave trade. The former still has the dungeons, which became infamous under the Rawlings administration for holding some the government wanted to detain. In front of Trom Castle was a huge open space with a low stone wall – a relic of the old slave market. Unfortunately the slave market site has now been turned into a Total petrol filling station.

Osu Salem School

The last four years of my primary education were in the Presbyterian Senior School, known at the time as Osu Salem. The school was almost considered a military academy for juniors. It was a boarding school, though it did not cater for the pupils' meals. Food had to be brought from town. The boys of the first two years went into town daily to get food for themselves and for their "masters" in the top two classes. One famous or infamous rule of the school was the insistence that no one wore shoes. Even those children whose

parents could afford to buy shoes for them were forbidden to wear them; sameness would help diminish envy among pupils was the belief, I think. I certainly could not afford to have shoes. The uniform was a pair of khaki shorts and a white drill shirt worn over the shorts with a white belt. On Sunday, everyone wore long white trousers, an open neck white shirt and a navy blue blazer. The joke was the wearing of long trousers and no shoes. But the pupils really did shine in their uniforms at all school gatherings.

A problem I had in my first year was how to wash and iron my own clothes. I had not done this before, either in my mother's or my father's house. Being small also did not help. One of the big boys of my class became a true friend and my saviour: he helped launder my clothes and taught me how to deal with them. Anum Dorhuso remained a true friend even later in life until his untimely death while working as an electrician in the Kwame Nkrumah University of Science and Technology.

The infant and junior schools had been mixed, but the middle school, Salem, was only for boys. Our female class-mates of earlier years had to continue their schooling elsewhere in Accra. although it was during my time in Salem that the Presbyterian Church started to build a senior girls' school. So between the ages of say 12 and 16 or even 18, or older for a few, the opportunity to interact with female pupils disappeared somewhat.

The puritanical nature of the discipline was famous. Boys got up early, had some exercise or drill, as it was called, then followed a routine of assembly and classes. While the medium of instruction had been the local language, Ga, in the first six years, in the senior school English was the medium.

The literature available in Ga during my time was quite restricted. There were a few starter ones like *Sowah tee faa le naa*, Sowah went to the stream. More serious ones were a collection of stories in Ga, often translations from English. But the Ga literature par excellence was the Bible in Ga, a truly amazing translation done under the Basel Missionaries. For the ten years of Presbyterian education I came to know my Bible rather well. As was to be expected it was also the standard for morality: sex and sexuality had no place in the education curriculum. Yet there was a great deal of peer education, or shall I say mis-education.

Sex and sexuality

Two things happened in my second year which must have burned deep into my mind's innermost recesses. One morning during assembly one of the senior boys was asked to

us a lot that could be classed as politics. I have no doubt that my affair with politics of all kinds developed from his influence. Mr. Adu was to become one of the first Africans together with K. A. Busia to be elevated to the very high administrative position of District Commissioner in the Gold Coast.

Daniel Chapman, who later changed his name to Chapman Nyaho, was a famous geography teacher, but he earned the nick-name of "Good Food", because he insisted that the three most important things in life were "Good food, good English and good geography" in that order. He became the first lay head of Achimota school. In the religious sphere a man of great influence was the Rev. Fr. Persico who hailed from the Caribbean. A quote from one of his sermons still comes to my mind is, "the rain it raineth everyday both on the just and on the unjust, but chiefly on the just because the unjust has taken the just's umbrella". Achimota school was built on very strong religious principles and accommodated all the major Christian groups.

Of the junior masters of the time George Sowah was impressive as a science teacher. He was later to study in the United Kingdom for a degree and return to Achimota as one of the key teachers. His untimely death in an accident was a blow to the school. A never to be forgotten senior master during my final years was the Rev. Dr. Simpson who taught senior level biology. It was simply a joy to be taught by him.

Wartime menu

True enough, Achimota in those days fed us very well. Those of us from poorer homes enjoyed the regular access to bread and butter, to lamb chops, even if presented in a sauce we described as "Khaki soup". As the war turned sour, some of our culinary delights disappeared but were nonetheless replaced by well-balanced meals. The war taught us how to eat corn bread. Ablemamu – roasted cornflower porridge – joined the menu, as did fried plantain, which followed the arrival of the Nigerians. They called this preparation *dodokyi*. Fried plantain and bean stew has now been christened "red red" throughout the country.

Tuition at Achimota was good, in fact very good. We benefited from a large contingent of dedicated teachers from Britain and other parts of the British Empire, together with a sizeable number of Africans Some of the teachers of the time were to become truly great in their field. Ephraim Amu who taught us music comes to mind. Some of the Africans were junior masters. My understanding was that they were yet to get their degrees. I was to join this band of junior masters when I completed my London

intermediate BSc. English was the fundamental language, and good English was truly the maxim. For youngsters there was a good library and we had access to the English classics, not only Shakespeare and his like but stories including *Kidnapped*, *King Solomon's Mines* and *The Prisoner of Zenda*, various Dickens' novels and Lamb's *Tales from Shakespeare* were available. These helped to make some of us avid readers and lovers of literature.

Science and mathematics were only second to English. Compared to what I heard about other schools, we were very lucky in Achimota to have laboratory facilities. I believe it was this and perhaps the size of faculty that made Achimota the school to which students came from other schools for their intermediate London BSc. courses and exams. So until the introduction of the A levels, Achimota was the centre for the best Ghanaian students. This assemblage of Ghanaian leadership material helped provide a cohesion that is not too visible in other parts of Africa.

School Certificate

Achimota was an incredibly forward looking institution in many ways. Whereas the Christian religious groups and other institutions were concerned to separate us, "the natives", from many aspects of our culture, Achimota insisted on retaining these as part of our education. The cloth was accepted as good enough for going to chapel and major functions. Tribal drumming was institutionalized. Tribal groupings were not discouraged, although our first loyalty was to the school. So it was that a student had a choice of tribal allegiance in Achimota which was not necessarily his or her birth tribe. In fact many students followed friendship when choosing their tribal allegiance in school. The native languages were taught and allowed as school certificate subjects. In fact I offered Ga at the Cambridge School Certificate examination and that made me learn much about my culture including topics such as birth and death rites, marital rites and rites of passage, knowledge of which stood me in good stead both in medical practice and in family dealings.

Right from the beginning I did well in Achimota. I topped my class both in many individual subjects and overall. Because of the war the school had to economise, so the end of year prizes became certificates rather than books. I must confess I do not know what happened to the bundle I collected during my four years in the secondary school.

In final months of the fourth year, late in 1943, we had to sit the Cambridge School Certificate Examination. With the war still on it was necessary to be sure the answer papers got to the United Kingdom for marking. We therefore had to write the

whole examination in duplicate using carbon paper and a pencil. What was even more depressing was that we had to wait for almost a year for the results to be declared; and without the results there was no schooling. I passed well enough to get another scholarship to enter the next level which was called "inter". For the school certificate I had offered seven subjects; for inter I had to do three, physics chemistry and biology. The course lasted two years, and again we had to wait for a long time for the results to be announced.

Teaching experience

During the first wait, after the school certificate examination, I gave some voluntary teaching service to the Osu Salem School and was later invited to teach the final class of the Osu Presbyterian Senior Girls School. It turned out that the English syllabus for the standard seven examination had been altered – the long essay had been replaced by reading, comprehension and précis writing. The teacher in charge was not comfortable with these and in any case she was either sick or had to go on maternity leave. With weeks to go before the examination the class had no teacher. So there I was hardly older than some of the class, the sole young man among 30 or more teenage girls. The two main subjects I taught were English and maths. But it turned out to be a most rewarding period. My horizons were widened and I gained a lot of experience in temptation. Incredibly to me all the girls passed the standard seven examinations.

Soon after the examinations I learnt that, in a class below mine, a girl who had been to school throughout the term had given birth to a baby. She was such a quiet girl, to me anyway, that I was most surprised at what I heard. I wondered what it must have cost this young lady to hide a full term pregnancy from other girls and from the teachers. This experience must have etched itself on my brain for the future.

Meeting Florence

Florence Dzani, whose older sister had married into the same family as one of my aunts was among the bright girls in the class. She did very well in the standard seven examinations and was given an interview for a teaching scholarship at Achimota. Rather than being made to do the straight category A teacher's course for which the scholarship had been offered, the programme was changed and her group had to follow a full secondary course prior to doing their teacher training. So it happened that I taught her twice, because when I finished my inter examinations I was invited to teach some of

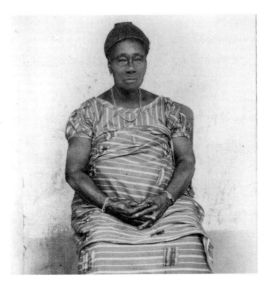

Above: My paternal grandmother.

Below: My Uncle 'Papa'.

Above: My mother, Shormeh (left) and her sister Korlei.

Below: My wife, Florence, our daughter Oboshie and my Uncle 'Papa'.

the junior classes science and Ga. Unbeknown to me she was to become my friend when we met again in the United Kingdom and then my wife.

The school certificate results were finally declared and I was given a science scholarship for the intermediate BSc. The houses for the inter students in Achimota housed quite a few youngsters from other schools. I had next to me in the dormitory Smiley Chinery, from Adisadel, who was reading arts. His subjects included English literature and his books enticed me. So it was that I devoted a great deal of time to reading all his books, often before he finished them.

The course took two years. In the first year my group did a lot of naughty things. We were quite noisy and must have disturbed the senior class, including Silas Dodu, K. B. Asante and others who were busy preparing for their exams. Once, they were so exasperated that they said "if you keep on playing, this time next year you will know what it is like". No one made us curb our excesses but when we saw how intimidating past examination questions were, we settled down and worked hard. I finally completed the total second cycle education in 1946. It had taken six years, not because we were dummies but because of having to wait two years for my exam results.

The waiting started again after inter. Fortunately I was invited by the Achimota authorities to join the staff as an assistant master. Though not at all well paid it was a good job. It kept me fully occupied and away from the temptations around my area of Osu. I shared a flat with A. A. Armar, who also later became a doctor and a gynaecologist. It was during this period that I was invited for an interview by S. T. Dunstan, acting as headmaster, and asked if I would like to be offered a scholarship to train as a teacher. After a day's thought, I declined the offer. It was perhaps a little foolhardy as the exam results had not yet arrived and had I not been awarded a scholarship later, my family would never have been able to send me overseas to study.

Fortunately when the results came out I had passed well enough to be interviewed for a medical scholarship. I have never been too sure even today why I had chosen medicine. It was partly the glamour of the white coat, but also perhaps because of what I seen while doing social service in the villages round Achimota.

Social service, in those days, involved teams of students under the guidance of a master, trainee teacher or a senior student. The villages covered included, Anumgle, Apenkwa and Achimota. We dressed sores, advised on hygiene, especially of food and water, paying particular attention to the control of mosquitoes by covering all stored water. We even performed little educational skits.

Arriving in the UK

The evening of the eleventh night on the *Almanzora* the captain announced that we would land in Southampton the next day. There was great excitement and merry making well into the night. I reflected on the lessons I had learnt on board, and the acquaintances that were to end. One lesson which stands out till today was table etiquette, largely because of the way it was taught. Very few of us knew that English table manners demanded that cutlery be placed in a particular order and in different positions to attract service. So it was that during the first few nights of the voyage some of us got plates removed before we had finished eating – we had put fork and knife together, implying then that we had finished. Different types of cutlery were for different foods; for example fish required using different knives and forks from meat. The stewards taught us how to handle the choice of cutlery. This stood me in good stead for the rest of my stay.

After a fitful night I woke early to find the boat anchored. We had breakfast and were told that disembarkation would begin at 10 a.m. Everything had been organized for our reception at the dock. Under the supervision of Colonial Office personnel our boxes were placed on to the train, after we had cleared through customs and immigration controls. Compared to today I would say we were treated like diplomats, if not royalty. Many of us were bound for London as the first stop. One thing which amazed all of us was to see white people handling our luggage and doing other menial jobs around the port and the train station. This just didn't happen in the colonies.

After the pleasant train ride we poured out at Waterloo and were bussed to a holding dormitory somewhere in West London. It was here that we were given our briefing on the colleges we were going to and the dates of departure. Before departure the important business of getting various allowances had to be organized. My friend Claude Ennin was heading to Leeds whilst I was to stay in London. So just a few days after landing in Britain we were dispersed. I found myself in a hostel in Hallam Street, behind the BBC's central London building.

2 medical school in london

It was truly marvellous the way the British Colonial Office looked after us. Just a few days after settling in the hostel behind Broadcasting House, we reported to the Students' Office at 1 Pall Mall East, SW1. There we got us all the instructions about London life and were issued with our settlement allowances. They also pointed us to the Barclays Bank on the floor below; and into that bank I went and deposited my money – and I have banked with Barclays ever since. What was most interesting for me was the size of the £5 note. This was a white sheet of paper with various things written on one side only in addition to the £5 and one had to sign the back if one wanted to use it. It was then the highest note in circulation – now £50 notes are not out of the ordinary.

The Pre-clinical and Medical Schools were in two separate buildings in Gower Street attached to University College. The college was quite extensive but had suffered a great deal of war damage, and we saw many buildings which had been bombed during German air raids.

We started classes in early October. Even though the weather had turned cold, we had no heating. Just after the war, England was still suffering from shortages, and there were rules about when the heating could come on and when it had to go off. Fortunately, having bought some warm clothes, I was able to survive until the heating was turned on.

Anatomy

The first subject that we started was anatomy, and one Dr. Aitken, the Dean of the pre-clinical courses, gave us all the necessary instructions. We were divided into groups and sent down to the anatomy laboratory or dissection room. Each group consisted of eight students. The total body of students was about 50 with only about half a dozen female students at that time. We were then shown rows of white-covered objects. At first, I thought under the sheets would reveal a sculpture or clay model of some sort.

Each group of eight was divided into two, one set of four on the right and the other on the left. Then we were asked to take off the sheets. We were told then that these were the bodies that we were going to work on for our anatomy course for the entire duration of the second Batchelor of Medicine (MB) course.

We were given quite a long lecture about respect for the bodies as these had either been donated or been obtained by the hospital because they could not be buried. But the essential points that were driven home to us were that we should treat these bodies not only as very, very important gifts to the school but as deserving the utmost respect and perhaps even reverence. We should not, we were told, handle any parts lightly or refer to the bodies as a joke. And for most of the 15-18 months that we spent there, the smell of formalin in that laboratory was really very high. Yet, despite the lecture and despite the smell, we had a lot of fun, not at the expense of the bodies but the anatomy room was a place for exchanging many very earthy jokes.

Two weeks after our first meeting with these bodies with which we were to stay for so long, I was invited to take an IQ test and have an interview. I found this strange because normally one would have thought that the interview and the test would come before the admission, but in this instance, I had been admitted and then I was being given the test and the interview.

The interview went extremely well. I remember being asked questions like why coming to medical school when I was so relatively old. Most of my British classmates were in their late teens but I was already into my 20s partly due to the lengthy nature of our primary, secondary and pre-university education, and partly the result of the war-time delays in getting our exams evaluated and the results returned to Ghana.

The IQ test unfortunately did not go well at all. Although I was not told what the test showed, I felt I had done particularly poorly because the type of things that were used for that test were not things or models I knew anything about. Fortunately, however, nobody threw me out and I stayed and completed my medial training.

The Professor of Anatomy at that time was J. Z. Young. He had become the professor at an early age and everyone said how bright he was. The pre-clinical course consisted of anatomy, physiology and biochemistry mainly. The Head of Physiology was the famous Professor Lovat-Evans, who, with a colleague, had developed method for demonstrating various functions of the heart and the lungs. He was very proud of it and I got to like physiology very much. To me, at the time, physiology was much more of an academic exercise than anatomy although I had to revise my thinking later.

I finished the courses in the University College and at that time, there was an offer of a scholarship for a one-and-a-half year course to complete a BSc. I opted for this without expecting to be offered the scholarship, but, for some reason, I got it.

Hostel life in the UK

Life in the student hostels in the late 1940s was remarkably enjoyable, despite the post-war restrictions and rationing. I was in a students' hostel in Hallam Street which, although small, had very good accommodation. I had the privilege of sharing rooms with quite a character, King Bruce. He had come under the sponsorship of the Accountant General's or Audit Department, but as soon as he got to London, he decided he wanted to learn the trumpet. At first, he practised in the basement of the hostel but somehow the noise managed to get out and he had to look for a studio elsewhere. He persisted and, as they say, the rest is history. As his course was only a three year one, King Bruce got back to Ghana way ahead of me. There he established the Black Beats Orchestra which reigned supreme for quite a long time. His example was one which I like to put forward to be emulated: a man taking his hobby to a very high level.

During the week, we ate breakfast and evening meals in the hostel; at weekends we got all three meals there. These, however, were nowhere near as appetizing as the ones we had been served on board ship as quite serious rationing was still in operation in '47/'48, even though the war in Europe had ended some two years earlier. The thing which most of us Africans or West Africans found very difficult was the way the English cooked vegetables. Cabbage and Brussels sprouts which were often in abundance, managed to come out of the kitchen with smells that completely put one off. However, for that time in Britain, we were not badly off at all. This was a time when rhubarb reigned supreme as the basis for puddings, and we got used to it. Strangely enough, many of us did not get that used to the way green salads were made. What we knew as salad before we came to England was what could be considered as the rich mixed salad. made with baked beans, sardines, and everything else – almost a meal in itself. The British salad – just fresh soft lettuce leaves with an occasional slice of tomato – did not appeal to us at all and took a long time to get used to.

Social life

There was a reasonable amount of social life among students in London at that time. Our hostel had only a small living room so our socials were restricted to playing music

and a little bit of learning to dance in which I took an enthusiastic part, mainly as a teacher. On Sundays, I hardly got out of bed as I occupied myself with several of the British Sunday papers. I developed this habit which turned out to be a bad one and I had to get rid of it by the time I had finished my BSc. degree. Other hostels for students in London were Knutsford House and Hans Crescent. Knutsford House, in west London about a mile and a half from ours, had a huge hall for weekend socials and it was there on Saturday nights that many of us would gather and have the time of our lives. We did not have to invite any girls. Women, both white and black, invited themselves to the socials in Knutsford House. The other hostel, in Hans Crescent in Knightsbridge, came on board later but it also had facilities for socials and there too we enjoyed several Christmas Eve and New Year's Eve parties.

In the second year, 1948, I was elected chairman of the Hallam Street Students' Hostel. As such I had to organize various functions and one which I remember with great pleasure, was a visit to the hostel by the great Dr. J. B. Danquah, sometime in 1948. Dr. Danquah was invited to bring the students up-to-date on happenings in the Gold Coast, as Ghana was called until independence in 1957. He gave an excellent dissertation of what had happened from the time of the strikes and demonstrations which led to the deaths of the three people and how they had managed to keep the fire burning; the progress of the United Gold Coast Convention and happenings since Nkrumah arrived on the scene. It was a marvellous lecture and I received many congratulations for organizing it.

When I finished my second MB, I got a fellowship to do the BSc in physiology. Of course, I thought I could take this course as leisurely as I had taken the pre-medical course. The Fellowship was additional to my student's stipend from the colonial government and therefore I had a little more disposable income than the average colonial student. The first thing I did was to send some money home to my mother to be used to buy a sewing machine for my sister who had gone into dressmaking and was doing quite well but needed a brand new machine. Beyond that, I was able to enjoy life a little bit more than previously. I took to a study of the London theatre, including operas, plays, and music. I also discovered the opposite sex and had lots and lots of female companionship during this period, to an extent that once I broke one of the laws of the hostel, namely that girls should not go upstairs into the rooms of the residents. Soon after that, I had to leave the hostel and find accommodation outside.

I moved into a flat in Maida Vale and shared it with Mills Odoi, then a law student, later to become Mr. Justice Mills Odoi. We were great companions, but he

finished his course before me. Searching for digs, as we called private accommodation in those days in London, was not at all difficult. I found a Nigerian who wanted to rent two rooms with a bathroom and kitchen in Kilburn. There I stayed with Albert Tackie who had come to London to study pharmacy. Tackie and I had a great time; we had female friends taking turns to come and cook for us and help clean the flat. Things went on like this for quite a while till I was invited to go and live in North London with the Blighs.

John Bligh was one of my classmates on the BSc course, as was Harry Cleave, who came from Portsmouth, I believe. The three of us and Tony Bligh, the youngest of the Bligh children, were very happy together in the house. We had to come to University College together and I developed the habit of getting up very early, taking the trolleybus and getting into college long before business started. I also stayed fairly late and had a shower before going home. At this time, one could not have a shower in the digs except on specific days, usually once a week; so I was particularly lucky to have showers and baths which one could use whenever one needed in college.

Disappointing result

It went on like this till we finished the BSc. I must confess I took it very lightly and suffered the consequences by getting a bad degree, the first disappointing exam result that I had ever had. For some reason, I completely mishandled the practical which required me to give the approximate composition and strength of a material in solution. The muscle would hardly move and the drum which I prepared was in a sad state by the time I had finished the practical. Anyway, such was London and its exams, that no matter how well I had performed during the course, the exam results decided what degree I got and so I considered that I had done extremely poorly. But it made me resolve to start doing better. So it was that I went on to undertake studies for the final medical MBBS from 1950 to 1953.

Unwanted pregnancies

It was late in 1948 and early 1949 that I came face-to-face with the problems of young women in foreign lands. Once or twice as a medical student, I was approached by this or that young woman who had a problem with a pregnancy. I did not know then what to do; but I felt quite sad for them. It was not too long before I myself found myself in trouble so I tried to find out from one of them how she "solved" her problem. I was

directed to an African doctor living in the Kilburn area. He agreed to help but at quite a fee – almost a third of my then monthly stipend. Of course I had to pay, the operation was successful and a load taken off my shoulders.

At this time, although one knew about condoms and all that, trying to get a condom was quite a palaver. Frequently, one just went to the chemist, waited till there was a male serving at the counter, whisper and the object would be produced disguised with a newspaper covering. Of course, many of us didn't take the trouble. I am mentioning this simply to show how I came face-to-face with some of the problems that are confronting people who have unsafe abortions today. In this particular instance, the two or three girls who had directed me had been safely helped. Unfortunately, my girl-friend had another friend, a Ghanaian. This girl got pregnant, and instead of telling her friend, she kept it to herself. I do not know whether she asked somebody and could not find the right place where she could get help. Over a weekend, in 1950, I heard that the poor girl had been taken into a hospital in South East London and was in a coma. I went and saw her. She was in a very poor state and died the same evening. Several weeks later, I heard of another death of another Ghanaian woman. This time, not because she had tried to commit suicide but because her abortion had been botched. These problems rankled with me for a very long time and helped shape my own views on the laws against abortion.

Clinical experience

The undergraduate clinical course was probably the most demanding I had undertaken thus far. During the three years, one could not have any meaningful holidays. Of course a few days here and there over Christmas and various bank holidays were permissible. I was lucky enough to be clerking, as we called it, for some of the best physicians and surgeons in the medical school at the time. Of course, we had arguably the best Professor of Medicine at the time, Professor Sir Max Rosenheim. He was a wonderful, affable man and he remained very charming to me even long after I had qualified. One example of his kindness that I would like to record is when we later attended a dinner celebrating the Lancet's 150th anniversary.

I had written a chapter for the book which had been produced for the anniversary. Sir Max had made one of the speeches at the dinner. We had a chat and he asked me where I was staying. At that time I was staying in a nice little hotel in St. John's Wood. He said, "oh, I'm going that way", gave me a lift and dropped me at the

hotel. We had quite a long conversation, including my asking him about how to set about getting my MD, the second part of which I had left hanging for a long time. His response was that I had already reached a stage in life where the MD would not add to my progress. It was wonderful of him.

One boss of mine at medical school whom I grew very fond of was Dr. John Stokes, consultant physician, and his wife Joan. Joan also taught microbiology in the school. They invited me to their home on a couple of occasions. Sometime after I had left and was practising in Accra, Dr. John Stokes, who had became one of the consultant physicians of Dr. Kwame Nkrumah, made it possible for my wife and I to have dinner with the Nkrumahs in Flagstaff House. The very private dinner, for just the President and Mrs. Nkrumah, my wife and I, and John and his wife Joan. It was a most pleasant evening.

Problem of colour

I recall very vividly the only occasion as a medical student that I had an overt problem with my colour. One afternoon, I was assigned a dear lady, who could be described as small. I am a small man, but she was smaller – less than five feet tall, slim, outwardly charming aged around the 60. I was to clerk her, meaning take her history and examine her. As soon as I went into the clerking room to talk to her, she screwed up her face and when I asked her a questions she would not answer. I looked at the nurse who was accompanying me for help. The nurse kindly tried to say to her that I was a medical student and advised her, please to answer the questions. The patient replied that she would not talk to a black man. So the nurse and I left and told Dr. Stokes of the situation. He calmly came and sat with the woman, and in my hearing started asking the following questions:

"Madam, have you heard of our empire?" She said "yes".

"Did you hear that we were training people there?" She said "yes".

"Did you know that when your boys went there, these people were the ones who dealt with them?"

She said yes and then he immediately switched the questioning around and asked

"Did you sign any form when you were here for registering?" She said "yes".

"Did one of the questions say that you agreed to be examined by students?" She said "yes", and then the final question was landed.

"Did you ask what colour the students would be?" She said "no", but then Dr.

Stokes said, "Well, ma'am, let me tell you that this is one of our very best students, and I can assure you that the skin colour is not what makes a doctor and you will learn to respect a person irrespective of colour. Just permit him to ask you the questions he wants to ask and we'll see how we get on."

The woman relaxed a bit. Dr. Stokes left us and we started the questioning. By the end of the session, the patient had become very friendly and she wanted to have me do her follow-up whenever she came to outpatients throughout the period that she was under our care. It was a wonderful example to me of how to handle the rather small and ticklish problems of colour. I considered them small because although in the fifties those of us who were in Britain had problems of colour, in retrospect, these were nowhere near the problems of colour that we came to see in the '80s, '90s and even now.

I finished my course in late 1953 and took the exams. I found these quite reasonable and did well. In the end, I got an honours degree with a distinction in obstetrics and gynaecology. I then had to go and register as a provisionally registered doctor. During the registration in the General Medical Council offices in the same Hallam Street where I had lived during my first couple of years, I went to the desk, gave my name and college and asked for the registration office.

A young lady came up with the list from London University in her hand and I gave her my name and asked to be given a form for registration. She took a look at the list, ran a pencil through from somewhere in the middle, down. Because of my name Sai, she thought, I should appear towards the end. She did not find my name so she looked up and said, "Sir, but your name is not on the list." I asked, "are you sure?" I noticed that she was running her pen from the long list which was lower than the short honours list above the one she was using. So with a little grin, I said, "would you kindly look at the first list, at the top list?" She looked and there was the name and she turned completely red and apologised. Then we finished the registration. I could not help thinking that she could not imagine that a small black man could be among those with an honours degree from London University. Pity, but I hoped it taught her something.

3 returning home

By the time I'd finished my examinations, a law had come in which required that everybody who completed their medical graduation should do a year's housemanship before being completely registered. That was to be a provisional registration year.

I did the first six months in Poole, Dorset, having failed to secure a house appointment at University College Hospital (UCH): I had found Poole a most exciting place when I did my obstetric clerkship there. For completing the clerkship in obstetrics a student had to perform, I believe, 20 normal deliveries. UCH could not give all its students such exposure so it had arranged support from different hospitals. Needless to say, I was able to learn a great deal, particularly the obstetrics part of my surgical training. Even during my housemanship, I was still not too sure whether I wanted to specialize in clinical medicine or in obstetrics and gynaecology, a subject which I truly loved.

It was from Poole that I applied to do my second internship in Accra, Ghana. London University had agreed that it would look at some hospitals in the empire and decide if they were to be approved for pre-registration or not. Fortunately for me, Accra was approved. I was very excited, because I had married before my graduation and my wife, in fulfilment of her contract, had returned home before me. She had produced a daughter Oboshie, whom I had not seen at all and I was anxious to see my wife and family. It was therefore with much excitement that I received my papers to travel to Accra in late July 1954.

I was very surprised to find on the warrant that I would be travelling by the *M. V. Sangara*. As far as I knew, the *Sangara* had been beached in Accra in 1941 or thereabouts by a German U-boat. Unknown to me, in the same year that I had left for England. 1947, the *Sangara* had been salvaged and brought back into service after repair.

Florence

So many friends and family members have wondered about my courtship and marriage that I feel compelled to write something about it. Though I had known Florence both as

a little girl among the external family by marriage and had taught her twice for short periods, she was not a special friend of mine. In fact I had a couple of girlfriends in the Osu Presbyterian Girls' School at the time I left for England, one of whom my family believed I would marry. When Florence was coming to England in the summer of 1949, she wrote to me informing me of her good fortune and asking if I could meet her when she landed in Liverpool. She was coming by one of the Elder Dempster Line boats from Accra. I was so involved with another Gold Coast girl at the time that I did not even reply to her letter; and I did not meet her at Liverpool. This has been used, perhaps not so playfully, as a major black mark for me ever since.

Anyway she arrived and went straight to Glasgow for her studies in domestic science as the subject was then called. I was told her college was known in Scotland as The Dough School. To her credit she wrote another letter. For the Christmas holidays she decided to visit London. I arranged for her to stay in the students' hostel in Collingham Gardens and for my girlfriend to help show her around. Obviously she must have noticed that my girlfriend and I were not getting on too well. So although she went back to Glasgow without saying very much, we developed quite a correspondence. She came back down during the Easter holidays when my friend and I had almost completely parted company. She, Florence, was to tell me later that she had had a one on one with that girlfriend of mine culminating in their agreeing that the other was not interested in marrying me and Florence saying she was.

The Student Section of the Colonial Office and the British Council managed to get students some very good vacation deals in those days. Through them, in 1948 I had watched the FA Cup Final between Manchester United and Blackpool which United won and I have remained a supporter ever since. In the summer of 1950, after my BSc exams I managed to arrange for the two of us to join a group touring the Lake District. We had a wonderful 10 days or so and it was in those beautiful surroundings that I asked Florence to marry me. The wedding itself had to wait till we had obtained permission from the Colonial Office since we were both government scholars.

I also had to make my family perform the traditional "asking of the woman's hand from her father". My folks got together some drinks, as custom demanded, and went to see A. Abraham Dzani, Florence's father. He refused to accept their drinks or entertain their request on my behalf. His statement to my folks was that he had not sent her daughter to Britain to get married there. Both Florence and I were unhappy about this but she said her father was being obtuse and was prepared to get married with or without

his blessing. So till now, some 57 years since we married, no traditional function has been completed on our behalf. We had a church wedding in the North Kensington Presbyterian Church on 19th July 1952.

Fortunately friends of ours who were with a group known as Moral Rearmament had managed to get us invited by a French couple as their guests for a fortnight or so. Therefore a day or two after the wedding we went off to France and stayed with a middle-aged couple in 23 Rue de la Bonne Aventure, in Versailles. I always thought that was a very good omen or sign, though I am not normally superstitious. Our daughter, Oboshie, was definitely conceived there.

Florence left for home some three or so weeks after we married. And it was to be almost two years before we saw each other again. I had a year of medical studies and a year of housemanship ahead of me.

Voyage to Ghana

I boarded the ship in Liverpool and was pleasantly surprised to find that this relatively small cargo boat of five and a half thousand tons had been nicely renovated and had cabin space for about a dozen people. I shared a cabin with Mowbray Nicholas, a very fine gentleman, who later became an Assistant Director General of the Food and Agriculture Organization (FAO). We became good friends during the voyage and remained so for a time until I lost touch after his stay with FAO.

We settled in and had as company the captain, a charming man at whose table we sat throughout the 14 or so nights that we were on board. He told us many stories and asked us a lot of things about home. As we got closer to Ghana, the captain wanted to know what would happen when we landed. Rather interestingly, I told him about all the customary rites for welcoming people who were returning after a long overseas trip. He asked me whether I expected such a reception which, of course, I did not. Little did I know!

We berthed during the night but it was not till about 10:00 a.m. that we actually were allowed to disembark. There were my mother, my Uncle Papa, my wife Florence with my daughter Oboshie who, as she was not too anxious to see me, greeted me for a couple of minutes and then went back to her mother, my cousin Sophia and a whole crowd of friends and relations, several whose names I could not remember. They poured *krōbo*, a white clay powder, on my shoulders, neck and so on and poured perfume on me and there were hugs from everybody. There were yells of *Wō na eko, wō na eko,*

shidaa aha Nyomō, meaning we have got one, thank God; libations were poured and a prayer was said. All the while, the ship's captain was standing by taking it all in and delightedly cheering the group on. Customs and immigration were easily cleared, my luggage collected and we headed for home. We parted and I was taken to Papa's home, where a sumptuous feast was awaiting me.

By the tradition at that time, a feast would consist of light soup and *fufu*, cassava and yam paste; palm nut soup and *kpoikpoi*, a steamed maize meal preparation; followed by rice and stew and then pancakes. The feasting over, and after a lot of storytelling, bedtime arrived. As Papa's home in Takoradi was rather small and was also home to relations who had come from Accra, it was a cousin from my paternal grandmother's Obosumasi family who offered Florence and me a home. We stayed in Takoradi for the night and the next day another relation called Paul Steiner came and drove us to Accra.

We were driven to Accra by my cousin whilst other members came by Florence's little car or by public transport. On the way, we had to call on my Aunt Afua Dzaa, a first cousin of my father's and a very nice woman. One of her family, Obeng Bekoe, was not only a relation but a personal friend who later became a principal of the Takoradi Polytechnic: sadly he died since I started writing these memoirs. At the Bekoes' house we had another sumptuous meal; this time it was not a feast but a most delightful *fufu* meal. We continued to Accra arriving in mid-afternoon to a reception that had to be seen to be believed. I had not expected anything like it. From the junction of the Labadi Road and Cantonments Road to our house, there were crowds – I do not know how they got to know that I was coming – and everyone was shouting: "*Wō na eko, wō na eko*". I went to the family home where there were even bigger crowds. The entire extended family in Osu must have been there and I was received with a great deal of merry making.

As I had a week of rest given me for returning, I reported to the Ministry of Health/Medical Department and then started making arrangements for getting settled.

House appointment

During my week's holiday, I had reported to the hospital in Korle Bu where I would be working and been allocated one of their small bungalows. Mine was a one-storey building near where the old bungalow used by the Medical Association as its temporary offices still stands. It was one of those called sweat boxes in those days because they

had full cage netting windows and were very warm nearly all the time. We had to use ceiling fans – air conditioners were almost unheard of back then. As I had been given a resettlement allowance, Florence and I used it to equip our bungalow with bedding materials and household necessities of various kinds. Without the allowance I doubt whether we would have been able to start life without getting heavily in debt, since my family had absolutely no way of helping me establish a home. But I am not sure whether the allowance I received would go very far today.

The other thing to think about, despite the fact that I was a houseman, was a car. Fortunately, the Medical Department decided that the work I was going to do was not very different from that of a registered medical officer so I was given the loan for a car. I had next to no information about cars. One thing I knew from hearsay was how the Peugeot 203 had been the campaign workhorse for Kwame Nkrumah's campaigns. I decided to get one as it was about the cheapest car on the market and SCOA who were marketing it then had a good salesman. And so it was that as a houseman, I could afford to get and run a car. Fortunately enough, with the maintenance and travelling allowances – known as T & T – the car was able to pay for itself without any difficulty whatsoever.

I went to Korle Bu and reported to Dr. Neils Hesse, who was then the Medical Officer-in-charge. This hospital, which had been built in the early 1920s under the governorship of Sir Frederick Gordon Guggisberg,was quite a different place from today's hospital with the old buildings that are still standing now completely overwhelmed by new six-storey buildings and many other additions. Then, in 1954, the hospital only had beds for something like 350 patients and although it had all the major departments, there was no Paediatrics Department. I was assigned to work as Dr. A. J. Hawe's houseman. Other doctors who were in the Medical Department at the time were a Dr. Ray from Rhodesia and Dr. Silas Amoo Dodu, later Professor Dodu and Dean of the Medical School.

As Dr. Hawe's houseman, and with no other medical officer between the two of us, I had first-class teaching and training from him. He was a charming man, who had been in the Ghana medical service since the 20s or 30s. He was very much a workaholic and a hard taskmaster, seeing to it that notes were prepared on time, ward rounds were ready and all the nurses knew to a tee what he expected and carried it out. He was well versed in general medicine and particularly in tropical medicine. He also had a lot of historical anecdotes to tell, both about Korle Bu and happenings in

the Gold Coast. It was Dr. Hawe, for example, who told me that before the days of the sulphonamides and particularly before the recently introduced penicillin, Ward G used to be full of young men with lobar pneumonia, during the cooler seasons – late July, August and September. All one could do then was to watch them till the crisis; meaning a sudden drop of their temperature. If the crisis arrived and the patient was alive, they would survive. And he told me what the mortality rates were. I wondered as he told me this whether or not people in my father's family had died of similar infections? Ward G was one of our three wards, the others were A and C.

He taught me practically everything I knew about tropical diseases and their diagnoses. Every Monday morning he did a complete ward round. But as he was frequently in the hospital with me on Saturdays, I had to be in the hospital on most Sundays to get patients' notes ready so that the ward round could go without any hitches. Of course there were other rounds and we had to do out-patients work several days in the week too. During these sessions he saw cases that had been referred, and I clerked for him. Old patients that came for repeat prescriptions were mostly dealt with by me. He always addressed his patients by name and he insisted that I should do the same, a habit that was to win me much admiration later in life.

Superstition

There were instances of tension between what one had learnt as the text book medicine in Britain and what was happening in the Gold Coast. The patterns of the diseases seen were different. I also came face to face with what superstition and misinformation could do to medical care. One instance of waste of police time which stands out in my mind clearly was when I was called by the CID to be interrogated about a certain death.

One of my extended family members, Sophia Doku, an important political figure, had re-married a man from Labadi, after her husband's death. This man was admitted on a Friday evening with severe cerebral haemorrhage which I diagnosed and fortunately Dr. Hawe confirmed the diagnosis the next day. The man sadly died sometime on Sunday and I signed his death certificate, thinking that was the end of the matter. When the family got to know that I had signed the certificate, instead of coming to see me or doing anything about how to get the body out of the morgue, they went to the police and claimed that the man had been murdered.

The police called me and faced me with the allegation that, as a relation, I had connived with Sophia Doku and that the man had been beaten to death. And that as a

doctor, I had been able to stitch up his wounds to such an extent that nobody would immediately notice the wounds. I showed the case notes to the police and then they went to Dr. Hawe and asked him his opinion. Dr. Hawe was really furious with the police, telling them that even if they had nothing better to do, he did and there was absolutely no reason for them to follow up on such nonsense. To dispel any doubt, he suggested that if they liked, they could bring the body back for a post mortem examination. Nothing like that was done and I never heard of the case again.

On many occasions one was confronted with very seriously ill patients who obviously had been suffering for a long time, only to find that they had been trying the treatment of fetish priests, herbalists and other types of medicine men and women. Sometimes the patients believed so strongly that other human beings were behind their problems that even when the disease was cured the patient remained unwell. Typical was a young civil servant who presented with a raging fever which turned out to be typhoid. He recovered rather rapidly with appropriate antibiotic treatment, but he was mentally quite difficult as he and his immediate family were convinced that the problem was related to his ex-wife.

He had married his current wife after unceremoniously getting rid of the previous one. A major relation of his ex-wife had threatened him with death and he firmly believed that this was happening. In the end his people pleaded with us to discharge him and grant him a reasonable period of sick leave for them to take him away and get him truly cured. We gave him a fortnight, after which he came back from his village completely cured. This taught me something about the struggle between belief and physical evidence in medicine, and the fight between tradition and modernity.

Fevers of unknown origin

It was during my work with Dr. Hawe that I also realized the seriousness of many illnesses we dealt with relative to those that were presented at University College Hospital where I had trained. There, we largely saw the diseases of older people. Here, we had to deal with diseases in young, active ones. Dr. Hawe was also responsible for the children's ward, so I had the opportunity of learning paediatrics quite seriously. At one stage, I thought that this would be my calling, but it was not to be.

We saw a lot of typhoid fever, a lot of cases of convulsions in children and most upsettingly quite a few instances of household poisoning, mainly the result of children

drinking kerosene mainly. The unfortunate thing was that when a child drank kerosene or something like it, instead of the child being immediately rushed to hospital attempts were made at home to make the child swallow things like red palm oil and frequently, when these children died and a post mortem carried out, the immediate cause of death would turn out to be aspiration of palm oil which had been forced down their throats rather than the result of the poisoning.

Of the fevers of unknown origin which I had to deal with, quite a few turned out to be related to unsafe abortions in young women. Of course, tuberculosis which people did not accept in its early stages underlay quite a few fevers, too.

One thing which irked Dr. Hawe was the handling of diabetes by patients and their relations. Then as now. diet was an important part of the management of late onset diabetes. We would advise our patients of the kinds of foods to eat and not to eat in relation to their care; yet, almost invariably when the women, particularly those who worked at Makola Market, were closely questioned about their diets after their urine had shown the tell-tale signs of lack of control of their diabetes, they would tell the full story. It turned out frequently that, for breakfast, many were having large quantities of Quaker oats with a lot of sugar and, in some cases, almost a whole tin of evaporated milk. Sometimes the milk was not the unsweetened evaporated milk we see today, but sweetened condensed milk. Dr. Hawe would turn round to them and say, "Each time you put this milk into your breakfast, you put one nail in your coffin because by the time the milk is finally finished your coffin will be ready". But it did not seem to frighten the women very much.

Sudden deaths of women were noteworthy and it was not till I came into practice myself, after my specialist qualification, that I realized how serious and common sudden deaths from hypertension were in my country.

Move to Kumasi

I finished my six months' stint in the Korle Bu Hospital and got my full registration. I was then appointed a medical officer and immediately started applying to be transferred to Kumasi. As stated earlier, my wife, Florence, had come home ahead of me in 1952, after we married, and she was comfortably settled as an Assistant Lecturer in the then Kumasi College of Technology, now Kwame Nkrumah University of Science and Technology. The Home Science Department, where she worked, headed by Ms. Sproat, was considered quite important in those days. By the time I got to

Kumasi a new government hospital called G had been completed, and I was posted as medical officer in charge of medical patients. So it was that early in 1955 I arrived in Kumasi. There was no bungalow immediately ready for me, so I stayed with my wife on the compound of the college.

The community there was most affable. There were several who had been senior students or teachers in Achimota during my secondary school years. In Kumasi, generally, the medical group was also very friendly and we had a good social life. Dr. Evans Anfom was a surgeon, Dr. Kwamla Cofie, now Nana Kwadwo Ababio of British Accra or Jamestown Mantse, was a Dental Surgeon and the whole crowd had known each other in one way or another for some time. Dr. Nikoi Robertson was also there as a medical officer, as was Dr. Awuku Asabre, who was very interested in obstetrics and gynaecology. The Medical Administrator was an affable Englishman, Dr. Hughes. I happily joined this crowd.

In Kumasi, I had to handle a ward, do medical duties as an outpatients' medical officer, and also take my turn in casualty. As there was no physician specialist to supervise the department or me, I had to do the best I could for all medical cases that I saw. Of course, as some of the specialists like Anfom and Bowesman had a lot more experience, it was possible to discuss cases with them, but by and large one had to develop the courage to consult textbooks and make decisions which would have been far above one, even in Accra.

Laboratory facilities were also rudimentary and I could not help but think what courageous people doctors in private medical practice were. We had been trained to depend on whole groups for consultations before arriving at diagnoses and here I was, on my own, a young doctor, taking very serious decisions of life and death, on my own.

It was sometime in 1955, while in Kumasi, that the *Mate me ho* problems erupted: this was the equivalent of the Ashanti part of the Gold Coast seeking separation. A curfew was imposed. For some reason, it did not occur to me that curfews applied to us, doctors. One evening, when I had been called to see a patient who had arrived as an emergency, I gaily got into my car and drove from the College of Technology towards the hospital. Strangely enough, although I could hear a siren, I never thought that it was trying to get me to stop; so I kept on and went into the hospital, immediately followed by the car which also came to a stop. There was a British police officer in it. He came out angry, and demanded to know why I did not stop when I heard the siren. I said I honestly did not know that the siren

was asking me to stop. It was only later that I realized how close I could have come to death and when I heard how brutally people who disobeyed curfews were treated, I shuddered. Certainly, I feel had this been in post-independence days, or even now, I might have been killed without my realizing that I had been doing anything wrong whatsoever.

It was also during this period that there was a huge fight between the National Liberation Movement (NLM) and the Convention Peoples Party (CPP) people in Ejisu, Ashanti. This was a Saturday afternoon and unfortunately for me, I happened to be on casualty duty at the time. When the emergency cases were brought in, I decided to go strictly by my medical practice of triage – those who were most seriously hurt had to be looked after first. Of course this did not go down very well with the members of the CPP who felt, as governing party people, they had to be treated first. I was foolish or naïve enough to try to argue with them. They nearly tore me into bits. Some of them were saying "as Kwame Nkrumah sent you to England, now you have come back, you have to look after his followers". I said, "I was in England before Kwame Nkrumah became the head of this country so please …". Before I could say "please" I was surrounded, and fortunately some of them kept the angriest of their colleagues away from me. Luckily, Dr. Hughes, the medical administrator, came in, quietly asked me to go home and took over the treatment of the injured.

I do not know what would have happened if the medical administrator had not intervened. It was on that day that the well known CPP activist called Kofi Banda died. As I was treating the outpatients, I had not heard that the CPP had suffered what their members considered a very serious decapitation of their organization.

As I was living in the College of Technology, whenever I was on call duty, casualty duty, I had to sleep at the hospital. Frequently, I was called to see emergencies which would require surgery and I would refer these people. For obstetrics, it was my friend, Dr. Asabre, whom I called. The friendship developed in such a way that I was able to lay before him the problems of my cousin, Comfort, and her husband David Batsa Azu who was a classmate of mine from Osu Salem. Although they had married before I left for England they had not been able to have any children for seven years. Dr. Asabre decided that my cousin needed an operation for fibroids, which once carried out successfully, enabled Comfort to conceive – she went on to have Akutey Azu, his two sisters and brother. Comfort, as I said before, was one of the closest of immediate family to me until she recently died.

Social life

We had quite a social life in Kumasi, both around the College campus, in town and around the hospital. My wife and I regularly enjoyed dancing at weekend events at the Hotel de Kingsway in town. The owner, Collingwood Williams, was really very well known in Ghanaian circles at the time – I believe the present Minister of Religion of the Action Church is a relation, if not his son. The dancing and the music were good and the atmosphere was most engaging.

But of course, the activities we enjoyed most happened in colleagues' and our homes. Usually one of the medical officers would convene the party and provide food; others would bring different kinds of drinks and we would have a really good evening . But as we worked on Fridays and Saturdays too; these parties usually happened on Saturday night.

It stands out clearly to me now, that some of the most enchanting things about life in Kumasi were the relationships between patients and doctors. The patients were very anxious to show their gratitude. Even chiefs, as patients liked to show appreciation by giving the doctor some money or cloths, fish, chicken, and things like that. This was not at all common in Accra at the time; there, people from Osu who were in the extended family, or even friends of people in the extended family, had a habit of coming to consult us and then asking to be taken home. However, this did not happening in Kumasi.

Another endearing thing which happened to us while I was in Kumasi was my introduction to the then Asantehene, Nana Sir Agyeman Prempeh II. My maternal family uncle, Carl Reindorf, was related closely to Dr. C. E. Reindorf and worked as an assistant to him. They had both worked in Ashanti and knew the Asantehene very well. In fact, Dr. C. E. Reindorf had been a physician to the Asantehene for some time. So when my wife came back and settled in Kumasi, my uncle took the trouble to get her introduced to the Asantehene and his family. My wife and family were soon adopted and joined other families around the Asantehene. The matriarch to whom she became closest was Madam Nana Ama Dapaah, mother-in-law of the Asantehene, and the mother of President John Agyekum Kufuor. This bond was strengthened because the elder brother, Dr. Francis Addo Kufuor, my classmate from Achimota College, was lecturing at the College of Technology and was another link to the family. As my wife had been introduced to the Asantehene and been in and out of the Kufuor household for sometime; I was immediately introduced to the Asantehene when I was posted to Kumasi. His first words to me were "oh, so we have finally met Mrs. Sai's husband". I found this particular

41

expression most interesting because I never ever thought that I was going to be introduced as somebody's husband. The Asantehene had sown another seed for gender equality in my mind.

The campus of College of Technology itself was also extremely interesting. Some of the major Ghanaian characters who were closest to my wife and me were Silvanus Amegashie, who lived a couple of houses away; and Mr. and Mrs. Bertie Opoku – both of whom sadly have passed away.

As Florence had made numerous friends in Kumasi, I was very well received on the campus of the College of Science and Technology. She had a beautiful two-bedroom bungalow on Buroburo Road and we visited and were visited regularly by many of her colleagues. Of particular attachment was her Head of Department, Miss Sproat, later to become Mrs. Eden, whom she had known in Achimota and also Ms. Authors. These two British ladies treated Florence like a daughter and Oboshie as their special grandchild. When I arrived, I was received with open arms. But our joint special friends at the time were Mr. and Mrs. Albert or Bertie Opoku: he later changed his name completely to Mawere Opoku and became a Professor of Music and Arts in the African Studies Department.

On July 19, 1955, the Opokus invited us to dinner, because it was our wedding anniversary and they decided to give us a treat. When we got there, Bertie, as usual, was not ready, but he was sitting by his easel, painting furiously. I went close to him and upon inspection, found that he had a painting of three women standing under some trees and a man with an apple in his hand, sitting in contemplation. I looked at it and asked him: "Bertie, are you trying to depict the judgment of Paris?" He turned round and said: "Fred, you are extraordinary. How did you know?" I said, "well, when you have three women showing different views of human beauty and a man with an apple, if one knows any Greek mythology, it could only be an expression of the judgement of Paris that led to the Trojan Wars." He was truly amazed but he said nothing more. So, we had our meal and then went home.

In the night, Florence said she felt the baby was coming. I took her to the hospital and within a short half an hour or so, Adai, our second daughter, was born. The afterbirth, placenta, took a while coming, but instead of calling the obstetrician, I decided to assist the midwives by doing an external massage. It has always been my belief that children do get born with the assistance of trained midwives but the extent of training is the important thing. In this situation I was quite comfortable with the

midwives and I did not think it necessary to call the obstetrician, who I was told had been in the hospital till about an hour before we got there. Of course, he was not very happy when I told him what had happened. He said, as my colleague, that it was my responsibility to see to it that he was there just in case anything went awry. Maybe it was wrong, perhaps for a right reason, not to call him, but I did not think he should be disturbed when things were going so normally.

Florence came home a few days after the delivery, and we had the out-dooring ceremony for Adai the week after her birth. We combined her christening with her naming ceremony. After this, the Opokus came round with a huge parcel in their hands. We opened the parcel and it was Mawere Opoku's painting of the Judgment of Paris. He made a little speech and said, when we married in 1952, he was a student and had nothing to give us, so now that he had finished this painting and because I had identified what he was doing, he thought that the picture would be a perfect wedding present for us. It remains one of our most prized possessions, hanging in our sitting room wherever we have been from Kumasi, to Accra, London, the United States and back.

Work in Kumasi Hospital continued to be exacting. I was the Medical Officer in charge of Medicine. The only other person I remember who was a general duty medical officer was Dr. Nikoi Robertson, who left fairly soon afterwards on transfer back to Accra.

I felt I needed more training and as the conditions of service also required that anyone who had trained outside Ghana undertake tropical medicine training, before really becoming fully acknowledged as a medical officer, I was granted a scholarship to go to Britain to train in tropical medicine and hygiene. So it was that in 1956, when I had hardly finished a year in Kumasi, that I went back to England. This time, I flew by one of the planes that stopped in Lagos and Tripoli before getting into London.

With Florence on our wedding day.

4 tropical medicine and nutrition

I got myself a flat in Alderman's Hill, in Palmer's Green, quite a pleasant location overlooking a huge park. To get to the London School of Hygiene, I had to get up very early and take the trolley bus, the same one I had used when a student at University College Hospital. This made me an early riser; and because of the heaviness of traffic, frequently, I stayed in the library and came home fairly late. I had nobody waiting for me, as I was cooking and looking after myself at this time.

I found the Tropical Medicine Course fascinating but not particularly exacting. What I really enjoyed was the laboratory sessions, peering down microscopes. Sessions at St. Pancras Hospital, where we had clinical presentations, were also quite exciting. Although some of the cases were relatively difficult to diagnose, they seemed to pose fewer problems than cases I had faced in Accra. What was even more interesting was the small number of cases that were being used for our training compared with the size of clinics that I had run both as a houseman and later as a medical officer in Accra and Kumasi. Some of our professors – Leonard Bruce-Chwatt and Alan Woodruff – later became good friends, as did B. B. Waddy, who had worked in Ghana before and during the time I entered into practice.

The exams came and I passed, but before passing, I had gone back to my interest in human nutrition which had featured in the course as the major background cause of the high mortality of infants, children and mothers during pregnancy. I therefore applied to be allowed to do a short course in human nutrition. I was accepted and so stayed another six months in the School of Hygiene in the department of Professor Ben Platt, mainly studying nutrition policy. And before the course finished, I had decided to try my luck at the Part I MD of London University.

Sometime, before my time, the London University MD could be taken by examinations only or by an examination and a thesis. By my time, the first idea had been dropped so I had to do the Part I exam and then try to find out how I could do a thesis and on what subject. I undertook practically no special studies for the exam. I had a look at

some of the previous Part I papers and found that they would be manageable with the work that I had done previously, the work that I had done at the School of Hygiene, plus re-reading of the major medical textbooks. I found that there were a couple of requirements which were important and these were major essays on subjects some of which bordered on the philosophical – such as "A Little of What You Fancy Does You Good" or "The Skin is the Mirror of Health of the Individual – Discuss". Fortunately, I passed the Part I exam and decided to return to Ghana. Homecoming was fun and this time, I went by air and my luggage followed me later.

My wife had been able to get her annual leave and visit London with the two children, Oboshie and Adai, during the summer that I was there. They found living in my flat very interesting, climbing up and down the stairs. They also found walking and playing in the park very amusing. We had quite a good time. The other colleagues who joined us in the holiday period were Mr. Joe Ahia Lamptey and his wife, Mrs. Comfort Ahia Lamptey, née Ashietey.

Interestingly, the College of Science and Technology had very good terms and conditions of service. Apart from summer leave with full pay and all fares paid, including fares for children, staff could ask for an advance with which to buy a car. Florence asked for one and she bought a Ford Zephyr while she was in England. As Mr. and Mrs. Ahia Lamptey bought a similar car, we two couples were able to travel around much of southern England quite freely. After the holiday, we took the car back to Ghana where it was registered as AS 8100 – AS was for Ashanti. I mention this because of the part that it was to play during the independence celebrations in Accra in March 1957.

Accra

When I returned home, I was immediately, and unexpectedly, posted as the Medical Officer in Charge of Nutrition. I was to be stationed in Accra, whilst my wife was in Kumasi. This meant I had to start commuting back and forth; but as each of us had a car, this did not prove too difficult a situation and we endured it.

There was really no Department of Nutrition. There was a lady called Mrs. Elsie Sowah, who had been appointed as the Dietician for the Ministry of Health and it was she and I who formed the unit of Human Nutrition in the Ministry of Health. Our main task was to plan nutrition education programmes and train others in conducting personal advocacy and things like that.

Soon after I arrived, the Ministry decided that they were short-handed in the

Pathology Department; so I was asked to do part-time work under Dr. later Professor Eddington and others in that Department, undertaking post-mortem examinations. I was mortified, as I had never done one anywhere. I had to observe a couple of post-mortems before I could understand what was happening. What proved most valuable was that practically all the assistants, who were not particularly well educated, were able to help and lead me through the examination. How they had been trained, I did not know, Here, I must confess, that I did learn a lot by the time I had finished my six or so months carrying out these procedures.

I tried to pursue a few research lines at this time but I was not very successful. One of them was to try to find out the length and head circumference of new-born babies and try, if possible, to relate these to the nutritional status of the mothers. The other was the hæmoglobin situation of the children in relation to those of their mothers. I did not get very far with these because I myself was unsure whether or not the methodology would be accepted as ethical as time went on, since it was not likely that the people from whom I was taking blood samples and performing the measurements were likely to benefit from the results of my research.

Ghana's Independence

1957 was also Ghana's year of destiny. All of the struggles for independence, especially since 1948, were coming to an end. Ghana was finally scheduled to have its independence from Britain – the first African colony to achieve this. Through the researches of Dr. J. B. Danquah, the Gold Coast, as it then was, had been preparing to change its name to Ghana on independence. March 6, 1957, was declared the day of independence and the city of Accra really celebrated.

I was then working in Korle Bu and my wife was visiting from Kumasi. So early on the night of 5th March, we went to the old Polo Ground to watch the celebrations. We had hardly parked when we heard a huge noise coming from the direction of our car. Right in our hearing, we could hear three or four Gas saying, *"Ashanti mei mini nye feo ye biẽ?* You say you have left and do not want independence. Why should you bring your car here?* They had bashed our Zephyr because of its having an Ashanti registration number. That was my real first confrontation with anything approaching that kind of situation. We said nothing, just took it in our stride and when later I came to think of it, I laughed a great deal; without even trying to find out who owned the car, merely having a car registered in Ashanti outside the independence celebration was

enough for some ruffians to try to smash the car. Fortunately, the damage was pretty small so it did not really spoil our enjoyment of the independence celebrations.

Meeting with Kwame Nkrumah

While Medical Officer in charge of Nutrition, I had one singular opportunity to address the nation. This was April 7, 1957 when the focus of World Health Day was nutrition. I went on radio and made a powerful speech on the nutritional status of children in Ghana and how unsatisfactory it was. This apparently was heard by Dr. Kwame Nkrumah, the Prime Minister, and a couple of days later, when I had left Accra and gone to Kumasi, a message came from the Castle that the Prime Minister wanted me see him as soon as possible.

Without wasting any time, I went back to Accra and went to the Castle to meet the Prime Minister. He invited me to take a chair and sit with him on the parapet outside the offices overlooking the beaches of Christiansborg. It was a most charming reception which I will never forget.

Dr. Nkrumah started by asking whether I was well settled and whether I was happy with the job I was doing. I confirmed that I was although I had only just started and frankly did not know what I was going to need. He said "Well, when you are settled, whatever you need, let me know directly. Don't go through the Ministry of Health hierarchy." I found that a little odd, but kept it to myself. And then, he also stated that he had been told that I had taken to nutrition very well and he wanted to know what my views were about the malnutrition problems which I was discussing on the radio. He listened quite attentively and when I mentioned what I knew about the geographic spread of malnutrition, how among children we had malnutrition everywhere, how in northern Ghana there was malnutrition even in adults; particularly weight loss during the hungry seasons as we called them; and how loss of weight accompanied pregnancy in much of that part of the country, he really appeared very concerned and interested and he said we would have to discuss matters further. So after about 45 minutes, I was dismissed. Little did I know that he was going to contact the UN system, and through them my professor in London, to ask for assistance to tackle the problems of malnutrition in Ghana.

Formation of the Ghana Medical Association

My next meeting with the Prime Minister was in early 1958, during the launch of the Ghana Medical Association (GMA). Dr. M. A. Barnor has described the formation of

Florence with our daughters Oboshie and Adai.

Above: With Dr. Easmon in Prague, 1961.

Below: With visitors during the building of the clinic in Danfa, 1969.

the GMA in detail so I will just state a few points which concerned me directly. During much of 1957 we, young doctors in Korle Bu, had been worrying about our inclusion with the hospital and allied health workers section of the Trade Union Congress. This meant we were in the same group as the sanitarians, cleaners and other hospital staff. What was even more important, since the group was in existence before doctors were added, our voice was to be quite small. We did not know how the support staff could really represent us. Deductions of dues were being made from our salaries.

There were two organizations which could speak for doctors, if government would listen to them, but this was not the case. The Gold Coast Branch of the British Medical Association had as its members the majority of those trained in the UK most of whom were working in the government service. The second organization was the Gold Coast African Practitioners' Union about which I personally knew practically nothing (ref. Barnor MA, A Socio-Medical Adventure in Ghana 2001).

Towards the end of 1957 we learnt through the grapevine that there were plans afoot to form a medical association which was to be the only one the government would recognise and deal with. This was confirmed through reports in the press. It turned out that one Dr. Adjei Schandorf who had been in Lincoln University with the Prime Minister was behind the moves to form the new association. The government doctors felt that this was a plan to strait-jacket us into a group that would toe the line of the party in power, and we, junior doctors, held meetings trying to decide what to do. We realised that our more senior colleagues were wrestling with the same problem. Dr. Barnor was the one who seemed to be most conversant with what was happening. In the end, he and Dr. Easmon, among others, convinced all of us that the best thing to do was to join the new association and take it over.

True enough on the 4th of January 1958 through the efforts of Dr. Schandorf and the Ministry of Health a meeting was convened at the Ambassador Hotel in Accra to launch the new Ghana Medical Association. Dr. Kwame Nkrumah performed the launching ceremony and made it clear in his speech that the GMA was the only doctors' organization that the government would deal with from then on.

After the ceremony and a suitable break for interaction, the Prime Minister and his entourage departed. The doctors then reassembled by themselves for the first business meeting of the new association. A unanimous resolution was passed establishing the GMA. After a short discussion it was decided that officers should be elected and charged with the development of the association's constitution among other matters. Of course with

the numerical strength of the government doctors our wishes prevailed. Dr. Charles Easmon was elected the first president of the GMA and I was elected the first honorary secretary. Then the first meeting was adjourned for more consultations. The second meeting was convened a week later and the rest of the officers elected. Dr. Schandorf was became vice president, Dr. John David, treasurer, Drs. R.H.O. Bannerman, D.B. George, Mrs. Susan de-Graft Johnson, Silas Dodu and E. M. Brown, a dental surgeon, were elected as members of council.

The council started functioning and one of its major tasks was to develop a constitution. This was allocated largely to a small group consisting of Drs. Easmon, Barnor, Bannerman and me. We worked truly well together. Of course the young association had practically no funds so we just met in the home of whoever invited us, usually Dr. Barnor's, until the Ministry allocated a bungalow to the association. I enlisted the help of a relation, Miss Vida Magnusen, to help with the secretariat. She also worked mainly *pro bono* for me. We approached Mr Akufo-Addo, a famous lawyer and one of the "big six", who became the ceremonial president of Ghana during the Busia administration, for legal help . Our work went on for most of 1958, but it was nowhere near finished when I had to leave for the UK for my post graduate studies in internal medicine. Dr. Barnor took on the mantle of Secretary after me.

FAO/WHO Mission to Ghana on Nutrition

I was surprised when, a few months after my first meeting with the prime minister, Professor Ben Platt sent me a note, saying that he would be leading a World Health Organization (WHO) mission to Ghana to advise the country on its nutrition problems.

I was told by Professor Platt that the first approach made to the WHO was a request for a nutritionist to come and help in Ghana. He claimed to have told them that he had got a young person who had trained with him who could easily give government all the advice needed. However, it was agreed, that WHO would lead a mission to Ghana, which would lay out the plans and give broad-based advice for fundamental changes in the national food and nutrition situation. Upon hearing of this development, the FAO decided to send somebody to join the team. The French-American Professor Jean Mayer from the Harvard School of Public Health was sent. The Platt-Mayer team came to Ghana in 1958 and I was to midwife the mission. After general discussions and visits to various southern regions, it was decided that the team would be divided into two groups, one with Professor Platt would look after the

southern portion and work with government officials in Accra, whilst Jean Mayer and I went up north to see what was happening there.

In those days, people of my status did not have access to government vehicles for travel. I took my wife's Ford Zephyr and drove Mayer to northern Ghana. We had a pleasant exploration of many of the major areas of northern Ghana, now divided into the three regions. We visited Tamale, Damongo, Bole, Wa, Tumu, Lawra and Bolga. It was in Bolga that one of the funniest incidents happened because that was the only place where we had to sleep in two of their round huts, joined with a single corridor which also passed for a dining/sitting room. Jean Mayer said nothing to me at the time, but the next day, we were driving towards the northern parts of the country on very rough roads. I had to drive at a speed which I had been taught would make the car more stable. He said nothing until we arrived in Accra two or three days later; and then, he started telling stories of how we had had a wonderful time, how in every village or every town we went to, there was at least one woman who would say, "Hello, Dr. Sai, how wonderful to see you". And then he said, "But you know Florence, one thing which I was very frightened of was when Fred was driving at top speed on this rough road and he was whistling the spiritual *Lord, I am coming home*. I thought the man was interested in sending us both to the Almighty."

The other story that he told, which, much to my discomfort, was based on the fact that when the team had a meal with us at home, I went through the chicken bone like bones were my only food; so this man said to Florence: "When we were given two adjacent rooms in Bolga, I had to stay awake because I did not know when your 'friend' would start thinking of having my bones".

Jean became a very good friend and during the debriefing in Accra, he insisted, and at the time I thought he was joking, that I should come to Harvard to "finishing school". Despite Professor Platt assuring him that my training under him and the London School of Hygiene Tropical Medicine was enough for what I was required to do, Jean would not stop. So it was that when, later in the year, I asked for a scholarship to go and study for my membership, he also wrote to me saying when I finished the membership, I would get an invitation to Harvard.

The mission's report was written, and it was this report which recommended the formation of the Nutrition Board or Nutrition Council as an intersectoral organization, having the ministries of Health, Agriculture, Education and Information

as the major line agencies and other ministries and NGOs as members. The Board had not been formed when I left for my further studies.

The report also made recommendations for the establishment of a meat packing plant in the north as well as the development of horticulture and a vegetable processing plant. This latter was the basis for the tomato processing plant in the North. The reason for suggesting the meat packing and corned beef manufacturing plant was the finding that by the time cattle had been walked down to the slaughterhouses of Kumasi and Accra, they had lost a lot of weight. The owners or the sellers of the cattle, we surmised, were definitely losing by driving them 'on the hoof' rather than transporting them dead and packaged.

Both of these recommendations were implemented in the establishment of the Volta Meat Packaging Plant in northern Ghana and the Tomato Factory. Some people of my age or younger would remember that for several years Ghana produced probably the best corned beef in Africa, Volta Corned Beef. This was simply because the Volta Corned Beef was being manufactured from really good beef rather than using a lot of gristle and fat as some of the imported corned beefs did. It is a great shame that this particular factory was left to rot after the end of the Nkrumah regime.

I later found out that the meat factory was actually losing money. After independence Ghana's borders were no longer as open to our northern neighbours as previously. The seasonal movement of cattle from outside Ghana had to stop or be quite severely restricted. Prices changed and the factory could not survive. In addition to the political change it became obvious to me later that our recommendation had been incomplete. We should have taken more note of activities further downstream such as handling of offal and skins for leather that could have supported the cannery.

Edinburgh – my first Mercedes-Benz

By the end of 1958, I had been awarded a nine-month scholarship to go to Edinburgh and study for my membership of the Royal College of Physicians. The passing of a membership examination signified that one was on the road to becoming a specialist or a consultant physician. I took my wife and my then three children with me – Obodai our son had been born in September 1958. As I had received a loan to buy a car, soon after we reached the UK I went to Germany and took delivery of my first Mercedes Benz. I bought it, not because of its reputation as a luxury car but for its durability in our terrain and for the excellent after sales service provided by its agents, R. T. Briscoe.

I drove this car through Europe to Dover where I had to answer a lot of questions from both immigration and customs authorities – my work, how I managed to get the money, what else was I carrying in the car, and so on. When I said nothing, the customs officers were really surprised, because they could not imagine a young man having the wherewithal to buy a Mercedes in Europe and then declare that he bought nothing other thant the car. At this time I was not to know that Mercedes were seen un the UK as cars for the very well-off or those who were involved in some very unsavoury activities. So it was that my car was searched thoroughly. When finally they asked me how I could afford such a car and I told them that it really belonged to my government as I had got a loan as a government officer, and was going to use it on government service they relaxed and I was finally allowed to go.

In Edinburgh, too, we were treated as really special because of the car and the fact that an African like me could afford to be the the UK with a wife and three children. We settled ourselves in a nice flat and I registered for the three-month course at the Royal College of Physicians. The examination for the membership came on and fortunately for me, I passed easily. As soon as this was communicated with the Ministry, there was a clamour for me to return and join the workforce. This was something I understood, because suddenly, with independence and the opening of the health service to everybody, there was increasing pressure on the service.

5 harvard and the united states

Fortunately for me though it turned out that Professor Mayer's efforts had yielded fruit. WHO had agreed to give me a fellowship to do a Master's degree at the Harvard School of Public Health. So, after a short break in the UK, my wife, the children and I took a flight from London to New York and then from New York to Boston. When we arrived, Professor Jean Mayer was at the airport to welcome us and he made us feel very good indeed. We were put in an hotel in Huntington Avenue, which was just opposite the School of Public Health.

Finding accommodation

The next day, a representative of the Society of the Wives of the School of Public Health professors and senior staff had a representative came to see that we were comfortable in our hotel and to ask what we would like by way of permanent accommodation. She promised that getting something for us in the area should not be difficult as they had a list of very cooperative property owners who were happy to take in students and their families. It was obvious that these very good ladies were oblivious to two facts which were significant at the time. Firstly, we were black and then we had not one, not two but three young children.

For a fortnight, these ladies tried very hard to get us somewhere to live. They would get a promise that some suitable accommodation with at least two bedrooms had become available. When we went, we were greeted usually with the statement, "Oh, but you didn't come early. It was taken yesterday". This went on for a full two weeks, during which they, and we, were getting rather upset as it had dawned on everyone that the colour issue was involved and where it was not colour, an antipathy to small children was at play.

There was a black Baptist Church in Western Avenue, Cambridge and soon the members heard of our plight. So they sent some of their elders to see whether we would like to live in their community, staying in their pastor's house as he was having a

sabbatical and the house was completely empty. Of course, when the Harvard professorial wives, all of whom were whites, heard about this they felt quite aggrieved and redoubled their efforts to get us a house. Of course, my friend Jean Mayer felt particularly completely cut out, because he knew the level at which we were living at home as a medical officer, or university lecturer, in a government bungalow and the friendliness and openness that we had in our community. This was late 1959 in the United States of America and colour was a major national issue.

In fact in the same Western Avenue from which the black Baptist Church members had come to offer us their pastor's house, there was another Baptist Church, but that was for white Baptists. Of course the Harvard wives felt they could not let us stay in the black community, but we had been so upset by the to-ing-and-fro-ing in search of a house that we readily agreed to go and stay there. On examination we could not have made a better choice. The detached house had seven rooms in all – four bedrooms upstairs and three rooms downstairs in addition to a kitchen and the other necessaries. We moved in very quickly and I must confess that assistance of the level we received after moving in had never been showered on me before or since.

The Harvard wives collected bed sheets, crockery, pots and pans – everything that was to be needed to make us set up home and settle in. They found it quite upsetting, though, to see us surrounded by the black community, but we found it wonderful because the church groups saw to it that they looked after the house precisely as they would have had their pastor been living there; so we had very little hard work to do on the property. In fact when, soon after we moved in, the snow started to fall, it was the church group who came to dig us out of the snow. There was absolutely no question that we had made the right choice.

Unfortunately, the relationship with the church members, although it was quite nice on the surface, became a little difficult at some point, although we managed to survive the difficulties and continued with good personal relations. They were surprised at the number of our visitors who were white. They were also surprised that my wife insisted on putting on the African attire to the extent that some of them queried whether she wanted not to be identified with them by putting on the "African fancy clothes" – we let this pass. All in all, we had a most enjoyable life among the communities there.

We had arrived in Boston in late August and finally got settled after school had really started in the first week of September, right after Labour Day. The class was rather

large, composed not only of doctors but also of nurses, epidemiologists and even people who had first degrees in the biological sciences. There were also one or two economists. It turned out that whilst those with medical degrees completed the course in one year, the majority of the others were to take more than a year. Thus those of us with a medical degree, plus holdovers from the previous year, constituted the Class of 1960.

Fall in New England

As we had arrived towards the end of summer, the first noticeable change was fall, as the Americans call it or autumn as it is called in Britain. The changes in the leaves were spectacular, more than anything that I had ever seen in the United Kingdom during my seven years there: they have to be seen to be believed. Leaves of all shades of brown, gold and red, giving a panorama which was just breath-taking. Towards the middle of October, we had a pleasant trip to other parts of New England to see this but I had to do the trip again to be finally satisfied that I had seen as much as I could.

Unfortunately, winter came quite early to Massachusetts that year and sometime in mid-November, practically unannounced, we had our first severe snowstorm. As bad luck would have it, this snow started about 4 p.m. just as we had finished classes. As we were living in Cambridge, Massachusetts, but had to attend classes in Boston, it was quite a trip and we really had our first experience of driving in the snow. The snow came on a Friday so we had Saturday indoors and then tried to go to church on Sunday. On Monday morning the church members came with their equipment and dug us out of the snow which had settled around the house. It was, however, very fascinating for the children to see this great sheet of white lying all round the house and they had quite a ball.

Classes had started in earnest and the first thing I noticed was that the relationship between staff and student was quite different from Britain. It was more relaxed and more collegial, despite the fact that I had also been in a post-graduate school both in London and in Edinburgh. First names were used very, very freely and some of the staff would ask students who had particular expertise to give seminars or lead workshops on various topics..

The major core courses were epidemiology and biostatistics taught by Prof. Brian McMahon and Dr. Hugo Muench. Both McMahon and Muench were excellent teachers and I enjoyed their classes immensely. Several of my classmates who found biostatistics particularly difficult, joined me to study the week's course in biostatistics again, in my home, over the weekend.

Of course, my special interest was nutrition and the chairman of department at the time was Professor Fred Stare with whom I got on extremely well. His home was also open to us as was the home of the Mayers. A surprising but pleasant occurrence that we joked about was the fact that after an eight year gap the Mayers had had another baby less than a year after Jean's visit to Ghana. Needless to say, I did well in nutrition too. The most exciting area was tropical medicine under Professor Tom Weller who had by then won the Nobel Prize and was extremely well-known. Initially our relationship was rather cool for reasons I did not understand as I enjoyed the tropical medicine lectures and whenever he gave the class test, which he did frequently, I came top. So I was not sure why the relationship between us was cool.

One day, he had quite a chat with me and I was amazed and amused at the same time. He asked how, from what he could see, I never took any notes whilst he was lecturing and yet, whenever he set a test I came on top. I told him that I had learnt quite early on in my student days that it was much better for me to listen to the lecture, only noting reminder words, and then make my notes later after I had absorbed the lecture fully. That seemed to satisfy him because the next time we had a chat, it was about my English and how it was that a person from the colonies spoke such good English. In fact, his knowledge of British colonial rule was relatively limited; he thought the British did not give us the freedom to be as well educated as they themselves were. He was disabused of this and we became very firm friends, I can say, from then on.

Of course, as student life would demand, I had some especially close friends from the group. The top were Charlotte and Al Neumann. Al had a medical degree and masters in economics too of which he made great play. Charlotte, his wife, is a very bright woman. They had two children at the time and we had three children. They also lived in Cambridge as did another member of our group, Dirk Spruyt and his wife. This group met periodically to study epidemiology and biostatistics in particular. The friendship continued right through the year of the course and well beyond. And we would come across the Neumanns again during my work in the Medical School in Accra.

Throughout my stay at the School of Public Health, there were occasional references to the accommodation problems we had had. These were quite apologetic and the staff wives, as well as the members of staff, tried to find ways and means of preventing such a situation arising again. I learnt before leaving that plans for building an international house for the accommodation of students in my kind of situation were well advanced, so that the embarrassment would not happen again. I learnt after

leaving the school, that in the following year, the International House was completed and others who followed me, including my good friend, Prof. Ofosu-Amaah, attested to the usefulness of the facility.

Hotel problems

The year ended in May and we decided that we would try and have a trip across the United States of America, so we would see something of this huge country before returning home. Of course, back then, neither my wife nor I had any inkling that we would be in and out of the United States for practically the rest of our lives, or that at some stage in our lives, we might go and live there again. We believed we had had a once in a lifetime opportunity.

So we asked our friends the Neumans how we should set about it. This pleased them greatly because they had two cars with them in Boston and they wanted to go to San Francisco with both cars. It was agreed that Florence and I would drive one car and they would drive the other and the whole trip was to take something like ten days so we could give ourselves a chance of seeing the country. We chose the northern route and stayed as close to one another as possible. We set out and for the first few days of the trip there were absolutely no problems. In several of the northern states we enjoyed the overnight stops, at some points staying in the same hotel together. But as we progressed, however, problems arose.

The area outside of Chicago, Evanston, was one such problem spot. We drove for miles trying to get accommodation. We kept on being turned away without understanding why. It later was explained to us that the area in which we were was one of those where residents would rather not have black people in their hotels.

Another area where the problem stood out was in Utah where we tried to go into a motor restaurant to eat. My wife and I were ahead of the Neumans so we went in and asked for seats. The person allocating seats looked at us and said, "You mean, to take out?" We said "No, we want to sit down and eat". He repeated "You mean, to take out?" and this was repeated the third time. Then I came to my senses, pointed to my arm and said "You mean the 'tar brush" is not allowed inside but can eat your food?" We were about to leave the restaurant when our friends came in and we told them what was happening. They turned round, looked at the man we had been speaking to and said, "You are not going to have our custom either", and the four of us drove off to find food somewhere else. Of course, you can imagine what I have felt

about Utah and the Mormons ever since. The episode rankled so much that a few years ago when some Mormons came to try and talk with me about religion I turned them off my property quite rudely. Of course, in the US at this time irritating episodes of discrimination did happen in spite of the movements against racial segregation having started in earnest. But as none of this had existed overtly for us in Britain, I kept on forgetting where I was.

Wisconsin and Wyoming

After Evanston, Illinois, we arrived very tired in Wisconsin, at the home of Mrs. Neumann Senior, Al's mother. It was quite an interesting house and it was the very first time I saw an automatic gate responding to a long distance signal from a radio wave. We thought we were seeing magic at the time. It was in Wisconsin also that we visited a small lakeside retreat of the Neumans. It was very serene but what amazed us was the sizes of the armies of mosquitoes that greeted us. In almost a year spent in the US we had seen nothing like that and we might have returned home thinking the US somehow had very few mosquitoes. It was good though that unlike our mosquitoes in Ghana these ones carried no malaria.

The trip went on and we arrived one day in the state of Wyoming. Two things stand out from this visit. One was the never-to-be-forgotten visit to the Yellowstone National Park and the Grand Tetons. The Yellowstone National Park, a very well organized reserve of trees and animals and the most marvellous geyser that I had ever seen which I learnt was called Old Faithful.

On the day we visited, the whole park was wrapped in sunshine and it was extremely warm. We went up into the Grand Tetons, climbing up into the hills to celebrate my birthday which was on 23rd June. We had hardly started our picnic when it started to snow – dry snow which did not last for long . I was certainly amazed, as was my wife, to have snow in midsummer in any part of the world. Little did I know that my own mountains in Africa, Kilimanjaro and Mount Kenya, could be wrapped in snow all the year round. This was not wrapped in snow, which was quite surprising, because it was quite green when we went there.

In the evening we went into town to have a steak. We ordered T-bones and the portions arrived. They were much larger than any that I had ever seen, even at celebrations in either London or Accra. Neither Florence nor I could eat more than a third of our portions, so there we were, wondering what to do, thinking how we would

need some food as we continued our travels the next day. We called for some paper napkins and started wrapping what we could not eat. The waiter saw what we were doing and came over, asking, "Do you need doggy bags"? "Yes please", we said, rather sheepishly. We never knew that you could ask for a bag and take food home from a restaurant. So we took the meat home, kept it in a fridge and used it for sandwiches, enough for the whole of the next day.

San Francisco

We continued with our trip and finally arrived in the beautiful city of San Francisco. I fell in love with San Francisco. Its hills and buildings were really impressive, so were its trams which were everywhere. Truly, until I visited Cape Town recently, San Francisco was the city I would most love to live in if I were to leave Ghana. What made our stay even more attractive was the fact that the home that we were given for our stay in Palo Alto, belonged to Charlotte Neumann's brother, who was away. It had a very nice orchard with apricots, green pears and peaches - all in all we had a wonderful time there.

6 guatemala and korle bu

My fellowship included a travel allowance for a visit to an institution, which could give me insights into the practical problems of nutrition. Before leaving for the trip to San Francisco, it had been decided that I would undertake a six-week travel fellowship to the Institute of Nutrition of Central America and Panama (INCAP), in Guatemala City. So early in July, my wife and I separated, she to Ghana, to join our children whom we had sent home by Pan American Airways prior to our undertaking the trip across America, and I to Guatemala.

Sending unaccompanied minors home in those days was quite a palaver. The children were seven, five, and two years old so we had to pay the fares for all three plus an adult fare for a caretaker to be supplied by the airline. All went well and the children got home into the care of extended family relations, Mr. and Mrs. Cronjie. Mr. Cronjie was then the head of the West African Examinations Council.

Guatemala

The trip was fine and I was very well received by the staff in Guatemala. Moise Behar, who had been a classmate of mine during the MPH course in Harvard, met me at the airport and saw to it that I had a comfortable accommodation. INCAP at the time had some very well-known nutritionists; the best known perhaps, was Professor Nevin Scrimshaw, who became a close friend and remains a friend till today. Approaching 90, he is still travelling the world and working to improve the nutritional status of the less developed nations.

Drs. Bressani and Aroyave were big movers in my areas of interest, which were protein-energy malnutrition or kwashiorkor and allied nutrition problems of infants and young children. At this time, INCAP was developing a weaning food for children with this type of malnutrition. They had concentrated on oil seeds and cereals. The oil seed they were working on was cotton seed oil, which, because of its high content of gossypol, turned out not to be as good as could be expected. For a time the product was made up of cotton

seed oil, mixed with maize and sorghum, plus some yeast and vitamin A. This product was found to be good for treatment. It was cheap and could be distributed widely; so it was the major product for treatment and prevention of protein-calorie malnutrition for a period – other oil seeds were tested and finally a soy-base mix became the major product. The life was fun and I had a lot of opportunity to visit the country and its ancient ruins.

Alas, although I had been given six weeks to stay on the visit, by the end of the third week, I had a note from Ghana saying that I was required to come back home as soon as possible and join a group that was going to the Congo. At this time, the Government of Ghana had decided to send a contingent to the Congo, which was in flames. Civil war, stoked by all kinds of foreign interests, was raging, as well as the political infighting between Lumumba and Kasavubu.

I quickly went back to Boston through New Orleans to pack my things. It was in New Orleans, again, that I came face to face once more with the unfortunate black-white problems of the US at that time. I had to change planes in New Orleans Airport and as it was a long wait, I had been given coupons for a meal. I went into the airport restaurant only to be told that I could not eat there. I had to go outside and be given my food. The result was, I went out of the airport and instead of eating took a bus ride through New Orleans to see what the town was like. I joined the plane, got to Boston and then, after a couple of days or so, I packed my things and returned to Ghana, only to find my services were not needed in the Congo after all.

Medical officer in charge of human nutrition

Back home again to work in Korle Bu, I was given one of the new bungalows close to the Nurses Training College. It was not a particularly good one but it had enough accommodation for my family, so I accepted it. This time, my position was Medical Officer in charge of Human Nutrition. I had offices in the Medical Research Institute as it was then called, now the Department of Pathology. My staff consisted of Mrs. Elsie Sowah, who was married to one of our judges. Prior to my coming, Dr. Susan Ofori-Atta had been handling nutrition and she was the head of the newly-formed Nutrition Council. The Council had been formed as a result of the recommendations made by Platt and Mayer.

I took the nutrition work seriously, trying to form a group and also to find out, first-hand, what the nutrition problems of the country were. This involved visiting schools, trying to measure the heights and weights of some of the younger children and comparing them with international standards, as well as finding out birth weights

of children born in the maternity hospital and relating them to international standards. I was fortunate, in another year or so, to be joined by Dr. E. A. Asiedu, who also was interested in nutrition. The two of us really formed the nucleus, since Mrs. Sowah had left about a year after I arrived.

We had technical assistance in the person of Ms. Pauline Whitby, a hard working woman, who was mostly interested in secondary desk research, which she did extremely well. She gave us very good insights into the situation of Ghana as it was known up to that point. I also took the opportunity to travel all around the country and see for myself what the situation was. Of course I had been around with Dr. Mayer earlier; but I had learned a lot in the interim so my eyes were more open. It was during these trips that I came to confirm the very high prevalence of thyroid goitre in parts of the north and some of the more hilly parts of Ashanti Mampong. I made recommendations that we should start on iodine supplementation, if at all possible, but nothing came of this.

Nutrition Board under Ministry of Food and Agriculture

After the formation of the Food and Nutrition Board in 1959 it was decided that for a properly grounded nutrition policy and programmes a national survey was needed. The Board recruited Dr. Peter Davey to assist with the task. The lead team for the survey after my arrival was Davey, Whitby and me. The survey reports were published in 1962 and formed the basis of nutrition thinking in the country for a long time.

In a Cabinet discussion of where the subject of nutrition should fit in government, it was decided that the Nutrition Board should be placed under the Ministry of Food and Agriculture, although the Ministry of Health could continue to have its own Nutrition Unit or Division, too. So it was that as Secretary to the Nutrition Board, I was answerable then to Mr. Kojo Botsio, Minister of Food and Agriculture, whilst as Head of Medical Nutrition I was responsible to the Ministry of Health. It was an interesting position, which in my view, could have advanced the subject of nutrition as a practical issue very far in the country; but this was not to last.

Somehow, Cabinet made other decisions and instead of the Board being under Mr. Kojo Botsio, it was decided that a minister who had been moved from another ministry was to be the Head of the Nutrition Board. This gentleman took it upon himself to be not only minister and chairman but also the chief executive of the Board. He had a friend, a lawyer from London, come to be his main adviser and between them, they took on the job of not only recruiting quite a few young women who had done

catering, dietetics or any other remotely related subject onto the board staff, but also ostensibly to help them acquire cars. Several of these women were therefore made to buy Volvo cars with government loans. Unknown to me, these cars, new to Ghana, had been sold on some concessionary basis and the discounts had been pocketed by my then minister and his lawyer adviser. Of course, when Nkrumah heard of this, he was furious and the minister was given his marching orders in no time at all.

Physician Specialist, Human Nutrition

Whilst the nutrition education work went on, I had by this time been appointed Physician Specialist, Human Nutrition and had been given permission to supervise the nutrition work going on in the Princess Marie Louise Hospital. This is the hospital from which kwashiorkor was described by Cecily Williams in the 1930s. It gave me very good insights, not only into the disease syndrome of protein energy malnutrition, but also into its social and cultural backgrounds and also afforded me the opportunity of trying to see how women could be made to help other women and to look after their children.

By this time, I had arranged for the employment of Miss Victoria Bright Davies, who later became Mrs. Victoria Adomako, as my Dietician Assistant. She was responsible for helping the women to prepare the food that was to be given to their children and to see that they gave it to them properly. She also developed a small vegetable garden in the hospital compound, and this was used to teach the women about the use of green, leafy vegetables of various kinds and how important these were in the cure of their children. She also helped in raising funds from commercial firms and well to do individuals so we could provide small amounts of money to women who really needed financial help

But above everything else, the one innovation that she and I brought into the hospital, of which I am very proud even today, was getting the women organized into groups so that they could do a rotation. Some women would go and continue with their commercial activities, others would remain particularly on the market on a given day, whilst a third group would remain and look after all the children. So on any given day a third of the mothers of the malnourished children would be feeding and handling all the patients, with supervision from nurses and the dietician, while the others were pursuing economic activities. Much to my surprise the women agreed to this quite quickly because it helped them.

Those women who had nothing at all were given portions of oil and various articles, that we were being given by United States Agency for International Development (USAID) and the Catholic Relief Services (CRS), to sell and out of the profits to try and make their own mirco-enterprises grow. The women were most enthusiastic about all these things. Unfortunately there was no expansion of this from the hospital into the community and as soon as I left even the hospital gave it up.

Kwashiorkor

In the clinical sphere, it was at this time that I learnt how closely much of the malnutrition of children was related to closely-spaced births. As written elsewhere, by Konotey Ahulu first, and then by myself, because I did not write what I had been talking about for a very long time, the name kwashiorkor was almost certainly derived from the names of the Ga people.

Kor or *korkor* is found either as a prefix or suffix in practically all Ga-Dangme family names for second born females. The expression *kwashiorkor* therefore suggested to me that the child was being deposed from the breast as another was coming. So closely did my people believe in this idea, that when a woman with a clearly malnourished child was given the diagnosis some of them would say, "Oh, but doctor, I am not pregnant" implying that in Ga understanding the kwashiorkor syndrome should only follow a pregnancy, which was not the case at all. The truth was that fully one third of the cases that we were seeing at Princess Marie Louise Hospital had mothers who were either pregnant or were carrying another child less than two years older than the index child.

It was from my observation of the close links between kwashiorkor and child bearing that I started to help my patients' mothers accept some family planning. At this time, President Nkrumah had declared that no family planning equipment should be brought into the country. I was able, however, to get some rings and diaphragms and to know where diaphragms could be obtained. So I started a kind of clandestine clinic, helping women to space their pregnancies. Since the husbands did not come to the clinic even to see their sick children, and there were no important female methods available in Ghana at the time, the only methods I advised were the diaphragm or foaming tablets – at that time, I think the only major tablet was *Gynomin* which has quite a smell. In any case, it was from this small beginning that I developed my major interest in family planning, population and reproductive health.

Assistant at the Ministry of Health

Sometime in 1961, Dr. Charles Easmon, as he then was, called at my house with his wife. It was most unlike him to visit without a previous invitation or announcement so I was quite surprised. He had a story. He had been invited by President Nkrumah, to take on the post of Head of the Ministry of Health and he had been given the authority to bring anyone he wanted into the Ministry. He had given thought to this assignment and he felt that I was the only one that he wanted to assist him in this endeavour.

I was dumbfounded, because at that time, I had not considered myself either as going into administration or senior enough to take on the responsibility of trying to work at this level. I knew my country well and I knew that in the civil service generally and in the medical profession, seniority, meaning the number of years of service, was more important than ability, and certainly more than documented qualifications, when it came to promotion. What was being considered now was going to be a complete departure for me. I asked for time to think about it and later events taught me that perhaps, at that time, I should have said no. But maybe, agreeing to go to the Ministry also did contribute to my rapid development in other fields – it certainly contributed to my being noticed internationally and opened up links with the WHO and African ministries and ministers of health.

After a few days, I called Dr. Easmon and told him that I could not refuse his offer and I hoped that I would be able to give him the kind of service he wanted. I moved to the Ministry of Health and was asked to look after the nursing section, the posting of doctors and all training programmes supported by the Ministry of Health, both within country and externally.

I had not been there long before various situations arose that indicated how careful I needed to be particularly with my seniors not only in age but in length of service. The reason I mention aged seniors is that doctors in the Ministry of Health administration were mainly holders of the UK Diplomas in Public Health. Apart from Dr. Eustace Akwei, who after heading the ministry worked for WHO and later returned as health commissioner, none had selected Public Health as their first option for specialization. It was when they could not, for some reason, take up their chosen speciality that they had gone into public health. To me, the strangest thing in this service was that the people who could not attain the clinical speciality of their choice, managed to do the public health diploma, which they did not necessarily want to do; and then the public health diploma assured them of a career in the ministry and various regions. Fortunately the current situation whereby the Director

General of Health Services is a presidential appointment heralds a more sensible approach to the headship of such a technical institution. I am not sure the maintenance of a separate set of medical advisers inside the Ministry should be continued. To me the Director General of the Ghana Health Services should *ipso facto* be the chief adviser to the Minister.

I am afraid the older or more senior doctors felt affronted by my appointment. Some of them felt their pathway to glory, being Assistant Directors or even Chief of the Ministry, was being thwarted. There was a lot of background noise and underhand dealings that I chose to ignore. In one instance, simply because I was accompanying the Chief, Dr. Easmon, on a visit to a region, the Regional Medical Officer refused to meet us at the airport as convention demanded. Of course, I was angry enough to write to him about it and he did not speak to me for many years. Nevertheless I enjoyed the work and I threw myself into it enthusiastically.

I was bolstered in my determination to stay on by what I had learnt of the US administration. The technical headships of the major ministries were political appointments. They came and went with their appointing presidents or secretaries, as the US describes its ministers.

In the nursing field, I worked very closely with Miss Docia Kisseih, then the Chief Nursing Officer, who was a most active and thoughtful individual. She was full of plans for changing the face of nursing in Ghana and one of her plans was to see to it that nursing education was also raised to a degree standard. It was during her term that we succeeded in getting nursing accepted in the University of Ghana as a university programme. I helped her also to get the level of the head of the nursing service raised to the same level as that of the pharmacy service. It was not a thing which endeared me to the pharmacy chief; other department heads were also quite antagonistic to my arrival in the Ministry of Health. Many though changed their minds after working with me for a few months. Whilst some of the technical staff were not happy with my presence, the managerial and administrative staff were. They found in me someone ready to learn and understand their difficulties and hopes and to lead them in arguing their positions with other ministries and departments. I learnt much about human resource management and the national budgeting process during this short period.

President Nkrumah's prestige and influence led to our having a lot of technical assistance – for example Israel provided a team of physicians led by Dr. Brachott who was at the time the number two in the Israeli Ministry of Health. He was to assist with forward planning.

Brachott Report.

Dr. D. Brachott was appointed by President Nkrumah directly and charged to produce a ten year health development plan. He consulted widely and had the support of the whole Ministry of Health. He mentioned in his acknowledgement Dr. Easmon, me and Ms. Docia Kisseih. The report though brief, made some very far reaching recommendations. He stated: "this 10 year programme will not deal with all aspects of the health service nor with many existing health problems but it will direct attention to three main aspects of a health service. These are:

1 an efficient rural health service, with full integration of the hospitals, health centres and other medical units;

2 a country-wide hospital plan based on the health needs of the population and having regard to sound medical and economic considerations;

3 a training programme for medical and para-medical personnel to permit the effective implementation of the 10 year development plan."

He went on to point out why there was such an urgent need for an accelerated development plan for health and identified three issues which could easily apply to today. These were

1 rapid growth of the population;

2 progressive urbanization, particularly in the major towns of Accra, Kumasi, Tamale, Sekondi-Takoradi and Cape Coast;

3 growing awareness and demand for modern health services.

Some areas for emphasis which he mentioned are still challenging the country. These include environmental sanitation, child and maternal welfare, food and nutrition, control of endemic diseases and health education. The plan also called for the rapid implementation of proposals for new hospitals and the renovation of old ones, the development of both urban and rural health centres, and the distribution of all these to respond to the development of the health area concept on which we were working. It also endorsed and called for an acceleration of the establishment of the medical school, and the National Institute for Health Research, as components of a health tripos with the National Health Service.

Needless to say these were exactly the views of the top management of the

Ministry of Health, as proposed by Dr. Easmon and me, and so implementation was planned in earnest. Health areas were demarcated to replace the old concept of districts. The NGO run hospitals, especially the church-related ones, were included in the demarcation to minimise mal-distribution of hospital services. The renovation of Korle Bu, including new surgical medical and paediatric blocks, was started in earnest. The medical school programme and the establishment of the National Institute of Health were on course.

The report's emphasis on food and nutrition, water supplies and sewage disposal still remain challenges today. Even though an Israeli firm constructed some underground sewers for parts of Accra there is no evidence that these are functioning.

A truism which Brachott states has to be repeated for all interested in health in the developing countries today. "It must be stressed repeatedly that the long term health programme cannot be adequately fulfilled unless it is an integral part of an overall master plan for economic and social development of Ghana."

In this regard, too, I must state that Ghana, under President Nkrumah, tried hard to make such integration a reality. I was a member of the committee appointed by the President to develop a seven year development plan for Ghana for1963 to 1970 but its implementation was curtailed by the overthrow of Nkrumah in 1966.

I firmly believe that the Brachott report, produced by a man who sought what the people themselves wanted and needed and tried to support the directions of their health leaders, remains a good example of technical assistance and needs studying by our students.

One of the Israeli physicians with whom I developed a firm relationship was Dr. Daniel Katsnelson, a paediatrician from Tel Aviv University. He was a great teacher and nice human being, ready to answer a call to help. In one case I called him to help with a child who was having fits brought on by post-vaccination encephalitis. Though he was himself ill, he came out with me and attended to the child. He was great fun and full of stories and jokes, largely at the expense of himself or Jews and Israelis in general.

One of his jokes or funny stories which I remember is "how much is that fish over there?" The circumstances in which he told the joke were interesting. My wife and I were hosting some of the staff at our regular New Year's Eve party. Because of the presence of several of the Israeli physicians at the party we had taken the trouble to provide some very large baked grouper fish. We also had the usual barbecued pig

turning on the roasting pit. My friend Katsnelson and another Israeli went towards the roast when invited to serve themselves, so I gently went and told them that was pork and there was much fish available. He stopped me and then said: "Let me tell you a story. A Jew went to a butcher's shop, claiming he was going to buy fish. He saw a beautiful leg of pork on the shelf and asked: 'How much is that fish over there?' The butcher was perplexed and said, 'Fish? There is no fish.' The Jew repeated the question twice more pointing to the leg of pork. Then the butcher said 'That's no fish that's pork.' The Jew shook his head and said, 'Who asked you?'" This story was his introduction to educating me on the differences between an Israeli, a Jew and an orthodox Jew. As part of this technical exchange I visited Israel a couple of times and expanded both my medical and general education greatly.

Negotiations to establish a Medical School

Much has been written about the medical school (see particularly S. K. Addae) so I will only go into a few points. At one point the British government had agreed to help Ghana develop a medical school. Arrangements had reached the point at which a dean designate had been appointed. This dean designate, Prof. Norman from Sudan, arrived in Accra one day to learn that the Ghana Government had entered into other negotiations with the US for assistance. I believe the determinant factor in changing horses so suddenly was financial – the US had promised funding for facilities which the British had not. Poor Prof. Norman went back to the Sudan on the same plane.

The American Government had agreed to help Ghana establish a medical school. A group from Philadelphia, consisting of representatives of seven of their universities which had formed a consortium entered into serious negotiations with us. Plans were made to build a medical school facility and a teaching hospital on the University of Ghana Legon campus. Unfortunately for all of us, at this time also, Dr. Nkrumah had received as exiles from South Africa, Dr. Joseph Gillman and his partner, Dr. Christine Gilbert. These were both very bright individuals and Gillman had arrived with his laboratory animals: mainly baboons and monkeys of various kinds for his own experiments. It turned out that Gillman was to have a very direct line to our President, a line which I certainly did not have, and Easmon had only occasionally.

Whilst we were negotiating, Gillman and others, I learnt, convinced the President that the Americans were going to bring in CIA agents and that they were not to be trusted. The official reason given for the breakdown was that the Americans

were asking for diplomatic privileges for the expatriate teaching staff which the Government could not grant. Since such privileges were being enjoyed by the research staff at the National Institute of Health and Medical Research I found the reason difficult to accept.

But before the negotiations broke down irretrievably, we had several visits from the consortium's leadership. A potential Dean, Dr. Richard Cross, had been nominated and I, as secretary to the committee, charged with making arrangements for the implementation of the programme, was secretary to the group that was to interview many of my colleagues for scholarships overseas for positions in the medical school. However, Dean Cross was busy recruiting core American staff for the school

It had been agreed that since we had not specifically dealt with medical education in any of our previous studies it would be useful if some of the future Ghanaian leadership of the various departments were to undertake courses and understudy programmes in various universities in America noted for their particular excellence in medical education. In addition to this programme, we were to take the opportunity, to recruit younger doctors, who had still to undertake their graduate and post-graduate training. So it was that within a short space of time we managed to send some thirty or so young doctors to undertake various fields of study. As things turned out, with the breakdown in the negotiations with the Americans, it was these doctors who managed to help keep the medical school going when it was finally established by presidential fiat in 1964.

As soon as the negotiations broke down, there was a movement from some of the doctors to get Dr. Easmon and me out of the Ministry of Health. This was successful and in late 1962, the President decided that doctors were needed in the hospital and not as administrators. Dr. Easmon was told he would be Surgeon in Chief in Korle Bu. I was simply to be dropped. I went back to Korle Bu and this time reverted to the position of physician, joining Silas Dodu and others in handling medical cases. Mr. Afla Addo was appointed head of the Ministry of Health with the title of Chief Administrator.

He was a rather opinionated individual. He immediately made it known that he would brook no nonsense from any of the doctors who had been involved in administration, essentially meaning me. He simply could not dare openly antagonise Dr. Easmon who was rightly held in very high national esteem for his pioneering work in surgery and his general charm as a human being. The chief administrator did not fare too well either and he had quite a few problems, finally, landing in jail.

Death of Obetsebi Lamptey

One challenging situation with which I was personally involved during my last weeks in the ministry was the case of Mr. Obetsebi Lamptey. Known affectionately as Tsebi, this political figure had been one of the six Ghanaians goaled by the British as insurgents following the 1948 riots. They had earned the appellation the Big Six and currently feature on all the national paper currency. One Saturday afternoon in November of 1962 I was working in my office when the telephone rang. It was a request from the Medium Security Prison at Nsawam asking that the Ministry of Health sent a doctor to see a political prisoner who was very ill. I asked for the name and was told it was Mr. Obetsebi Lamptey. Because of the name and the circumstances of his detention for subversion I decided to go and see him myself.

What I saw upset me a great deal and gave me many sleepless nights afterwards. When the patient appeared, I saw what must have been a tall well built man now extremely wasted. He was just skin and bones, and he was in chains, like someone from the World War II pictures. His head looked disproportionately big and his eyes were blazing and penetrating. I went through his notes and examined him. He was febrile and sweating profusely. He had a huge lump in his abdomen and very loud pathological chest sounds. He obviously had to be diagnosed further. My immediate impression was that he had an advanced cancer of some sort. But since he was a prisoner I was not prepared to rule out some form of tuberculosis. Furthermore the possibility of a treatable condition would be more likely to help in asking for his transfer to Korle Bu for further investigation and treatment. His one plea to me which was repeated several times, in the Ga language, was "Doctor, please don't let me die in prison".

Upon my return I contacted Mrs. Vardon, the mother of my class mate and friend Mrs. Hilda Ayensu, a dental surgeon. Mrs. Vardon was widely known as one of the women who had influence with Dr. Nkrumah. I asked her to intercede with the President to get the prisoner transferred to Korle Bu for diagnosis and possible treatment, making it clear to the President that Tsebi's death would be assigned to the government if he were to die in prison. The transfer was agreed but on condition that he remained under my care until he died. When he came to Korle Bu I realised that he was still in chains. He had day and night guards and he was not even allowed a toothbrush on the grounds that he might do himself harm with it.

Back to Mrs. Vardon to ask for removal of the chains and permission to use a toothbrush. I maintained that the gentleman had no intention of harming himself and

was incapable of fleeing from the hospital. The diagnosis of cancer of an abdominal organ, possibly the kidney, with widespread metastases was made. The condition was totally incurable and I was simply providing terminal palliative care, waiting for him to die. Everyone in the hospital was informed of his condition and the agreement with the President that he was not to be discharged under any circumstances. I was asked by his wife for his discharge but I told her she was not being fair to me as she knew the conditions under which I was allowed to bring him to Korle Bu. Unfortunately for me I had to go on a consultancy of a week or so after the patient had been in the hospital for about four weeks. When I came back I learnt the patient had been discharged at the request of his family and taken home. He had been immediately re-arrested, had died and been buried. I was devastated.

I was not only sad that he died in prison, but also afraid that I might be accused of breaking an undertaking to the President. Fortunately nothing happened to me because of this. After the 1966 coup the commission looking into the issue of Tsebi's death among other things asked me if it was true that he was killed after his arrest. My response was that it would have been a most unnecessary murder. I said this because the man had more than enough to kill him naturally: even today I am not prepared to accept that he was murdered. The mere trauma of being re-taken from home to the cruelty he had been suffering in prison could have been enough to push him over the edge – he was definitely beyond any curative medical care available at the time, even by the time I got him transferred to Korle Bu. That he was in jail without trial and that his illness had to reach a terminal stage before higher level medical opinion was sought upset me every time I think about it. To me his death, as well as that of my idol, friend and patient, J. B. Danquah, who also died in prison without trial are among the major blots on Nkrumah's regime.

J. B. Danquah

Dr. J. B. Danquah, arguably one of Ghana's finest intellectuals, the doyen of Ghana politics and the man whose research underpinned the acquisition of the name Ghana by the independent Gold Coast, died in prison on 4th February 1965 after his second incarceration without trial. Many who should have attended his funeral were too afraid to do so, but I was able to attend it in Kibi.

As mentioned earlier my first real contact with him was when I invited him to talk to Ghanaian students in London sometime in 1948 or 1949. When I returned

home in 1954 I spent my first Christmas in his home; he graciously asked me to do the honour of carving the turkey. Soon thereafter I had the honour of being one of the doctors looking after him. Obviously I could not ask him to come to the hospital so I mostly saw him in his home. In 1962 my sister in law, Miss Matilda Dzani, now Dr. Mrs. Pappoe, got a USAID fellowship for study in the US and I needed a lawyer to help with the bond documents. I phoned Dr. Danquah for an appointment. He agreed to help but said I was not to come to the office. When I asked him why, he replied, "Doctor, when I need your services where do you give them to me?" I got his drift, kept quiet and we arranged for him to come to my bungalow with his stamp and execute the bond for us. To me that was a wonderful demonstration of humility and the utmost respect for a junior.

Dr. J.B. Danquah was one of twenty scholars Dr. Nkrumah selected to be founding members of the Ghana Academy of Learning and I always find it incredible that Nkrumah could consider that this fine gentleman could pose any terrorist threat or be part of an illegitimate effort to remove him. When I returned from my studies in Harvard in 1960 and in 1961, I was elected to the Academy and on a few occasions I had the privilege of driving Dr. Danquah to Academy meetings. I got to know after his death that in 1952 he had suggested the founding of an academy and had even donated some funds for it.

International delegations

The work in the Ministry of Health had been challenging and had exposed me to organizations, institutions and individuals to whom I would never have been introduced had I not been given that job. It was in this job that I visited Czechoslovakia with Dr. Easmon to negotiate for technical assistance for equipment for our hospitals and other facilities. I also represented Ghana in some international meetings, particularly the World Health Assembly. From all of these, I got close to many in the scientific world or the medical world who turned out to be major leaders in their countries and this gave me a major link to organizations and individuals, which was to prove most helpful to me in later life.

For example, in 1963, I had the opportunity to lead the Ghana delegation to the United Nations Conference on the Application of Science and Technology for the Benefit of the Less Developed Areas. It was quite a large and high-powered delegation with representatives from the Academy and the Council for Scientific and Industrial

Research. The conference had been convened in Geneva to analyse and plan for bridging the gap in the application of science and technology between the advanced countries and less developed ones. We all thought there would be a harmonious debate on what was needed to help bridge the gap but it turned out that ideological positions and divides between the Soviet block and the Western block were paramount. Discussions went on in a way which, at one stage, led some of us to say that it did not matter whether the refrigerator froze in Fahrenheit or Centigrade, as long as it froze the food. I am not really sure that, apart from the recommendation to set up a United Nations Advisory Committee on Science and Technology for Development anything much else happened. But this exposed me to the international politics of the time. Ghana was highly respected and, apart from being one of the few independent countries from Africa being represented, we had the late Professor Frank Torto as an Assistant to the Secretary General, which was a significant position. I became a member of the UN Advisory Committee which was formed after this particular meeting.

I attended a follow-up meeting in 1979 when I was with the United Nations University in Tokyo. The meeting was just as lost as the previous one and I do not think very much came out of it.

A rather sad issue in which I was directly involved as the Assistant DMS was the dismantling of the West African Council for Medical Research (WACMR) part of the West African Research Organization (WARO) set up by the British after World War II. The annual meeting of the Council was taking place in Accra in or around late 1961. As the leader of the Ghana delegation I was in the chair. The technical heads of all the former British colonies of West Africa were present as were representatives from Britain. I recall with fondness the presence of Prof. Brian Maegraith and my friend Dr. Herbert Gilles. I had heard on the grapevine that the President wanted Ghana to withdraw from the group and go it alone but the President had not informed me directly. When the subject of the future of the organization was tabled the first day of the meeting I was surprised and tried to temporize. Next day I was called from the meeting to see the President. No reason was given and my excuse that I was chairing an international meeting on Ghana's behalf was not to be accepted.

So I left the meeting and went to see the President in his office in Flagstaff House. The door opened and I was asked to sit down opposite him across an imposing desk. An Alsatian dog came from behind him and lay down at my feet. There were a few pleasantries as to how the meeting was going. In actual fact the meetings had been going extremely

well apart from the political bombshell from Ghana. When I mentioned this, his mood changed completely. He almost accused me of not being prepared to serve the nation's will. I was meant to lead a discussion which would make it clear that the group was not satisfactory for meeting the needs of West Africa. How could it without including even our immediate neighbours? The non-inclusion of the Francophone Countries in such a grouping was exercising the minds of us doctors, but we did not think breaking up the existing group should be the first approach to solution. Anyway he went on to state clearly that my patriotic duty in the circumstance in which I was operating was to completely support the government's position. He ended by saying that he expected all of us servants of the Republic to be like himself in putting the needs of the Republic first. I found such a statement difficult to understand but I had no opportunity to make a response. The order was now clear. Ghana was to be withdrawn from the group.

When he wished me good luck and I got up to leave I was confused both physically and mentally. Physically, because when I got up to leave I saw no obvious exit. All the walls seemed to be covered with books except the door behind him. He smiled at me pressed a button and one of the bookcases opened. I was mentally confused because he had obviously been informed of my temporising about Ghana's withdrawal, perhaps even with exaggerations. The only one who could have done such a thing was Joe Gillman, who simply could not stand my principled opposition to his various efforts to be the chief director of Ghana's health development.

Physician, Korle Bu Hospital

After my being unceremoniously moved from the administration I went back to Korle Bu as a full-time physician. As a matter of fact I had never truly left as I worked there part time during my period at the ministry headquarters. I now really came to terms with what were the major medical problems of the time. I found that we still had a major issue with fevers while tetanus was a challenging problem – for some reason, tetanus neonatorum, tetanus post-abortal and tetanus from all kinds of wounds. It was amazing. There was no real treatment and because of the few anaesthetists that we had at the time using anaesthesia to calm patients' convulsions was not an option and I was handling the majority of these cases with heavy sedation. Combinations of barbiturates and *Largactil* were the chief approaches then available to me.

I was also particularly interested in fevers of unknown origin and was struck by the number of young women who would arrive with fevers of unknown origin. On

close questioning, quite a few of these fevers turned out to follow two or so weeks after interference with a pregnancy or believed pregnancy. In a couple of cases, which are written large in my mind, these young women died. One of them had abscesses in her liver and in other parts of her body; another disclosed a couple of abscesses in the brain after death and post-mortem. These, plus previous experiences as I have mentioned elsewhere on suicides from despair with a pregnancy which the young women could not handle, were among the factors that made me finally decide that the laws on abortion in our countries were working against, rather than for, women.

It wasn't all so harrowing and we had occasional success with tetanus followed by quite happy recognition of God's and our medical inputs. One such led me to find out a little more about traditional healing practices, the charges levied and methods of payment. I looked after a rather handsome twenty-five year old woman with post-abortal tetanus. As the symptoms had started some ten days after the interruption of her pregnancy her prognosis was reasonable although she was very frightened. She made a full recovery and we discharged her. About a month later she appeared in my house early on a Sunday morning with an older male relation. They had brought a piece of imported *kente* cloth, a piece of Ghana print, some yams and some chickens. She had come to thank me for all that had been done for her. She had brought me the *kente* and my wife the Ghana print. Then the male spoke and said that as I had snatched her from the jaws of death she had come to offer herself as a co-wife to my wife and to serve us. Both Florence and I were dumbfounded. As politely as possible we informed them that the offer could not be accepted as we had no intention of adding another wife to the family. I never saw the woman again. But I later learnt that being a sexual partner to the healer in compensation for salvation was quite common. Such partnership extended to being a co-wife. At times another member of the family, usually a younger sister might have to be given. It is not surprising to find many of the more famous herbalists or traditional healers with houses full of wives of various levels.

African Nutrition Adviser for FAO Regional Office, Accra

In less than a year of my going back to clinical practice, I had an invitation from Chief Akin Deko, who was then the FAO Regional Representative for the newly formed Africa Regional Office, to become their first African Nutrition Adviser for the FAO's Regional Office in Accra. I was quite enthusiastic about this but I told him that I did not know whether the government would agree. Chief Deko

apparently saw Dr. Nkrumah who agreed, so I then applied to the Ministry of Health for my release to join the FAO. Unfortunately, by this time the Ministry had been told by the presidency that I wanted to leave the service and that I should be allowed to go but that all my benefits were to be frozen. I was a little upset but I accepted it and joined the FAO in 1963 as the first African Nutrition Adviser to the organization's regional office. I never got any separation or other benefits for my almost ten years of service to my country.

At the FAO, my mission was to get nutrition given priority, both in the rhetoric and in action, by all of the sub-Saharan African countries. I therefore had to travel very widely and discuss taking food and nutrition much more seriously with ministers of health, ministries of agriculture and of social welfare and education. I had to try and learn some French. Unfortunately I did not get on very well, but nevertheless managed to travel throughout Africa and discuss these problems with quite a few countries. I can say that my efforts yielded fruit in several, both Francophone and Anglophone, and we managed to get food and nutrition problems given a little more priority. Nutrition boards or councils were formed in quite a few countries. Nutrition rhetoric was fairly loud in political circles. Unfortunately these are not problems which are subject to one time or simple solutions, so up to today, I cannot say that my work with FAO was successful in terms of significant changes in the nutrition status or the food and nutrition statistics of the region. Yes, it was successful in that the subject of nutrition was talked about more and nutrition education at various levels was given some support, but in terms of whether we managed to affect the nutrition problems of Africa to any great extent, I am not sure.

An area of need that had been recognized and which was pursued vigorously during my tenure was that of education and training of nutritionists. The United Nations International Children's Fund (UNICEF), WHO and FAO were all very concerned and pooled their resources together to start programmes. An interesting one was the joint London-Ibadan Nutrition courses which lasted several weeks. Fellows undertook part of their studies in London and then followed with field studies and seminars in Ibadan. This course helped with the further development of the Ibadan University's Nutrition Department. As part of these developments Platt and others recommended the further development of food science nutrition and biochemistry in the University of Ghana. This beginning was to grow later into the separate departments of biochemistry, food science and nutrition and home economics.

The Danfa Project

Although I was enjoying my work as Nutrition Adviser to the FAO Africa Region, I always felt I would prefer working for my country. I had been deeply involved in the establishment of the medical school, so as soon as the Nkrumah Government was overthrown I wrote to express my interest in returning to national service either with the Ministry of Health or with the medical school. A meeting was arranged with General Kotoka, the leader of the group which overthrew Nkrumah, and it was made clear to me that with Dr. Eustace Akwei ready to come back to the Ministry of Health, my best bet would be to join the medical school.

I therefore applied to join the Medical School and resigned my position with FAO. After due formalities, I was appointed Professor and Head of the Department of Preventive and Social Medicine. Three ideas of mine which I wanted instilled into the students were:

1 public health requires a thorough knowledge of the structure and functioning of communities and societies just as clinical medicine requires detailed knowledge of anatomy and physiology of the individual;

2 the community is amenable to research, diagnosis and management just as in the clinical field;

3 the community should be the base for health promotion and disease prevention.

For all these to be attempted, I collaborated very closely with the Department of Sociology and Demography of the University of Ghana, with the Ministry of Health and with the Department of Social Welfare.

Drs. Kpedekpo and Nelson Addo, good demographers, helped with the teaching of elementary demography to medical students. They also helped introduce the students to research of a fairly elementary nature into the community. The first such was to study the number of under-five year old children in households and see how that related to the frequency of childhood febrile illnesses. Other studies followed relating to family size and fertility. But the most lasting innovation was the identification and negotiation of a rural area where students could get both training for rural health work and community health research. After a search I settled on the seven Ga rural villages around Danfa, just below the Aburi hills.

I got the Department of Social Welfare and Community Development to second Mr. Emmanuel Quartey-Papafio to help us; and with my wife and others visited the

seven villages. When we then invited the leadership for discussions on their needs. it turned out that they perceived their needs in the following order:

1 drinking water;
2 a health clinic;
3 a market.

We agreed that my wife would help them negotiate with the Water and Sewage Department for the supply of water while the Department of Social Welfare and Community Development helped with the development of a market. The medical school would help with the clinic provided that they, the villagers, supplied free the land for it and provided community labour for the building. Plans for the clinic were prepared by experts to reflect the fact that the clinic would function as a health centre for the community, a training place for students and a community centre for all of the villages.

The building started enthusiastically with the villagers donating their labour. However as soon as they realised that some of the technical staff from Accra received some payment they started grumbling. It took some time to convince them to continue giving their labour free, but the building was completed and opened with great pomp by the new Prime Minister of Ghana, Prof. Busia, on January 16, 1970. Up till today the community is still using the Health Centre for major social events.

While the building was going on. I was informed by the USAID Director that his government would be prepared to help with some aspects of the medical school's programme if the appropriate project could be developed. I was aware of the status of family planning at the time and the debates going on as to the best way to provide family planning generally and to rural communities in particular. I had to seek the collaboration of an American university to be able to access the USAID support. My first point of call was my old school, Harvard. The School of Public Health authorities, at the time headed by Dean Snyder, were interested in my project and ideas but claimed the School was not involved in this type of activity overseas. Whilst thinking of other possible schools of public health to approach I got a call from USAID to inform me that the University of California Los Angeles (UCLA) School of Public Health was interested in collaborating with us.

I agreed to work with them and negotiations started. It turned out Al Neumann, my old friend and fellow student at Harvard was the chief of mission. This sounded superb to me until well into the negotiations when I realised that the conditions of

their contract made for very unequal partnership. All the finances were to be handled by UCLA. In fact while talking of equality it was clear to all that the Ghana Medical School had to accept a very junior status if it was to get the project done. Al had changed quite a bit and his whole attitude was that of the lender distributing his largesse. An academic arrangement which I found interesting was the dual appointment by which I became a Professor of the UCLA School of Public Health. My staff and the UCLA staff involved in the project also had comparable dual designations.

For purposes of the project my original area had to be expanded to cover a district of some 200 square miles with a population of some 60,000. The goals and objectives of the project were stated as:

a investigating the state of the rural community and the factors associated with effective participation in health programmes;

b undertaking research into the most efficient means of utilising available manpower and other resources in the operation of health-post-centred comprehensive rural health services;

c training doctors, sanitarians, midwives, community health nurses and other health personnel, both separately and in teams, for their role in rural health work;

d providing manpower oriented and equipped to handle the problems of the community.

The most immediate objective of the project, however, was to help settle a controversy in international circles at the time as to the most cost-effective way of providing family planning services. A research proposal was developed dividing the project area into four sub-areas with different levels of services (See Sai and Quartey Papafio, or Danfa Final Report 1979 for a comprehensive description.) I was co-director with Al Neumann till I left in 1972. On my departure the department came under Dr. Julius Amorin who had been my classmate in Achimota and the head of Togo's health services. For some reason unclear to me, Dr. Amorin was not appointed co-director of the Project after me. I learnt some time later that after a disagreement with the Dean, Prof. Dodu, he resigned as head of department in1974. The Dean, who had been acting as the Co-Director of the Danfa Project then appointed Prof. Ofosu-Amaah as Head of Department and Co-Director until the project came to an end in 1979.

Prof Ofosu-Amaah's comment on the influence of Danfa was this: "I think that

before the School of Public Health was established, the Danfa Project was the seminal occurrence in the history of the formation of researchers and specialists in Public Health in Ghana. It made public health intellectually challenging and acceptable among doctors, from a period when Public Health was considered 'inferior'. It also attracted foreign researchers to Ghana and was the source of many publications from Ghana".

The Danfa Project helped train many health professionals at higher levels, mostly at UCLA who returned to the Department of Community Health. Many of these are among the public health leaders of Ghana today. Dr. Peter Lamptey, the internationally acclaimed AIDS expert, is perhaps Danfa's most outstanding product. Dr. Mrs. Pappoe a medical sociologist dealing with gender and sexuality, courageously undertaking research into commercial sex issues, is another. In fact the final project document lists almost twenty such.

A large number of research publications came out of the project and these influenced thinking on public health. Perhaps the most significant are the papers by Prof. Ofosu-Amaah and others which revised the epidemiology of poliomyelitis. These papers were acknowledged by Prof. Sabin of oral polio vaccine fame, and influenced polio immunization as a component of the WHO Expanded Programme on Immunization.

A major finding of the project was that the best uptake of family planning was obtained when comprehensive basic health care services were provided together with a strong family planning information and services, handled both by health service personnel and by specially trained family planning education staff. Uptake was also best if the services were offered within the villages and close to the homes of women. The surprising thing to me is how little use Ghana has made of this information.

The project area is still being used for community studies and training, both by the Medical School and the School of Public Health. The clinic is still functioning both as a health centre and community centre. I must concede that the fact that senior physicians of the medical school continue to use the area for research and training purposes continues to fill me with a great sense of satisfaction.

7 family planning and population

As stated elsewhere, my interest in fertility regulation and management was aroused during my days as a public health and clinical nutritionist in Ghana. I had to look after the malnourished children in the Princess Marie Louise Hospital (PML), as it was then called. The hospital which still exists is the one from which the renowned Dame Cicely Williams described the syndrome kwashiorkor, now termed protein-energy malnutrition, in the early thirties. As Cicely Williams pointed out, even the name that my people had given to the disease had a connotation of second child.

In looking at the histories of the patients with protein-calorie malnutrition at the time, I found that something like one third of them had their mothers either pregnant or they themselves were following within eighteen months or so of another child. The relationship between this condition and too frequent fertility or badly-spaced pregnancies was immediately obvious. The reason was not hard to find because my people believed that each child developed its own breast and breast milk; therefore, as soon as a woman found that she was pregnant, she had to stop breastfeeding the infant who was being deposed. The belief about the disease was that it was a symptom of jealousy: that the infant deposed was jealous of the one coming and that was why it was suffering. So strong was this belief that if the new child arrived and happened to be of the opposite sex, the deposed child was said to have been jealous for no good reason.

Because of this, I decided that I should try and help the mothers of my patients with family planning. I managed to get Ortho Pharmaceuticals to give me a set of measuring rings for the diaphragm which was then one of the most useful methods. With this in my own office, I was able to help a few of the mothers. At this time, our Prime Minister, Dr. Nkrumah, later to become President Nkrumah in 1960, had stated quite openly that the country was not overpopulated and it was not likely to be overpopulated. In fact, his belief was that we needed more human resources for Ghana and therefore, he had banned the importation of the condom and any other contraceptives; so we had to work on fertility regulation issues in strict secrecy.

I had also got a broader view of the situation during my Harvard MPH studies, where population and health planning lectures made it quite clear that population was a very important factor in all the work that I was intending to do. Finally, my nutrition studies themselves in Harvard also emphasized the very close relationship between population and food and nutrition, both at the micro and at the macro level. It was from these beginnings that I decided to add family planning to the issues that I was to be concerned with as a public health physician.

Planned Parenthood Association of Ghana

It was not too long after I had given up my job with the FAO and accepted the position of Professor of Preventive and Social Medicine in the University of Ghana Medical School that I heard that Drs. Barnor, Amar, Kwesi Bentsi-Enchill and Susan de-Graft Johnson (née Ofori Atta) had been invited by the International Planned Parenthood Federation (IPPF) to a meeting in Copenhagen. This delegation from Ghana, after listening to the discussions and being involved, decided right there and then, as stated by Barnor in his memoirs, that upon return to Ghana, they would form a family planning association and would get it affiliated to the International Planned Parenthood Federation.

They had started holding open meetings soon after the overthrow of Nkrumah in early 1966. I heard about this. I met Dr. Barnor and asked him how they could be discussing a major issue like family planning without involving the Professor of Preventive and Social Medicine. He was quite surprised, because, according to him, he did not think people in my position would be interested in the area of family planning. I discussed extensively with him why and how I could be interested. He invited me to join the group, carrying with me the strength of my department and, in some ways, of the whole medical school. Dr. Barnor has described the formation of the Planned Parenthood Association of Ghana extensively in his memoirs, *A Socio-Medical Adventure in Ghana*, so I will leave that here. A major step which Dr. Barnor did not mention, however, was the actual establishment by resolution of the organization. The Planned Parenthood Association of Ghana (PPAG) was launched by resolution on 3rd March 1966 in the lecture theatre of the Department of Obstetrics and Gynaecology in Korle Bu by the following, as the founding members: Dr. K.G. Konuah as chairman, Dr. M.A. Barnor, Mrs. Jean Forrester Paton. Dr. K.K. Bentsi-Enchill, Dr. A.A. Armar, Dr. Susan de Graft-Johnson, Dr. K.K. Konuah, Dr. D.B. George, Dr. F.T. Sai, Mrs. Jean

Pinder, Mrs. Clara K. Quarcoo, Mrs. Elfrida Nettey-Marbell, Mrs. Rosina Aku Acquaye, Mrs. Fredrica Aryeetey, Mrs. Valencia Cofie, Mrs. Dorothy Barnor, Mrs Rosina Konuah, Mrs. Comfort Akrofi, Miss Docia Kisseih, Mrs. B.B. Asrifi. The majority of the men were doctors and the majority of the women nurses. Mrs. Jean Forrester Paton and Mrs. Jean Pinder were foreigners. The new association was accepted as an affiliate of the IPPF and received some funding. From this we recruited our very first full time executive secretary, Gladys Mills-Odoi, who had recently concluded her master's degree programme in Legon. I provided her with office accommodation and facilities in my department for quite awhile.

The Association was formed and it was launched in March 1967. Dr. K.G. Konuah was the Chairman for the occasion. The guest of honour was Mr. E. N. Omaboe, Commissioner for Economic Planning. I was assigned the role of giving the keynote address and I delivered one which gave a broad view of the importance of population, not only to individuals and families, but to the country as a whole. I ended by saying that although the whole basis of human reproduction was a private decision made by individuals and couples, the outcomes were definitely a responsibility for the state as a whole. Therefore the state had a right to intercede with individuals and couples to plan their reproductive behaviour. Of course, I made it quite clear that nothing that the state did should be of a coercive nature, that our approach would be to educate individuals and couples and to try and make the services available to them, but in the end, it was they who had the choice to make. I added, which I believed at the time and I still believe, that unless and until we could expand the social services available to our people, particularly the education and health services for women, children and mothers generally, we would not be very successful with our family planning approaches.

Something which the association took upon itself to do immediately was to convince government to come out with a population and family planning policy. Happily, Mr. Omaboe did not need too much convincing. He, as commissioner, got a committee together in or around early 1968, to start developing a population and family planning policy for Ghana. This committee, which consisted of Ghanaians from the university and from the economic sectors, met under his chairmanship, initially, before splitting up into groups, to develop the policy.

The newly-formed Planned Parenthood Association was asked to send a representative and Dr. Barnor decided that I should be its best representative. When I was assigned to the Committee, Mr. Omaboe agreed that I would represent the PPAG

87

but he also decided to make me a consultant to the committee. The committee was also assisted by Dr. Lyle Saunders and Dr. Gordon Perkin, consultants supported by the Ford Foundation. They came and with courage and great perseverance, the policy paper, entitled *Population Planning for National Progress and Prosperity* was completed in 1969. Parts of Mr. Omaboe's preface are worth repeating since he clearly stated Ghana's main reasons for wishing to undertake population activities until today:

> *"The size of our present population does not pose immediate problems for us. However the rate at which the population is increasing will very certainly create serious social, economic and political difficulties before the turn of the century. If we want to alter the rate of growth, even marginally, in two decades' time we must initiate action now."*

He went on to discuss population size and national recognition stating:

> *"Huge populations alone do not make nations great. We are moving into an age in which quality rather than quantity determines the power of nations and their influence in international affairs. By choosing to emphasize quality in its policies on population, the Government has taken a decision which will have a major impact on the lives of future generations of Ghanaians."*

Population policy

These words spoke volumes about the previous administration's position that Ghana's population was too small and it therefore did not need a population management policy.

Although the policy document was ready and issued in March 1969, its official launch and dissemination were however delayed till the National Liberation Council Military Government gave way to a civilian administration. Elections had been held towards the end of the year and a new government had been formed under Prof. K. A. Busia. This government decided to accept the population policy and launch it in the Ashanti Region early in 1970.

The basic elements of the policy document have been summarized as follows:

- the policy and programme were to be integral parts of social and economic planning and development activity;
- the vigorous pursuit of ways to reduce the high rates of morbidity and mortality would be an important aspect of population policy and programmes;
- the specific and quantitative population goals would be established on the basis of reliable demographic data and the determination of demographic trends;

- the government would encourage and itself undertake programmes to provide information advice, and assistance for couples wishing to space or limit their reproduction to do so safely and effectively;
- the government would seek to encourage and promote productive and gainful employment for women; to increase the proportion of girls entering and completing school; to develop a wider range of non-domestic roles for women; and to examine the structure of government perquisites and benefits and, if necessary, change them in such ways as to minimize their pronatalist influences and maximize their anti-natalist effects;
- the government would adopt policies and establish programmes to guide and regulate the flow of internal migration and influence the spatial distribution of the population in the interests of the development progress, and would also reduce the scale and rate of immigration in the interests of national welfare;
- the government would make provisions to establish and maintain regular contact with other population programs throughout the world through intensified relationships with international public and private organizations concerned with population problems.

Programme goals and processes mentioned in the document include the following:

Article 5.1

"… that the population problem must be recognized as a principal element in long range national planning…";

"… that the great majority of parents desire to have the knowledge and the means to plan their families; that the opportunity to decide the number and spacing of children is a basic human right…";

"… that the objective of family planning is the enrichment of human life, not its restriction; that family planning, by assuring greater opportunity to each person, frees man to attain his individual dignity and reach his full potential…".

5.2 goes on to say

"With these considerations in mind and with the conviction that present rates of population growth are detrimental to individual and family welfare and constitute major hindrances to the attainment of development objectives, the government believes that voluntary planning

of the size of families and reductions in rates of population growth are in the vital interest of the nation and proposes that a national policy be adopted to advance these interests."

These no doubt spelt out a very comprehensive approach to population policy development which differed from what was happening in much of the major developing countries. The stress on an holistic approach and individual choice was clear. Unfortunately there was no leadership to ensure that these objectives were properly translated into the development programmes and efforts in a planned way. It must also be emphasized that the Ghana document recognized the centrality of women's development and the need for equity long before this came to be accepted as an international principle in the population field. Translation of the policy into action was to be entrusted to a national secretariat.

The story of the National Family Planning Programme has also been told elsewhere. Unfortunately it has to be accepted, that, apart from our being able to raise the awareness of government, the programme has not chalked up too many successes. Caldwell and Sai have recently discussed this in their paper in *The Global Family Planning Revolution* published by the World Bank: they give a lot of background to the development of the Family Planning Programme and its successes and failures. Their conclusions are that the programme has achieved notable success, but state "*... although the total fertility rate has not yet fallen below 4.4 births per woman, and seems to have ceased falling in recent years, the fertility differentials point in a hopeful direction. In contrast to a total fertility rate of 7.0 in the northern region of the country and 5.6 in rural areas, it has fallen to 3.1 in urban areas and to 2.9 in Greater Accra*". They cite as constraints an average age at marriage of only 20, a change of only two years since the start of the programme; high infant and young child mortality rates and relatively low levels of education in the northern parts of the country.

Whilst agreeing with the conclusion above I am particularly sad that the programme has not achieved anything like the success some of us had expected, especially compared with the Asian countries in some of whose programmes I was involved while at IPPF.

Particularly upsetting was the very low key political support and leadership practically all Ghana's administrations since 1970 have given to the programme. This has translated into low levels of financing, lack of enthusiastic planning and involvement by the line agencies. My direct involvement in the programme came to an end with my departure to join the IPPF in London.

Speaking at the UN Habitat's World Urban Forum,
in Vancouver, Canada, 1976.

Above: The founding of IPPF's Africa Region, Tema, Ghana, June 1971.

Below: With Julia Henderson, James Grant of UNICF and his wife.

International Planned Parenthood Federation (IPPF)

My first true contact with the IPPF as a central organization was in my being invited to be a member of the Medical Committee. It was from this that I got to know Dr. Fernando Tamayo and I first met Professor Fairweather. In or around 1967, Dr. Alan Guttmacher, who was then the Chairman of the Central Medical Committee of the IPPF, had taken a trip through Africa and visited me in my office in Accra. It was during this visit that he spoke with me extensively about the IPPF and what it stood for. I managed to get him an audience through the newly-formed Planned Parenthood Association of Ghana and he gave us a marvellous lecture. Fairly soon after that, IPPF arranged the first African Family Planning Meeting in Nairobi. Alan Guttmacher was the overall chairman of the meeting which was very well attended. The conclusions arrived at were very far reaching.

Under the title *The Role of Family Planning in African Development*, more than 100 delegates from 16 African countries spent four intensive days studying the significant factors for future economic development in Africa; the present state and future prospects for health care in developing countries; basic needs and community welfare; and the contribution that voluntary family planning associations could make to African development.

I pointed out that malnutrition was a general problem and nutrition should be a central factor in preventive medicine. Family planning was one of the breaking points in the vicious spiral of population growth, malnutrition and maternal and infant mortality.

I was made rapporteur of this meeting and it looked from then that I was set for high positions in the international organization.

I was nominated to be one of the representatives of the Africa Region to go to the annual meeting of the Management and Planning Committee in Tunis in 1969. There, the status of the Africa Region, which was then tied to Europe, was discussed and it became clear that as soon as the region itself formed a regional council it would be given its own status as a separate region. Meanwhile, however, there was an agreement to nominate a vice president to be responsible for getting the region formed. Dr Fernando Tamayo of Colombia stood for Federation President and won. He then helped to fight for me to be elected Vice President for the potential Africa region. He had to do this on my behalf because I had to leave the meeting early as I was involved in electioneering at home and had to return to do some canvassing. I lost the election at home but was accepted as the vice president for the Africa Region.

The next year, 1970, we, the small Africa family planning associations' representatives, met again in Nairobi and this time discussed the preliminaries necessary

for the Africa Region and the formation of a council. The following year, in June 1971, we met in Accra and eight family planning associations of Africa – Ghana, Kenya, Liberia, Mauritius, Nigeria, Sierra Leone, Tanzania and Uganda – formed the organization which came to be known as the Africa Regional Council. The Africa Region has come a long way. It was originally simply a small secretariat manned by James Gregg, and became a Regional Office with K. J. Winton Lane as Acting Secretary. The first true Executive Secretary of the Region was Christian Gbeho, former Registrar of the University of Ghana Medical School.

The highest body of IPPF at the time was called the Management and Planning Committee – M&P for short. This was a group representative of all of the regions. As vice president for Africa, I found myself on this committee too. Below the M&P were various other committees, the most important ones being the Budget and Finance Committee, the Information and Education Committee and the Central Medical Committee. Apart from these there were several task forces or panels.

This was a period of rapid growth for the federation. By the time of its 21st anniversary in 1973, IPPF had 79 member associations and a budget of US$30 million.

There were always murmurings in the IPPF about the rights and responsibilities of membership and how these could be reflected in the governance. By IPPF's original constitution, the organization was simply a federation of autonomous family planning associations meaning that associations could be advised from the centre but they could not really be forced, as it were, to deal with things in a unified way. According to their own needs and perceptions associations were free to develop their priorities. At this time there was not in place what one might call a common strategy operating throughout the federation. Funding from the centre, which could be one avenue of identifying common priorities, was also restricted.

When I joined the IPPF Management and Planning Committee, Sir Colville Deverell was the Secretary General. After his retirement in 1969, Sir David Owen, Co-Administrator of the United Nations Development Programme (UNDP) and one of the principal architects of UN economic and social assistance to developing countries, was appointed. After Sir David's sudden death in June 1970, George Cadbury, as the Chairman of the Management and Planning Committee, headed what was constituted as a search committee to find a replacement. As a regional vice president I was one of the members. We interviewed one person only: that was Dr. Julia Henderson, who was then Assistant Commissioner for Technical Co-operation in the United Nations. She was not only very

knowledgeable about the field of family planning and population, but also very charming, very relaxed and very witty. We offered her the position of Secretary General and she accepted it, taking office in February 1971.

After she took over, Julia handled a few combined volunteers and staff meetings which I attended. We got on very well. Late in 1971, she mentioned to me the possibility that she was going to alter the structure of the secretariat. At this time, the secretariat had a Secretary General and one Assistant Secretary General, Don Lubin, responsible for finance and administration. There was Malcolm Potts as director of the Medical Department. Miss Henderson thought that she would arrange things so that the Secretary General had a financial and administrative assistant and a technical assistant. When she mentioned this to me I thought it was a good idea. I did not know that she had me personally in mind.

Head of the Ministry of Health

At this time, I had taken on the job of Director of Medical Services of my country. In 1971, I was Professor of Community Health, and also Director of the Medical Services, the technical head of the Ministry of Health of my country and at the same time, involved with IPPF as a volunteer, both at home and internationally. The story of my being the head of the Ministry of Health of Ghana might be of interest. I had been a member of the Consultative Assembly which produced the 1969 constitution that closely followed the British system of parliamentary democracy. This meant that no one could be appointed to ministerial office without being a parliamentarian. The Progress Party leadership approached me to stand for election as they wanted to have me as a minister. Unfortunately I lost the election.

Prof. K. A. Busia, the leader and soon to be Prime Minister, came to console me early the next morning after the results were declared and he promised to let me have any position in the setup that he could. At first I wanted to be assigned as an ambassador to the United Nations, but I gave up the idea and asked to be made the technical head of the Ministry of Health. Strange as it may sound today, as soon as the medical officers and the civil service leadership heard of this the opposition was loud. How could one who had declared his party affiliations be the technical head of a ministry? The prime minister and I stood our ground. The compromise was that the position would be that of a consultant. Even with that compromise some doctors actually managed to inform the prime minister that I was bent on diluting the practice

of medicine in Ghana as I had been advocating the use of medical assistants. Of course today many of them are wiser. But I was furious with this opposition and made it clear to them that they had absolutely no idea of the important medical advances in the care of the masses or in the effort to make some supervised quality care available for all. My position simply infuriated many. In hindsight my choice was not good for me. Perhaps I should have chosen the ambassadorial route and learnt to be a diplomat.

In actual fact I was asked whilst in the Ministry of Health to consider the position of Secretary General of the Organization of African Unity (OAU). The enquiry was conveyed by my friend and old teacher from Achimota days, Mr. William Ofori-Atta who was then Minister for Foreign Affairs. Diallo Telli's term as Secretary General was either over or he had been withdrawn by President Sékou Touré. Later on in life I have half regretted my decision – the appointment to such a high diplomatic level would, perhaps, have been very good for my *curriculum vitæ*.

Several issues of importance confronted me in the ministry. Perhaps the most disheartening was my having to deal with the effort to fire the Chief Nursing Officer, Miss Docia Kisseih. This lady was acknowledged in health circles as one of the most accomplished, if not the most accomplished nurse in Africa at the time. She had been rendering excellent service. In early 1971 the government of Prof. Busia decided to do a cleaning exercise of the civil service by dismissing those considered unsuitable for whatever reason. Some 568 or so persons were removed. The 1969 constitution had given the incoming government a window during which to do this exercise. But no one thought it would be done in one mad rush and so cruelly, without any kind of information or process.

I was informed through the grapevine that Miss Kisseih was to be removed. I was not only furious but saddened and felt betrayed by my prime minister, with whom I thought I had very good rapport. I went to see him and complained bitterly. He explained that some of his ministers and a small group among the nurses wanted the Chief Nursing Officer out. I told him it would be Ghana's disgrace in African health circles and that I could not defend it to my colleagues in the WHO. He asked for suggestions for a way out. I knew that Ms Kisseih had been offered a fellowship to undertake master's and doctoral studies in Boston University. She had not refused; neither had she accepted. I agreed with the prime minister that I should encourage her to accept the fellowship with full pay.

Now the problem was to convince Miss Kisseih. She maintained she wanted to be publicly dismissed knowing full well of the local and international embarrassment. Prof. Busia was very sensitive in this respect, unlike many African leaders. I had some ministers

of religion and mutual friends talk with her and finally she agreed. She went over to Boston and did exceptionally well. The completely inhuman way in which the dismissals were carried out remained a blot on the Busia administration for a long time and continues to be referred to, even today.

Cholera epidemic

Later in 1971 I was to confront a cholera epidemic. We had heard of a diarrhoeal disease epidemic in Guinea (Conakry) but it was not being admitted that we knew from the clinical descriptions it could only be cholera. None of us Ghanaian doctors in the health service had actually seen cases of cholera. As an historical disease we heard of it during training, but there were Indian doctors in the service who had actually seen and handled cases. My epidemiologists and I held discussions and agreed that if the disease was in Guinea and among fisher folk, it would be only a matter of time for it to reach Ghana as there were numbers of Ghanaian fishermen in Conakry at the time. We discussed the possible routes of entry and concluded that as soon as we heard of its entry into Côte d'Ivoire it would jump across to Togo and then get into Ghana from Togo, possibly carried by the fishing community. I therefore decided that the eastern coastal border should be a major observation point. No dead bodies were to cross without proper examination. I was to learn how meaningless such a decision was, given the social realities of the country. I also made it clear to government and through the press that we could not vaccinate everybody, that cholera vaccination was not very reliable anyway and that hygienic living, including washing of hands frequently and refraining from handshakes as much as possible, was the way to prevent transmission.

Vaccination was to be given in areas at special risk, particularly the south-eastern corner of the country, with priority given to the fishermen. School children were also to be given priority. The smallpox vaccination teams were with us in Ghana at the time and they joined the effort. I was unpleasantly surprised to hear that, contrary to my advice, those calling for vaccination and receiving it first included the members of cabinet, senior officials in the regions and the elite. Only the American smallpox officers kept strictly to the directives.

True to our expectations the disease arrived through the Ghana-Togo southern border. A small epidemic started there. Unfortunately one of those who died in that epidemic was from the Central Region. The fishermen took the body by sea to the Cape Coast Area and soon we had another epidemic centre there. Pretty soon the

illness got to Accra and other regions. The fear of the unknown which had led to the rush for vaccination abated a little. My then deputy Dr. Fred Boi-Doku and Dr. Gil Ashitey from the medical school did sterling service in leading the management of the epidemic in the Accra area. They set up a centre in Korle Bu Hospital, much against the wishes of many of the senior doctors there, and through their efforts the impact of the epidemic was minimised. Despite our action, cholera has become an endemic disease in Ghana and West Africa as a whole since that outbreak.

Medical and dental board

An uneasy task given to the Director of Medical Services at the time was to chair the General Medical and Dental Board – the overall supervisory and disciplinary authority for the practice of medicine and dentistry in the country. I had always considered the fact that it was within the Ministry of Health wrong and that it should be independent. Nevertheless it was my responsibility to chair it whilst I gave strong support to Dr. Barnor and others to canvass for change. The only time while I was in the chair that the Board had to cancel a licence to practise was in relation to a botched abortion by a doctor touting himself as a gynæcologist and endocrinologist.

This doctor had performed an abortion on a nurse with an estimated six month pregnancy and she had died in his clinic. He had transferred the body to the Mampong Tetteh Quarshie Hospital mortuary and telephoned one of her relations to explain where the body was . The whole board was truly upset about the callousness of handling the post-abortion situation and unanimously endorsed the cancellation of the doctor's licence. Some colleagues who know of my advocacy with respect to abortion asked how I could also agree with the decision.

My answer was that the doctor committed two unpardonable errors. He did an operation either beyond his competence or without due diligence. Secondly he tried to cover up what he had done in an offensive way without any consideration for the feelings of the dead girl's family. Had the law not been so restrictive at the time, a nurse working in the central hospital in Accra would not have risked her life. The best qualified gynæcologists in the country were available in Korle Bu and could have given her competent and safe care. The law which drove this unfortunate nurse to her death should be considered just as responsible as the doctor who lost his licence.

I had assumed office as the Director of Medical Services early in 1970. I was also chair of the medical committee of the PPAG and the Central Medical Committee of

IPPF as well as being the vice president for the Africa Region. Julia Henderson mentioned the possibility of my joining her once or twice in 1971 but I did not think of it seriously until January of 1972 when she asked me to consider it very seriously because she might have to look elsewhere.

I had met with my prime minister early the same month and he thought he would prefer me to stay on and help with the Ministry of Health. I also personally enjoyed what I was doing at the medical school where I had just recently managed to get all of the structures and logistics necessary to get the Danfa Research Project going. So I felt truly torn between staying at home and doing some research with the Danfa Project, or going international and being with the IPPF.

Acheampong coup

The decision was taken out of my hands when a very unnecessary coup overthrew the administration of Prof. Busia. I thought I had no other choice but to look for another job and leave the country. While I would have preferred just to stay in the medical school and forget about the Ministry of Health even the medical school was not a very friendly or congenial place for me at the time as some doctors there felt almost betrayed that a doctor of my standing had polluted his life by going into politics. Nothing that Virchow had written about politics being the social medicine of society convinced our clinically-minded doctors that they needed proper representation at the highest levels of government.

My reason for dabbling in politics as my major hobby or second choice of profession or may be the third one, was simply to make everyone understand that health was fundamental for development and therefore when the national development issues were being discussed seriously, it required the involvement of people who appreciated health in the broadest possible sense. Of course, since that early failure of mine the situation has changed to such an extent that we have had doctors as ministers, not necessarily of health, but of defence, or road and transport and we have had doctors vying for the position of flag bearer for two of the several parties that we have in Ghana. So far, unfortunately, none of them has won even the nomination to be a flag bearer, apart from Dr. Edward Mahama who is the regular flag bearer of the People's National Convention, a party which he almost owns. One of the serious gaps in Ghana's constitution, due perhaps to the inattention of the doctors to politics, is the omission of specific medical representation on the Council of State. In the colonial era, the Director of Medical Services was a member of the Executive Council which ran the colony. I find it

difficult that the constitution made provision for a former Inspector General of Police, a former Chief Justice, and so on but not for a former head of the Health Services.

Assistant Secretary General, IPPF

So when the coup of Acheampong made me decide that I had to move, I contacted IPPF's Secretary General and informed her that I would be available to take the position in the organization as an Assistant Secretary General. The complete designation was Assistant Secretary General for Technical Affairs. After a year or so, External Relations was also added to my title. In this capacity I worked closely with some truly wonderful people who among other things made me even more of a gender activist. Women like Frances Dennis, Nuray Fincancioglu and Penny Kane were so incredibly good at their professions in education and communication.

The secretariat was again reorganized in 1973 and the Information and Education Department was given its own assistant secretary general in the person of Patrick Crosse. I had obviously made clear my liking for advocacy and for interacting with various organizations, within and outside the immediate family planning fraternity, both in the United Nations and in the international community of non-governmental and governmental organizations generally.

Abortion debates

As Vice President of IPPF, I recall vividly the debates on abortion within the Federation between 1969 and 1971. They were intense, ranging from the genuine source of disagreement as to the inviolability of life and abortion therefore being a sin equivalent to murder, to easy abortion leading to promiscuity and libertarianism. There were some, mainly volunteers, who did not want an organization like IPPF soiled by dabbling in abortion or being seen even to be considering it. This surprised me greatly because the organization itself had originated from the righteous anger of many women – Margaret Sanger of the United States, Ottesen-Jensen of Norway and Sweden, Lady Rama Rau of India among many others – about the unfairness of biology putting practically all of the reproductive burden on women, and the man-made unfairness of keeping women in bondage through uncontrolled fertility. The title of Beryl Suitters' history of IPPF *Be Brave and Angry* reflects for me the raison d'être of the Federation.

I found it strange that an organization which could be described as rebelling at the inequities of the burden of human reproduction should find itself divided over

what I consider the most discriminatory law in the health field – a criminal law originating solely around the woman's womb and criminalizing her own actions over it. In my view, among the laws and practices that kept women down, the old laws on abortion introduced in Europe and the United States in the 19th century were the worst. That these laws should still be operating in the developing countries was bad enough but to find volunteers of IPPF from developing countries feeling that they should not do anything about them was most perplexing. So, I started trying to get IPPF to evolve some kind of a policy which might help advance the field. I found a ready ally in Dr. Attiya Inayatullah from Pakistan, a Muslim and a woman, who was very anxious to see that we did get some way with the abortion issue. After a lot of drafts, we managed to get a form of wording which was finally approved by the Management and Planning Committee and then the Governing Body at its meeting in October 1971. This confirmed the Federation's attitude towards abortion as follows:

Recognizing that

a   contraception is the first line of defence against unwanted pregnancy;

b   in those countries in which abortion is illegal, legislation which punishes a woman who has had an abortion deters her from seeking medical advice if she is ill after such an abortion and may inhibit her from obtaining immediate contraceptive advice;

c   the majority of incomplete abortions and other complications are the result of illegal abortions.

The Governing Body:

1   resolves that it is desirable that contraceptive advice should be readily available to a woman immediately after an abortion;

2   encourages member associations in those countries in which abortion is legal to seek to maximize the provision of contraceptive services immediately after an abortion;

3   urges Associations in those countries in which abortion is illegal, to seek, where appropriate, to bring their influence to bear towards ensuring that adequate and socially humane services are available to treat incomplete abortions and other complications, and that such services be linked with provision of contraceptive advice.

This policy really left it to the individual associations to try and do the best they could. I believe that it was not a very strong policy but at least it was a move from simply acquiescing to the situation as we found it. I find it sad that even with Roe v. Wade in 1973 and the changes in the British abortion laws in 1967, IPPF was unable to develop a more forceful position on the issue till the Secretary-General Dr. Halfdan Mahler pushed the organization to accept it within the Vision 2000 Strategic Plan of 1992.

Round about the same time, there was the issue of compulsory sterilization and very strong methods for advocating and carrying out family planning in some countries of Asia principally India and China, which was not a member of the IPPF at the time. The Family Planning Association of India (FPAI) was one of the founders of the IPPF. The FPAI, as well as the Asia Region, was represented on the boards by Mrs. Avabai Wadia, a formidable woman who had trained as a lawyer but who instead of going into practice had devoted all her life to the family planning movement in India and the world. She has written her own memoirs in a book entitled *The Light is Ours*.

Avabai brought the attention of the M&P to the issue of forced sterilization in India. Unanimously, the M&P decided that this was not acceptable to IPPF. Avabai was therefore given the mandate to inform her government that the FPAI objected to any compulsory approach to family planning and to sterilization most of all and that the FPAI would have nothing to do with it.

In March 1977, the IPPF M&P formally reaffirmed the principle that sterilization as a method of limiting family size was a matter for individual choice. The Committee recalled the determination by both the 1968 Teheran Proclamation of Human Rights and the 1974 World Population Plan of Action adopted at Bucharest that people have the right to decide freely and responsibly the number and spacing of their children. The resolution stressed that this free choice should be made with full knowledge of alternative methods of contraception and of the risks and benefits to health and welfare. It stated that:

> *"... it is the individual's right to choose a method of fertility regulation without coercion. No sterilization procedure should be performed unless the person concerned has given voluntary, unpressured consent. A counselling service and follow-up care should be an integral part of a sterilization programme."*

So for anybody to try to associate IPPF, at least in the 1970s, with forced sterilizations or coerced parenthood of any kind was and is wrong. It is a misrepresentation of where the

Federation stood. In fact, in many, many ways, some of us found the Federation as a body too timid to show itself in the front lines of the family planning movement.

People like General Draper, Sidney Swensrud, and George Cadbury were far more aggressive about what to do about family planning than the majority of those representing the developing countries. Of course, many of those representing the developing countries also were far, far too timid to stand up to the idea of extensive advocacy for family planning within their own communities. Whether it was the India and Asian situation generally or the old history of eugenics and population control, the debate raged during the early 70s – population control versus voluntary family planning – right up to the United Nations Population Conference which was scheduled for Bucharest in 1974.

This conference had as its Secretary General a former President of Mexico, Carillo Flores, a charming gentleman. He ran the conference with a gentle hand but one that did not prevent some very, very strong debate, accusations and counter accusations. In the end, the conference came to be known internationally as the one that decided that development rather than family planning was the priority – I quote from the then India Minister of Health, Dr. Karan Singh, "development is the best contraceptive". This became the line for most participants and continues to lead discussions and debates in some circles even today.

Despite the fact that China, which at the time had been lauded for her family planning programme, refused to support family planning as a major development input maintaining that "hegemonism and colonialism" were the major reasons for excess fertility and low levels of development; despite the many disagreements between the population community and the "development will solve the population problems" standard bearers, the conference managed to make some very far reaching programme recommendations. Yes, it was accepted that development was a necessary basis for enhancing family planning but it was also accepted that the ability to manage one's fertility or the fertility of a family is a right which should not be denied. The article dealing specifically with this issue was Article 14(f) of the Programme of Action of the 1974 Bucharest Population Conference. According to Jyoti Singh, most of the language of this article came from the International Conference on Human Rights (Tehran 1968), which had declared that

"parents have the basic human right to determine freely and responsibly the number and spacing of their children".

Bucharest advanced this and stated

"All couples and individuals have the basic right to decide freely and responsibly the number and spacing of their children and to have the information, education and means to do so, the responsibility of couples and individuals in the exercise of this right takes into account the needs of their living and future children and their responsibilities towards the community".

I personally love this recommendation and have quoted it extensively when advocating family planning and even when defending my stand on the issue of abortion. If those involved in family planning education and services were to interpret this correctly, they would have all the encouragement they needed for ensuring that all persons, male, female, young and old have access to family planning education and to appropriate services. Fortunately, despite many efforts by the Vatican and a few supporting countries, this recommendation has stood and only been strengthened by additions of what governments and society organizations have to do to implement it.

Fortunately for the population and family planning field, this particular article, which required a lot of nights of debate chaired by Carl Wahren to conclude, finally was adopted. The most important reason for the prolonged debate was that the Vatican and a few countries came together and did not want the word "individuals" included. They maintained that by giving individuals the same prominence as couples, the conference was encouraging promiscuity and was also encouraging extra-marital sex.

I personally do not believe the conference was encouraging either. What the conference was doing was recognizing that individuals had a choice either to have sex or not to have sex and whether to have children or not to have children. Nobody was going to force anybody to use a contraceptive and nobody should assume the right to deny anybody the benefits of modern contraception simply for ideological, political, moral or religious reasons of any kind. And fortunately, although this particular article has been examined and re-examined at subsequent conferences and meetings, it has only been strengthened, as we shall see when we come to deal with other international conferences on population and development in Mexico City and Cairo.

The Bucharest Conference of 1974, which I attended as IPPF's Assistant Secretary General with Julia Henderson, opened my eyes even more widely to the international community. At this particular conference, the non-governmental organizations were not made an integral part of the conference and a non-governmental conference took place

several kilometres away and preceded the main conference. So it was only those non-governmental organizations that enjoyed consultation status with the United Nations that took part in the main conference and their participation was strictly limited. We mostly had to work by lobbying our friends and country delegations.

Ghana was represented by Colonel Felli, who was sadly and most unnecessarily killed in one of our later coups (1979), and Dr. A. A. Armar, then Executive Secretary of the National Family Planning Programme. As a governmental delegation, they had the right to speak and recommend amendments to various parts of the conference document. I used my relationship with them to get them to support a lot of the changes that we, from IPPF, thought should be made to the document. Of course, other members canvassed through other avenues but I think Ghana's interventions were very valuable.

Implementing Bucharest

The Bucharest recommendations helped to re-examine an old problem. How much general development should a family planning organization undertake and how should the non-family planning activities be paid for. Strange as it may sound there are some who maintain that holistic means holistic, therefore any family planning effort should be included in a development effort. IPPF came to the conclusion that it should restrict its programmes funded with family planning funds to direct family planning activities plus an expansion into those fields which could relate directly to sexual and reproductive health. The latter to include the management of sexually transmitted infections (STIs) and some maternal and child health (MCH). Truth to say some of the family planning associations were already dealing with MCH. I was very surprised to find that some of the associations were against the inclusion of STIs. Their reason was that they might be considered to be associating with prostitutes, arguing that their normal clientele were "good women" and this addition would lose them both clients and status. A reminder that according the IPPF constitution associations were be free to choose what to add helped calm the situation.

The importance of gender equity and the role of women's development in the fertility arena were sensibly discussed. The decision was to set apart a fund for supporting pilot scale women's development and family planning projects. Mrs. Sai's women's development project was accepted and funded. The project was based on the Danfa Medical School field research area. Basically it was to provide small funds for the women of the area to further activities that they were already pursuing or to start new ones. Almost all the women did some small-scale farming and this was to be enhanced. Some added *garri* (a cassava

preparation) processing and still others added sewing. The project was well received by the villagers and it was expanded through loans from a couple of banks. Unfortunately the male spouses became jealous and asked that they should also be included in the loans and this was accepted for the sake of peace. But it was mainly responsible for the collapse of the project since repayment of the loans by the men, unlike the women, was most discouraging.

The other major discussion after Bucharest was how to expand contraceptive education and services so that all who needed and wanted them could have quality access. This led to the issue of community based distribution (CBD). Research had shown how successful some CBD projects had been and IPPF decided to demonstrate its soundness. Dharam Gupta of India had been known for a successful project in India so he was invited to help plan the project. Although it got off to a good start some of the central arrangements for supervising it created problems. It was being organized as a commercial venture and so Julia Henderson recruited someone from business, Hans Thykier, to head it. Those of us in the biomedical field found the high salaries paid to the project staff disturbing; indeed Malcolm Potts claimed this as one reason for his leaving the organization.

We were still digesting the Bucharest results when, in 1975, we went to the first World Conference on Women in Mexico City. This, as far as family planning was concerned, carried on with the agreements of the relationship of family planning and development, but it dwelt mostly on gender equality, gender equity, legal and technical issues. It was well-attended, but I do not think that IPPF's input was very great.

Centre for African Family Studies (CAFS)

IPPF and the Africa Regional Council deserve commendation for a particular effort which, at the time of its initiation, seemed to be outside the normal activities of the Federation and its associations. I am referring here to the Centre for African Family Studies (CAFS), based in Nairobi. John Muser, a philanthropist from St. Paul Minnesota, donated US$ 50,000 to IPPF in 1974 and requested that the money be spent to further family planning in Africa. As the assistant secretary general for biomedical affairs and also coming from Africa, I suggested that we should consider some kind of human resource development for the region. A team, including myself as the senior staff person, led by William Wamalwa, then chairman of the M&P, went on an exploratory mission to the region. After discussions with the leadership, it was agreed that a training programme should be developed with the funds.

Edgerton College in Kenya was chosen as the base for the training, which was to

Edgerton College in Kenya was chosen as the base for the training, which was to be short term and practical. Prof. Kivutu Ndeti was put in charge and CAFS started operations in 1975. It was also meant to mount peripheral training programmes. It was not too long before it was realised by the Federation that the location was influencing the programme towards the academic rather than practical training for the type of person required for family planning in Africa. The programme was therefore moved from Edgerton College to Nairobi and remained for a time directly under the IPPF Africa Regional Office. Governance problems stunted its growth and development as an integral part of the Regional Office and it was therefore made an independent, autonomous non-governmental organization in 1984, running both static programmes and peripheral and peripatetic ones in different countries. Now with a satellite in Lomé, Togo, it continues to produce good human resources for the continent.

Currently CAFS has its own executive director and its own board. Its brochure states the following:

"The original mission of CAFS was to develop the capacities and competencies of family planning personnel in sub-Sahara Africa. The initial objectives stemming from this mission were to inform and educate decision makers, opinion leaders, and professionals about the problems surrounding family planning and population growth. CAFS has since broadened its mandate to meet the demand for its training service and now includes programmes in research, information and dissemination, and women and health. Its mission statement today is:

to improve lives of African families through skills development, knowledge management and technical assistance in health and development."

Its overall vision is stated as:

the leading provider of training and technical assistance in health and development to organizations and individuals for the well-being of African families."

The development of CAFS and its progress through the years fill me with joy and pride. I believe it is one of the most inspired of the innovations in health in which I have been involved.

8 work at IPPF

Whilst in IPPF, many issues were raised which required answering, not only through the Information and Education Department, but also through public speeches and even papers. From about 1975, after the Bucharest Conference, it became obvious that those of us with responsibility to be the face and voice of IPPF in the technical area had quite a lot to do explaining the issues, showing the true role of family planning and related activities in overall socio-economic development, with particular reference to health, children's and women's issues and education.

It fell on me to give a lot of speeches, but Dr. Julia Henderson, the Secretary-General, decided that it probably would be a useful thing for me to put my ideas on some of these issues on paper. One area which I noticed had not been aired sufficiently by the Federation, or by others in the field of family planning at that time, was the ethical grounding of family planning in all of development. So, it was agreed that I should devote attention to producing papers explaining some of these things.

The very first paper that I produced in the *Occasional Essays* series, which came out in 1976, was on ethical issues in family planning. I still believe that contributed to the thinking in the field by drawing attention to some major ethical problems. Among other issues it tried to respond to the question of apartheid in family planning as observed in South Africa and what was then Southern Rhodesia.

Ethical issues

The Foreword that Dr. Henderson wrote to the first essay is worth quoting, as it set the stage for all of the things I wrote and speeches I made during the period I was with IPPF:

> *"The IPPF remains the biggest non-governmental organization in the field of family planning. Whilst receiving over 90 per cent of its funds from governmental resources, it retains its independence at both the international and regional levels. Naturally, its affiliates have to operate within national laws and practices.*

"On the other hand, the total Federation is one of social action and therefore affiliates within their national borders, are encouraged to be in the forefront of the social reform movement. This would mean that there are situations in which IPPF affiliates might be considered as disreputable, as long as such an appellation is in consonance with Brian Abel Smith's challenge to the Federation to be 'responsibly disreputable', it is fulfilling its objective.

"The whole area of fertility regulation is fraught with ethical and moral questions of grave complexity and it is impossible to arrive at a solution which satisfies all communities under all circumstances. However, it is necessary for organizations like IPPF, continuously to question the ethical and moral basis within which they operate. These will no doubt change from time to time, but such change must be accepted and understood.

"The period before Bucharest saw a great movement to challenge the aims, methods and practices of the population and family planning community. This culminated in the confrontation at Bucharest, out of which the consensus was reached, which can be summed up in the statement that family planning is a right of individuals and couples and the two further statements that this right should be exercised with responsibility for the needs of community and that countries should take appropriate action to harmonise their population growth rate, in relation to their economic development.

"Many people in the population and family planning community have devoted attention to some of the moral and ethical issues and I feel it is time for FPAs, to start a debate among themselves and with their leaders, which would help them clarify some of these for their programmes.

"It is with this in mind that I have authorized the publication of this essay by F. T. Sai. It is by no means a policy stand of IPPF; such a policy does not exist. It is largely composed of his own personal views, assisted in some ways by questions and criticisms that he has collected from some representatives of IPPF, international and regional volunteers and the donor community. It is my hope that this essay will form the basis of serious study and assist IPPF to evolve, what may be classified as a policy for the Federation and its various parts in the near future."

In actual fact, such a policy was never formally put down for the Federation although the ethical discussions and considerations continued for a long time. In the publication at the time I tried, directly and in a simplified way, to discuss the ethical issues raised by questions of the intentions of IPPF, our methods of advocacy, the technologies and even the way we provided services. In later papers I discussed more seriously the ethical principles which were really to be considered when thinking of family planning within the economic and development fields. These I put out in other publications later , through congresses in Thailand and IPPF's own congress in New Delhi during its 40th anniversary.

The introduction to the ethical issues volume of the Federation has the following:
"The IPPF is a Federation of 91 autonomous family planning associations. These associations have their own constitutions though they are required to comply with some general principles agreed by the IPPF constitution. These are stated as follows:

"In the belief that knowledge of planned parenthood is a fundamental right and in the further belief that a balance between the population of the world and its natural resources and productivity is a necessary condition of human happiness, prosperity and peace, the International Planned Parenthood Federation aims:

> *a. to achieve the education of the countries of the world in family planning and responsible parenthood in the interest of human rights, family welfare, community well being and international goodwill;*
>
> *b. to increase the understanding of the people and governments on the demographic problems of their own communities and of the world;*
>
> *c. to promote population education, sex education and marriage counselling;*
>
> *d. to stimulate appropriate research in the following subjects – the biological, demographic, economic, eugenic, psychological and social implications of human fertility and its regulation; methods of contraception, fertility, self-fertility and sterility and to collect and make known the findings of such research;*
>
> *e. to stimulate and assist the formation of family planning associations in all countries;*
>
> *f. to stimulate and promote family planning in all countries through other appropriate organizations;*
>
> *g. to encourage and organize the training of all appropriate professional*

workers such as medical and health personnel, educationalists, social and community development workers in the implementation of the objectives of the Federation;

h. *to organize regional or international workshops, seminars or conferences; and*

i. *to take all appropriate measures to further the above objectives.*

"Organizations and institutions are eligible for membership provided that they subscribe to the aims and policies of the IPPF, they are not controlled by commercial interests and they do not discriminate regarding race, creed, colour, politics or sex."

The paper itself dealt with some specific issues, particularly the accusations being levelled at the IPPF at the time and the major accusations that I turned my attention to were:

1 IPPF advocates family planning simply for population control and has no regard for other issues of development.

2 IPPF is in league with multi-national companies and some US foundations to keep down the population numbers of the developing countries in order to permit their exploitation. IPPF is an agent for genocide.

3 Apartheid South Africa and Rhodesia are included in the IPPF family.

4 IPPF advocates and promotes abortion.

5 IPPF has set up programmes for non-voluntary sterilization.

6 IPPF has no regard for proper follow-up of the users of contraceptives and encourages the use of unorthodox methods, such as threats of the withdrawal of social amenities and benefits, to encourage acceptance of sterilization in some countries.

I found some of these accusations outrageous and helped to provide many answers to them in the subsequent pages of the paper. This paper was one which gained great influence in the discussions and debates which took place after the Bucharest Conference. The Federation itself, unfortunately, did not make a major policy statement on its own ethical position.

The paper dealt with the accusations and then provided some answers, which helped to point out the extent to which family planning, when undertaken properly within the development agenda, is a morally supportable objective, even if other

development approaches were to be carried out later on. In some areas, comparisons with vertical programmes for immunizations and food supplementation were made. The major issues examined included the genocide question, the role and place of sterilization, the basis for abortion, the funding, the technological issues and many others.

Another in this series was, *Population and National Development: The Dilemma of Developing Countries*. This was largely based on a paper that I read to the London School of Hygiene and Tropical Medicine at the invitation of Prof. Bruce-Chwatt. Others followed. They were – *Food, Population and Politics*; then *Population, Health and Nutrition in Human Settlements* and the last one was *Defining Health Care Needs, Health Care Priorities and Standards of Care*. This last one drew heavily on papers that I had produced while I was still in the service of my country or at meetings that had been held since I left the service of my country. Editorial assistance for these papers was ably provided by Ms. Penny Kane.

The ethical issues paper also dealt with some of the basic reasons for family planning and how these reasons can be ethically and morally sound. At that time, one of the major questions was that of incentives and disincentives. The issue applied mainly to the Indian and some of the Asian programmes, where money was being given for people to travel to clinics for sterilization or family planning examination and services and where, like in the case of Bangladesh, some cloth was given to the acceptors. These, some purists considered, could, in some ways, be considered coercive to those people. Unfortunately I don't think this paper – only 32 pages long – is in print. Perhaps IPPF may find it possible to reissue it.

Apartheid

One issue which confronted the Federation in the early 1970s was the question of where we stood on apartheid judging by our own ideas of non-discrimination. It turned out that because of the apartheid laws the South Africa Family Planning Association was not treating black and white clients in the same facilities. The question was whether, because of this, the South African association should be allowed to continue as a member of the Federation. Of course, if the issue were to be stripped of its politics and considered on purely ethical grounds, trying to force the South Africa association out would be problematical. The question was whether we should, because of separate treatment, force black South Africans not to have any services at all? At the time only the association was providing any quality family planning services for the black population. I personally

Above: President and Mrs. Rawlings with IPPF Secretary General, Ingar Brueggemann during her visit to Ghana, 1997.

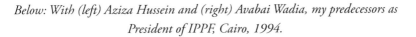

Below: With (left) Aziza Hussein and (right) Avabai Wadia, my predecessors as President of IPPF, Cairo, 1994.

Fred Sai, President of IPPF, speaking out in Cairo, 1994.

believed that it would be better for the South African blacks to get services; rather than not supporting the white-dominated South African association for political or ideological reasons. I felt that we should find ways of getting to the black community, which truly did not know where else to go, and provide them the service. The South African government did not make things easier for those of us holding the view of leaving the association to provide service for the black population. President Botha stated openly that he was against the white population controlling their numbers while he was for working to decrease the black population. Though the association was doing nothing wrong, the Africa Region could not associate with it, and it was therefore taken out of the Africa Region and attached to Europe till the end of apartheid.

By 1976, it had become obvious that IPPF needed to take another look at itself, to see how it was doing and whether it was properly organized and structured to face the various challenges that were increasingly coming up.

From 1973, for example, the budget of the Federation had increased tremendously because of the amount that USAID was providing. In 1973 also, the US Supreme Court decision on Rowe vs. Wade had been handed down. In the same year the Helms Amendment had been introduced making it necessary for organizations receiving money from USAID to keep accounts of these sums separate from any money that they were spending on the subject of abortion.

IPPF and its future

Suggestions were made by representatives of several donor governments and the M&P then agreed in 1976 that "a study of the roles and objectives of IPPF should be instituted." This, it was agreed, would be carried out by a group of volunteers and staff. They were to be assisted by a team of about 12 assessors drawn from experts in the fields of population and socio-economic development, the donor community and intergovernmental agencies. It was also agreed that the honorary officers, the Secretary-General and the Assistant Secretary-General for Forward Planning and International Liaison – that was me – should assume overall responsibility for the study as its steering committee. The steering committee was to meet with the external assessors and carry out group visits to three or four countries within each region and questionnaires were to be sent out to each IPPF affiliate, to obtain its views and to complement the task force report.

The external assessors were available for consultation throughout the study. They reviewed the findings and approved the final recommendations to be made to the honorary

officers. The study was of major importance to IPPF and its major recommendations provided the longer term perspective for the 1978-1980 plans and the guidelines contained therein. Ms. Nuray Fincancioglu did a superb job in technically leading the study and undertaking all the arduous analysis for the completed questionnaires.

In presenting the findings to the M&P, I followed the prior discussion of the chairman and urged the representatives to concentrate on the substance of the issues and to make recommendations. The conclusions were singled out for all subsequent discussion. Major recommendations for structural change were that the M&P should be abolished and be replaced by a Central Council. For better involvement by the associations in the programme thinking of the Federation there should be an association representative body called the Members' Assembly which was to meet once in three years. The Central Council, which would be regionally representative, would be the Central decision-making organ of IPPF. The Members' Assembly was to be consultative and advisory. An innovation was the recommendation that each association was to be represented by two people, at least one of whom should be female.

Comments and recommendations were made and a summary of the discussion on the report by the Management Committee was drafted. The summary was put to the Assembly for review and the following proposals were agreed by the assembly for recommendations:

> *IPPF AND ITS FUTURE: SUMMARY OF DISCUSSIONS ON THE REPORT OF THE STUDY BY THE CENTRAL COUNCIL AND THE MEMBERS' ASSEMBLY*
>
> *The report of the Study of IPPF and its Future was the central document for the November round of meetings of IPPF policy-making bodies and it provided a basis for discussion in all the meetings. In addition to the sessions entirely devoted to the discussion of the document, frequent references were made to its findings and recommendations during other discussions. The Members' Assembly also adopted a Three Year Plan, 1978-80, which provides the framework for the implementation of some of the most pressing actions recommended by the Study.*
>
> *The Central Council had a preliminary discussion on the report, which, at that stage, had not yet been discussed by the Members' Assembly. The Council transmitted a summary of its deliberations to the Members' Assembly for further*

consideration. The Assembly concentrated its discussions on Chapter III, Conclusions and Recommendations of the Study, and "being in broad accord" with these conclusions and recommendations, passed several resolutions and transmitted its commentary to the Central Council for "active consideration and guidance to development of policies and programmes" (Resolution 1). The Assembly recommended to the Council that, in its present form, the document should be used as an IPPF working paper.

The Executive Committee at its spring 1978 meeting will consider the policy and programme implications and follow-up necessary for the implementation of the Study findings and recommendations. These, together with the deliberations of the Members' Assembly, will be submitted to the Central Council, which is the IPPF policy-making body, at its next meeting. The Council will then be called upon to take those policy decisions that are necessary for further implementation of the Study recommendations.

The following is a summary of the main points raised during the discussions of the Central Council and the Members' Assembly, both at sessions entirely devoted to the discussion of the Study report and at other sessions. Except for those items on which resolutions were taken none of these points indicates any consensus of the Assembly or the Council. The resolutions passed by the Council and the Assembly are appended with cross references to the topics to which they relate.

SUMMARY OF DISCUSSIONS
IPPF Objectives

1   *There was general consensus of the "first flag" of the IPPF, namely the promotion of family planning as a human right, basic to the health and welfare of families. A point was made at the Central Council that one of the most significant revelations of the Study was the lack of knowledge among some FPAs of the IPPF's objectives. The educational aspect of the objectives especially that of the second one, was emphasised. It was stressed that this objective should not be called 'demographic' objective but rather an educational objective, i.e. educating peoples and governments con - cerning the demographic problems of their own communities.*

The discussion on the same point at the Members' Assembly showed that associations held varying views on this objective. The representative of one association considered the second objective as capable of Malthusian interpretation. Others felt this was not so. Nothing was imposed on FPAs from the outside. IPPF encouraged family planning where there was a demand and also tried to educate governments and people as to the realities of their demographic situations. This was not a Malthusian policy.

2 *A question was raised at the Council on the identification of the advocacy for social welfare as the third major concern of the IPPF. A point was made that since this policy is not included in the IPPF objectives listed in the Constitution, there might be a Constitutional contravention. The Council noted, however, that this policy was implicit in the first objective of the IPPF and that the Federation should not be restricted by the objects listed in the Constitution. It was recognised that there were many things the FPAs could do under the broad humanitarian aims. The IPPF was being called upon to expand its activities, with others, in the broad field of socio-economic development and not to change or add to its objectives.*

Strategies and Programmes

3 *Service Delivery: The Study finding that the IPPF still had an important service role was noted. It was pointed out that the continuity of service delivery had to be ensured by long-term commitment of funds without which clients would be let down and the FPAs would not be able to make long-term plans and train personnel.*

4 *Integration: It was suggested that integration should go beyond what is stated in the report and should include such activities as basic MCH services and immunisation. If the FPA cannot undertake all these services, it should encourage other organisations to provide them. It was stated that child care should be given special emphasis and that there were many ways in which the FPAs could contribute to the reduction of infant mortality: their own family planning work was a direct contribution to the solution*

of the problem; women who came to FPA clinics with their small children could be educated in child care and their children immunised; and FPAs could have a more active role in the planning and implementation of health and education services.

Active collaboration with other organisations and agencies as recommended by the Study was found a very important factor in the effectiveness of integrated projects. This collaboration was not only important at the international level, but also at the local level with informal groups as well as with governmental agencies and other nongovernmental organisations.

A call was also made for integration within IPPF programmes - the integration of the components which make up family planning services, including information, education, training and management as well as provision of contraceptives.

5 *Abortion: Concern was expressed at the Central Council that under the issue of illegal abortion, the recommendation that the treatment of incomplete abortion should be part of FPAs' programmes might be misinterpreted. To deal with this important health problem might be beyond the scope of FPAs and therefore should not be expressed as an obligation. There was a danger that the recommendation might be understood as a service to treat spontaneous abortion cases. It was pointed out that the recommendation was based on the observation that women who had had to resort to abortion were, in some countries, treated very badly and there was an urgent need to ensure humane treatment for them. FPAs could help with training, equipment and incorporation of contraceptive counselling and services for abortees as well as advocate their right to humane treatment.*

The Members' Assembly was also concerned about this recommendation. It was stated that IPPF should try to make abortion legal in as many countries as possible and FPAs should be more active in law reform. But IPPF should not deal with incomplete abortion which is outside family

planning and which is a health problem. Some FPAs are able by various arrangements to handle this problem directly. Findings from treatment of incomplete abortion are useful for studying abortion. It was decided that the Central Council recommendation on this issue should state that incomplete abortion should be treated "when applicable and necessary" (Resolution 2).

6 *Communication: A call was made that IPPF should intensify its efforts in the use of communication techniques. There was still a need in many countries to change public opinion about family planning. IPPF had to look at methods of disseminating views and achievements and results of research and evaluation using available resources. More advice had to be given to FPAs on how to reach the public (Resolution 3).*

7 *Sex education: It was pointed out that family life education and sex education activities should not only be directed towards youth but also to adults. It was also important that a sound system of sex education should be part of services and not be treated only as a means of demand creation.*

8 *Youth: It was stated that there should be much greater stress on the present and future problems related to young people. Teenage pregnancies caused a great concern in many countries and FPAs' activities in this field should include contraceptive, marriage and abortion counselling and information about adoption facilities. Most important of all, education programmes for youth should be strengthened and extended.*

Teenage pregnancies should not be regarded as a problem that takes place among unmarried girls only. In many countries, girls get married even before they reach puberty. IPPF should strengthen its efforts to raise the legal age at marriage.
[Members' Assembly Edinburgh 1977, Minutes]

Finding a new Medical Director
After the first year of my taking office in IPPF, it was obvious that Dr. Malcolm Potts

was not comfortable with either his position or other conditions prevailing in the Federation so he negotiated a separation from his staff position and obtained a consultancy direct to the Secretary General. His departure meant that I had to look for a medical director. I was determined to look for a one from the developing countries and if at all possible, the director should be a woman. We could not have international federation, which had been founded by women, being run so much by men, and men from the developed countries, when the majority of our work was in developing countries and with so much of our contraceptive activities based on women. I therefore got an understanding with the Secretary General that I was looking for a woman doctor, preferably from the developing countries.

We had several, but not many, applicants. In the end, I interviewed Dr. Dorothy Mahabir from the Caribbean. She was a delightful person and she agreed readily to take on the position. Unfortunately, it turned out, after a very short period of time, that she neither had the interest nor the capacity to really hold the job. What was more, the Medical Committee which I had previously chaired as a volunteer, naturally had to have another chairman when I became the Assistant Secretary General. The new chairman, Dr. Teddy Cummings also from the Caribbean, specifically the Virgin Islands, took it upon himself to have a direct supervisory line relationship to the medical director. This of course, in administrative terms, was bound to prove very difficult. It turned out in the end that he wanted to determine how the medical director would work. Finally the relationship between me and the medical director broke down irretrievably and she had to resign and leave us looking for a new medical director. This was to prove a godsend to both me and the Federation.

Another advertisement was put out and whether it was the advert he saw or through word of mouth, Prof. David Morley of the Institute of Child Health in London, found Dr. Pramilla Senanayake and sent her to see me. We had to have an interview quickly because she was on the verge of travelling for some work with the smallpox programme on which she was engaged. I believe the interview took place in an afternoon, probably a Friday afternoon.

She came in, not really dressed as one would have expected for an interview – she and I have found her appearance for the interview as something for laughing about since the interview. If I remember rightly, she was in a pair of khaki trousers and a blouse. She came across as very charming, very well mannered and extremely knowledgeable. She had finished her PhD with David Morley in the Institute of Child Health in London

and I was tempted to offer her the position on the spot. Later on, the position was offered and she accepted.

I don't believe I did IPPF a bigger favour than the day that I recruited the services of this young woman, now the very well-known international health champion, currently holding the chairmanship of the Global Council on Health Research among others. Dr. Senanayake asked for permission to go and finish her job and to take on the appointment when she had completed her then contract. I readily agreed. She came back and, as they say, the rest is history. She stayed with IPPF as the medical director and became not only medical director for the Federation's official work, but became in many instances the first point of medical call for practically all the headquarters' staff. Her output of work became prodigious, her calmness and her manner of dealing with others complemented my very sharp approach and made the IPPF team rather respected within the international family planning community from then on. She stayed in IPPF practically all her professional life, and although she is still in the health profession, she is not solely devoted to family planning. In fact she now runs a major NGO for young women in Sri Lanka which is making waves internationally. This very successful NGO takes care of young Sri Lankan women and girls of little means who might not be able to continue their education. Her organization is helping with their education, housing, and training in economic activities.

IPPF on abortion

For a very long time, IPPF has been accused, both verbally and in many publications, of being an abortion or a pro-abortion organization. As one of the IPPF leaders, I have also been personally accused of being either pro-abortion or trying to be disingenuous in explaining the position of IPPF on the issue. I must state categorically that IPPF continues to be a federation of autonomous national family planning associations. When I joined there were some 90 or so members, as of now, it is my understanding that it consists of some 140 national family planning associations and works in around 180 countries. So, apart from its own affiliates, IPPF is working in practically all countries which are members of the United Nations.

The issue of abortion has remained with the Federation for a long time and I am sure it was being discussed and debated even before I joined. But, as I have pointed out elsewhere, my own views on abortion were shaped not only by what I considered bad laws, but also by the experiences that I went through in London, as a student, or saw others go through in London and later, what I found in practice as a young doctor,

practising in my own country, and what I have found out in dealing with the issue internationally. In my own country, Ghana, today the misunderstood and unnecessarily restrictive law governing abortion was liberalised under the Rawlings' Provisional National Defence Council government in 1985. Though the conditions for legally performing abortions have been expanded there is still gross ignorance of the provisions by lawyers, doctors, the media, and the public in general. This situation leads to the agony of families resulting from either severe illnesses from unsafe abortion or the deaths of young loved ones, many of them leaving children and husbands behind. Getting this law properly interpreted and applied with empathy for women has been one of my major preoccupations for the last ten or so years.

The Ghana abortion law of 1985 which remains in force states:

"The Criminal Code1960 (Act 29) as amended is hereby further amended by the substitution for section58 and 59 thereof the following sections

'58(1):

i	*any woman who, with the intent to cause abortion or miscarriage and administers to herself or consents to be administered to her any poison, drug or other noxious thing or uses an instrument or other means whatsoever; or*
	b. Any person who administers to a woman any poisonous drug or other obnoxious thing or uses any instrument or any means whatsoever with the intent to cause abortion or miscarriage of that woman whether or not the woman is pregnant or has given her consent to causing abortion or miscarriage;
ii	*induces a woman to cause or consent to causing abortion or miscarriage;*
iii	*aids and abets a woman to cause abortion or miscarriage;*
iv	*attempts to cause abortion or miscarriage; or*
v	*Supplies or procures any poison or drug or instrument or other thing knowing that it is intended to be used or employed to cause abortion or miscarriage, shall be guilty of an offence and liable on conviction to imprisonment for a term not exceeding five years.*

'58(2)

It is not an offence under subsection (1) of this section if an abortion or miscarriage is caused in any of the following circumstances by a registered medical practitioner specialising in Gynaecology or any other registered medical practitioner in a government

hospital or private hospital or clinic registered under the Private Hospitals and Maternity Homes Act 1958 (No9) or in a place approved for the purpose by legislative instrument by the Secretary

    a   where the pregnancy is the result of rape, defilement of a female idiot or incest and the abortion or miscarriage is requested by the victim or her next of kin or person in loco parentis if the victim lack the capacity to make such a request;

    b   where the continuance of the pregnancy would involve risk to the life of the pregnant mother or injury to her physical or mental health and such a woman consents to it, or if she lacks the capacity to give consent, it be given on her behalf by her next of kin or person in loco parentis;

    c   where there is a substantial risk that if the child is born it may suffer from or later develop a serious physical abnormality or disease.'

'58(3)

For the purpose of this section, abortion or miscarriage means premature expulsion or removal of conception from the uterus or womb before the period of conception is completed'".

Unfortunately this revised Act was not properly disseminated so it is not being properly implemented, which is now the object of a major national campaign.

When I joined IPPF I noticed that Europe was ahead of the rest of the pack in many of the issues relating to abortion, and in fact, many delegates from Europe thought IPPF was being somewhat stodgy in respect of its own ambition to fight for the freedom, health and general development of women. They did not think that leaving women to die from backstreet abortions was one way of helping women and I had much sympathy with such a position. And I still have.

I have already mentioned elsewhere the 1971 resolution which I helped to draft. This resolution, in my view, was even less than the minimum to help save lives. It was based on the fact that we in IPPF genuinely believed that, except for total abstinence which is not a lifelong option for most human beings, contraception – preventing pregnancy – was the first line of defence in the management of fertility. Of course, for some of us who came to this from a health background, the illiberal stand on abortion, not even considering the ethical issues, looked to us as if we were saying that if we tried to help

our clients with contraception and the contraception failed, all we could say to them is "well you are on your own now". This to me went against our public health tenets and the teaching of primary prevention, secondary prevention and tertiary prevention.

So it looked to some of us, even going strictly by our own health codes of assisting with the next level of suffering, we might be doing something wrong if we withheld help from women who had a failure of their contraception and who did not want to carry on with their pregnancy. What was more, authentic information was reaching us within the IPPF Medical Department of what was happening to abortees in different parts of the developing countries, particularly in Latin America and in some of the more Catholic parts of Africa – sometimes, people bleeding or in severe pain from what was considered induced abortion were left just lying around clinics for hours without attention. Where they were given treatment, the quality of treatment was very poor and in many instances, unless they paid exorbitant amounts of money and provided for blood and other necessaries, they were hardly given a look in. Because of all this, I chose to pick up the issue of abortion as one of my main areas of concern, to discuss the call, legally and medically. I shall continue to advocate the liberalisation of the abortion laws in developing countries as long as I am able to. In fact my major stand has been to repeal abortion laws all together wherever possible . The subject then becomes one between the woman in need and her health care providers and any others she may choose to involve. And I am totally against the criminalization of women who seek or undergo an abortion.

The 1971 IPPF Resolution was therefore a landmark for the Federation. In the same year, the Medical Termination Act of India was passed and we hailed it as a very important tool for helping Indian women, particularly the poorer ones, since prior to the law most poor women in need of abortion had to resort to the back street and risk the consequences. The fact that abortions had been used in history as a major fertility limitation method and since World War II as the premier method available in the Soviet Union was known to us; but it was not a situation that we, in IPPF, agreed with. In 1973, the landmark US Supreme Court determination of the Roe vs. Wade case came and we were very happy thinking that with this in our armoury, our efforts to get countries to look at their abortion laws a little more humanely would not be difficult. Of course, nobody told us that things would get even worse.

As stated elsewhere, we tried first of all to get the African countries to appreciate what Roe vs. Wade meant, what unsafe abortion meant in their communities and the

ethics of withholding help from people who wanted abortion. The ethical issue of "coerced motherhood" was also discussed.

Meanwhile, abortion and the laws related to it, as well as laws relating to contraceptive practice generally, were being discussed by a law panel, chaired by Ms. Harriet Pilpel of the United States. It was during discussions with this panel that I did my best to put forward my arguments as to why IPPF as an international federation should take a more proactive position than we were doing on abortion.

The 1977 study, which was also led by me from the secretariat, gave thought to the issue of abortion and again stated IPPF's position that as an international federation, we could not take any stand on abortion as a right. Rather, the Federation should encourage collaboration with other agencies and organizations and if, within a country, there was found a need to change or review the law on abortion, the national association should be able to get help on literature, with examples of how to proceed, from the secretariat.

The study also discussed the question of collaboration with other agencies in terms of the IPPF's other programmes. The major effort advocated at the time was for IPPF family planning activities to be integrated, particularly integrated within maternal and child health services. The rationale for this was that family planning should not be seen as an activity which was an end to itself but as something which was supposed to promote family health and well-being, and as such it was particularly necessary for mothers and children.

There was a lot of evidence gathered during this period of the health benefits of family planning for women and for the child too. It had been found by nutritionists, as I mentioned elsewhere, that children who followed a preceding child by less than two years had more difficulty surviving than those who followed two or more years later. It had also been found that women who started child bearing before their early twenties, and particularly in the early teens, had more difficulties than women who started child bearing in their early twenties and finished before their forties. With these being known, if anybody who was having a problem with an abortion came to a family planning programme for help, I felt there was no reason why the programme should turn them away.

The proposal from the study that incomplete abortions should receive treatment as part of an integrated activity of an association was strongly opposed by some IPPF members. One of the arguments that I actually found strange and difficult to swallow was that this might mean associations treating spontaneous abortions as if this were part of their basic responsibility. Of course, we know that pregnancy, its supervision

and birth-related activities are part of the national health services, but if an individual woman felt more comfortable with a family planning association's services and came to it when she had an incomplete abortion, spontaneous or induced, it was my feeling that the association ought to provide whatever help it could. Anyway, the group agreed that although the ethics and logic were right, it should not be made a mandatory part of the IPPF Family Planning Associations' activities on which they would spend money, especially those family planning associations which were in, any case, not handling the full range of maternal and child health care in their clinics..

What was emphasised, though, was that whenever a family planning association had anyone with incomplete abortion, it should refer that person to the best possible point for treatment and that the patient should be counselled properly and when they had been treated, the association should see to it that they came back for contraceptive counselling and service. Thus, one can see that in a small way, IPPF was already advocating post-abortion care as part of its activities.

The Human Problem of Abortion conference

An important IPPF contribution to the guidance of associations was to come from a conference entitled the *Human Problem of Abortion*.

Although IPPF never developed a harmonised policy on its role in abortion, it nevertheless discussed the issue on many occasions, and one such was a workshop or seminar, which took place in Bellagio, Italy, in February 1978. This originated from joint discussions of the old medical committee and the law panel and Rockefeller kindly allowed it to take place in its conference centre in Bellagio.

The discussions were chaired jointly by the chairman of the medical committee Dr. Teddy Cummings and the chairperson of the law panel, Ms. Harriet Pilpel. The medical, epidemiological and legal issues relating to abortion were the background against which the discussions took place. There were discussions also on the abuses in abortion practice and how these prevented women from getting safe abortions. These abuses included things like unsafe procedures, lack of experience of the providers the lack of facilities, undue delay, over- charging, disapproving attitudes of family members as well as the medical profession, lack of follow-up services and misapplication or lack of public funds. The problems of adolescents with abortions were also taken up seriously.

The conference proceedings were edited by Ms. Rebecca Cook and Dr. Pramilla Senanayake. The point of departure for the discussions was the fact that, irrespective of

what the abortion laws were, abortions have been done and they would continue to be done; that all the evidence pointed to the fact that where abortions were legally restricted, the better off, as always, would manage to get their abortions safely and perhaps relatively inexpensively whilst the poor, less educated or those in less accessible circumstances could only get their abortions with difficulty and at great cost in both human and financial terms.

The group discussed the laws from papers which had been previously prepared which grouped the laws according to the levels of restriction. These included abortion laws in Commonwealth countries and others which helped provide a worldwide picture. It was concluded that, irrespective of the status of the law, some of the major problems were with interpretation and application. Therefore after due examination of all classes of the laws, the workshop concluded that it would be best for family planning associations to study their laws and even get lawyers to help the health departments and personnel appreciate the interpretation of the law, the limits to which they could go and how to conduct a defence in case of any legal difficulties.

In the end, the panel concluded that it was imperative for all associations to help interpret the laws in as sympathetic a way as possible, so that the women who were the most concerned did not face undue difficulties. It was agreed that one of the most serious impediments to making the law operate to the advantage of women in serious difficulty was the lack of understanding of the full implications of the law by both doctors and clients.

The workshop therefore gave examples to illustrate how different interpretations of the same law could lead to completely different conclusions about the extent to which abortions might or might not be legally permissible. It was concluded, for example, that where the law says health, this should be interpreted in the WHO's sense of not only physical health but psychological and social well-being as well, Thus where the law uses health as an exemption it has to be considered as relatively liberal as opposed to one which says saving the life of the pregnant woman.

The conference publication has an appendix which was agreed upon by the workshop. This aims at helping doctors and other health workers to maintain a good open and comprehensive record of the circumstances of their decisions to perform an which can be used to verify their own truthfulness and the reasons why they undertook the procedure. This record was presented as a physician's checklist for abortion .

The checklist starts with the usual medical items such as names, or code, age, address, nationality, citizenship, occupation of the applicant, the name and qualifications

of the doctor, and the location of the examination. The history has to include a comprehensive medical, social and economic history of the woman as well as details of her mental history, if any. This last does not necessarily mean whether she has suffered from any mental illness, but what difficulties she may have had during previous pregnancies, if any, her childhood experience, where she was born, whether she was fostered and so on. The welfare and economic history should seek to establish whether the woman's family is in a satisfactory condition and able to afford another child. Those who are economically dependent have to be examined carefully, for example, as to whether they have had any other children even though they are economically dependent, on whom they depended – husbands, boyfriends or are they going to be dependent on their parents.

Every bit of the history is needed. Sometimes it could be very difficult to get to the origin of the conception, particularly so with incest and rape. Was it within marriage, outside an existing marriage, widowhood or, for youngsters, just playing around – the question of rape or coercive sex needs to be examined carefully. The decision to terminate or not can then be supported by the written history. The extent to which the decision is itself a free and informed decision, whether there is any hint of coercion by a family member or partner or whether it is a social coercion because the situation might mean the person losing a job or losing a recognition of some kind – all need to be explored and as much as possible put on the record.

Another item of importance for the record is any others who are involved in the consultation – doctors or people who were there in another professional capacity such as social workers and/or friends.

Family members, with the permission of the pregnant woman, can be consulted if necessary. And an important issue to be covered is the history of contraception – whether the woman was using contraception and what the future would be if she wanted to be pregnant again.

Then the method of performing the abortion should be clearly stated, as well as the amount of money charged, if any. Unfortunately, for some reason, this particular document, which should have been a major contributor in preventing unsafe abortions, never received the distribution or dissemination it deserved and after a couple of years I don't believe that many people had heard of it. I am not sure that the associations even implemented its decisions extensively. IPPF, as a federation, certainly did not try to move to help associations to expand the availability of safe abortions in any of the

developing country associations until the Vision 2000 Strategic Plan was developed under Halfdan Mahler in 1992 when IPPF came out openly to state where it stood in the field of unsafe abortion.

The Depo-Provera controversy

In 1978, I was invited to appear before the US Congress to testify to a committee on a controversy regarding the contraceptive *Depo-Provera*. I learnt that the Upjohn Company which had developed *Depo* or DMP for short had made a first application for testing the drug in 1967. During the course of the tests, which had to be done both on dogs and monkeys, it was realized that beagle dogs developed nodule related breast cancers. No such cancers were developed in the primates, however.

In 1974, initial permission was granted for *Depo* to be given with some very strict restrictions. These included women, for whom other contraceptive methods were unacceptable or medically barred, or those who found other methods difficult to use and these included the mentally deficient or women who were institutionalized. Needless to say, these conditions applied mostly in the developed countries where the social and cultural barriers to contraception were not the same as those in the developing countries.

When I appeared before the Congressional Committee, chaired by Mr. James Schauer, my position was based entirely on my experience in the developing countries. In West Africa, for example, most drugs which were given by injection were found to be more acceptable and their effects more predictable than drugs which had to be given to the client to be taken at home. Secondly, in many marital situations the male partner was either completely unconcerned about contraception or antagonistic to it. In some families it was not only the male partner but mothers-in-law, sisters-in-law and even others who felt that they should have more control on family formation and fertility behaviour than the woman herself.

Depo, being a three monthly injection, would provide an avenue for a woman to have the injection somewhere outside of the home or even at a clinic and nobody would know about it. Sometimes, even the spotting that came as a side effect might be a useful thing for the woman to claim she was having her periods which she may not really be. Some of the criticisms of *Depo-Provera* were that it caused complete amenorrhoea and that when stopped, return to fertility was delayed – and the question of cancer remained. But by 1992, this question had been resolved.

My position on *Depo-Provera* was that it had been found to be the most acceptable of all of the short term methods of contraception by the women in my own part of the world and in many other parts of Africa. At about this same time, a furore was raised in Tanzania when a medical doctor who was a member of parliament stated categorically in Parliament that *Depo-Provera* had been known to make women grow hair like men, to make women have children who came out looking like monkeys because of excessive body hair and so on. The Tanzanian president was so incensed about this possibility that the central committee of the ruling party was asked for a special investigation into the Tanzania Family Planning Association's handling of *Depo* and to ascertain the true basis of complaint and advise Government.

I was able through the help of the IPPF Central Office in London to send Mrs. Christine Nsekela, who was then the executive director of the Tanzanian association, the papers which we had accumulated about *Depo-Provera* and the international controversy – we had details on *Depo* as used in Thailand and other parts of the world as well as results of experiments and permissions to use it in some developed countries.

The hearings of the central committee provided an opportunity for the Family Planning Association of Tanzania to show its contributions to national development. It was also able, with the scientific evidence at its disposal, to debunk the outrageous remarks of the doctor, much to his shame. By the end of the hearings, it was decided that *Depo* should continue to be used according to the instructions that had been given both by the manufacturer and by IPPF's Central Medical Committee. More importantly, the Central Committee endorsed the Tanzanian Family Planning Association as government's partner in the extension of family planning services to the whole population of Tanzania. So this is a classic example of good coming out of a difficult or challenging situation.

Although most of the developing countries that I know have approved *Depo* for use, there were either restrictions on its use or it was not registered at all in the United States and some other more developed countries – the United States finally registered *Depo* in 1992. However, the fringe echo of the difficulties over *Depo* together with the fact that it was one of the most provider-dependent methods of contraception led the Coalition of Women to fight for its total exclusion. This position was held largely in the period between the PrepComs and the full International Conference on Population and Development held in Cairo in 1994. Some of the women's groups mobilized their forces to come and ask for the complete international ban of *Depo-Provera* as a contraceptive.

I was quite alarmed at this and therefore managed to ask for a meeting with Ms.

Joan Dunlop who was then the head of the NGO, International Women's Health Coalition (IWHC). She and I had tea at the top floor of the Beekman Hotel in New York. She agreed with me that this issue might lead to unnecessary confrontation and really distance some individuals and institutions who were supporting the women's cause generally from being particularly active. She was able, I don't know how, to help tone matters down and in the end the women's caucus or the women's representatives did not ask for the banning of *Depo* or any reference to it in the plan of action or in any of the major decision making committees of the conference.

The Cosmic Joke

My continued efforts on behalf of *Depo-Provera* also led me into taking part in a documentary which discussed the pros and cons of contraception conditions for use and safety. I have seen a paper stating somewhere that Upjohn spent millions to bribe people to speak in support of *Depo-Provera*. I have to state categorically that Upjohn never gave me money for appearing in their film which discussed Depo-Provera and its role in family planning in developing countries. And no one ever paid me to speak on behalf of the product. I went simply by the observed facts and the preferences of women as I observed them.

Just about the time when I left the World Bank in 1990, I was approached by Dr. June Goodfield, a well-known writer, film producer, and documentary producer in the health field. She had written a story of the conquest of smallpox. The delightful woman asked me whether I would like to advise and take part in a film that she was going to produce and she at the time had the idea of entitling it the *Cosmic Joke*. I had not heard the phrase before and I found it quite difficult to understand.

She explained that the way mankind was going on and the way the population issues were being tossed around, particularly with the latest statements such as "population is a neutral in development", "development is the best contraceptive" and "technology and technological innovations would make it possible for the world to accommodate any number of human beings", were making it appear as if as humans we were not taking cognizance of the fact that many human theories might turn out to be wrong and turn out to be very costly. She believed that the way we were thinking about the population at that time might turn out to be a cosmic joke and very costly to the human race.

How right was she, because after all of the arguments that population was not important or it was at best a neutral, population facts have now found their way very

much into the arguments on climate change, the environment and the threats that the whole planet is facing right now. It may not be the single most important factor, but it is a very important one.

Parts of the film were shot in Ghana, Indonesia and elsewhere. I took part in the Ghana shoot and I remember appearing decked out as a sub chief in my *kente* cloth, talking about population, national development generally, and women's role in population and family planning. The documentary was produced in two parts and it made quite an impact in its time. In my own case, an English friend of mine, who saw the film, could not help writing to me to ask me what I had been doing in the blanket – actually my own *kente* cloth which I thought was very, very attractive indeed.

The Mexico City Policy

I have briefly mentioned the Mexico City Policy of the Reagan administration. Much of the controversy around this, from IPPF's point of view as a major recipient of USAID funds, has been discussed by Avabai Wadia who was then the President of the IPPF, in her memoirs *The Light is Ours*.

Briefly, the policy was that the United States government would not provide funds to any Family Planning Association or any non-governmental organization that used any funds to support or promote abortion anywhere. This, in effect meant, for some enthusiasts, that even an organization trying to gather abortion data could be misrepresented as promoting abortion and therefore would be denied funding, even if the money for such an activity came from non-USAID sources.

The United States claimed that IPPF was encouraging abortion, especially coercive abortion in China and therefore IPPF's funding was to be cancelled. In fact, ever since my first visit there in 1977, I had kept in close touch with efforts to strengthen a non-governmental family planning effort in China. One aim of IPPF's work in China was to showcase models of family planning activity that fully accommodated all human rights principles. No amount of discussion, factual presentation or otherwise, would make the United States change its mind and this 1984 policy stayed for nearly eight years until it was reversed by President Clinton in January 1993, only to be reimplemented by President George W. Bush in 2001 until the start of Barack Obama's presidency in 2009. This time, the reversal was done quietly and calmly and it is the hope of many of us in the field that this time the reversal of the policy will be permanent, that the issue will be taken out of the political football

field and made an American bilateral and bipartisan policy not subject to the caprices of the far right. But I am not sure this will prove to be more than a pious hope.

There is absolutely no doubt that abortions have been a problem for mankind since time immemorial and no matter what the law says, abortions will continue to be performed. The only definite issues are whether they are safe or unsafe. Where abortions are performed legally by trained persons, in proper facilities, there is practically no mortality. But when illegally performed usually by untrained persons in poor facilities, there are very, very grave consequences to the woman. Abortions performed by unqualified persons in unauthorized premises and under insanitary conditions are described as unsafe. Even where there are restrictive laws, the rich and the well connected are almost guaranteed safe abortions while the poor only have recourse to unsafe abortions and suffer the consequences.

To me, there is another reason why I am so much against any legalisation on abortion. The current legislation, as implemented in many countries in the developing world, repeats what happened in the western world before it woke up to the need and changed abortion legislation. When I look at the abortion map of the world and find that practically all the more industrialized parts of the world have unrestricted or only slightly restricted access to abortions while in the developing world, by keeping to old laws imported from those same northern countries, our poor are dying from unsafe abortions I shiver and increase my efforts to see what I can do from my country, as well as for the rest of the world.

Since 1984, I have been even more actively involved in the abortion debate, both internationally and in my country. First of all, in my country, I have tried to have my own people liberalise the law and, after that, to ensure as widespread implementation as possible. I cannot claim that it was my advocacy that led to the change of the law in Ghana in 1985: the great, late obstetrician Prof. D.A. Ampofo was also working at it in his own way but I know the extent to which I had called for such change.

The International Medical Advisory Panel (IMAP)

The IPPF Medical Committee had been a very peculiar mixture of some very well-known and brilliant obstetricians and gynæcologists or physicians and also some less well-known ones, largely put on the committee for regional or even national or political reasons. Working with the committee was quite complex and for several years it did not really achieve its objective of advising the whole federation and the world on technical matters,

nor was it really being accepted by organizations like WHO and the Population Council as an equal in the field of family planning. This was of great concern to several of the volunteers and management but nothing happened until Carl Wahren was made the Secretary General in 1978 and the Medical Committee was abolished and replaced by the International Medical Advisory Panel (IMAP). Unlike its predecessor, this was not to be representative of regions. Individuals were selected for their expertise and leadership in the biomedical and, especially, reproductive health fields.

IMAP was launched in 1981with Prof. Ulf Borell, an obstetrician/gynæcologist from Sweden, in the chair and a membership as follows:

Prof. Ulf Borell (Sweden), Chair;

Prof. Mahmoud Fathalla (Egypt);

Prof. Fred Sai (Ghana);

Prof. Lidija Andolsek (Yugoslavia – Ljubljana, Slovenia);

Prof. Shan Ratnam (Singapore);

Prof. Rodney Shearman (Australia);

Prof. Allan Rosenfield (USA).

As can be seen this very powerful group covered practically all the geographic areas of the world.

IMAP gave IPPF a major facelift in the reproductive health community, if not to general medical practitioners all over the world. As a group, it took over the policy issues related to most of the work of the medical department of IPPF and extended that to include even the working of the federation as a whole, its appreciation of the scientific basis of its work and the handling of controversies that arose. It helped to organise new editions for the various handbooks which IPPF had produced and which had made such an impact in the field, including the *Handbook for Nurses and Midwives*, the *Family Planning Handbook for Doctors*. It also made IPPF's *Medical Bulletin* an authoritative voice.

As a group too, it took the line that as IPPF was a non-governmental organization, it had the right to speak to the world freely without waiting for governments and the international institutions to approve of what it had to say or do. The approach of IMAP may be described as "follow the science completely and let other issues be considered by those country leaders who have responsibility for implementation". This means that it was able to react very quickly and effectively when

controversies arose.

A very important one was the controversy which arose about the alleged link between oral contraceptives and breast cancer. This, as can be imagined, was a very serious issue. The oral contraceptive pill, since its introduction, had become a major stand-by for women and it helped many women all over the world avoid unwanted pregnancies and unsafe abortion and plan their families effectively. So any link between these and breast cancer had to be of medical concern The IMAP took this seriously, looked at the risk/benefit ratios and came to the conclusion that, although the case linking the pill to cancer in certain conditions had been reasonably made, it saw no reason for the pill to be withdrawn from women other than those who had medical and other conditions which made it necessary for them not to take any of the components of the pill.

In looking at the developing countries, the question of comparison between the risks of pregnancy, delivery or unsafe abortion and the possible cancer risk from taking of the pill had to be considered. It was obvious that the risk from pregnancy and abortion in the least developed countries (LDC) far outweighed those that could be expected from taking the pill. IMAP issued a statement laying this out quite clearly and it helped considerably assuage fears in the field.

IMAP also worked closely with both WHO and the International Federation of Gynecology and Obstetrics (FIGO). In the case of WHO, IMAP members helped to develop two very important sets of guidelines: *Selected practice recommendations for contraceptive use* and *Medical eligibility criteria for contraceptive use*. These two were produced, within WHO, through the process of very wide consultation, peer review, and study of the literature. The study was led by Dr. Bert Peterson, a very energetic and highly regarded epidemiologist from the Centers for Disease Control (CDC) who was at the time working with WHO. IMAP members made major contribution to their publication and I was happy to be a member of the group that helped to put these documents together.

One of the areas in which they collaborated with FIGO during my period was when RU-486, also known as mifepristone, was invented and there was an international reaction led largely by the American right asking for the banning of this abortifacient or 'abortion pill'. Rousel Uclaf, the French company which had discovered the drug, was ambivalent about what to do. FIGO and the IMAP group of the time got together, issued a statement calling on the French Ministry of Health to ensure that this drug

was allowed after due scientific research and made available to women who needed it. Fortunately, the French Minister at the time, Claude Evin, came out boldly and said that the drug was the "moral property of women" and therefore could not be banned. This statement helped start RU-486 on its way as an early stage medical abortion drug – it is proving its value when combined with misoprostol right now.

IMAP was also involved in a major collaborative effort related to the *FIGO Manual on Family Planning* edited by Mahmoud Fathalla and Allan Rosenfield. In the week immediately following the 1984 Mexico conference, the editors and several members of FIGO assembled in Bellagio and went through the family planning part of this manual carefully, helping to review much of what had been written or making fresh contributions in several areas including adolescent sexuality and reproductive health. With Dr. Senanayake and Karen Newman I was a contributor to this particular exercise as well as to other parts of the manual and felt that the collaborative effort that went into this made IMAP and the IPPF proud.

9 un university

I had resigned my position in IPPF in 1978 and agreed to serve as adviser to the incoming Secretary-General, Carl Wahren, as well as to take a position as a Coordinator for nutrition activities to the World Hunger Programme of the newly-established UN University. The two organizations agreed to share in paying my salary. Prof. Nevin Scrimshaw, my friend since my 1960 visit to Guatemala with whom I had been serving on the Protein Advisory Group (PAG) and later the Sub-Committee on Nutrition of the Administrative Committee on Co-ordination of the UN (ACC-SCN), was the head of the programme.

The work with the UN University turned out to involve a great deal of travel. My main assignment was to examine the universities and training institutions in Africa and the Caribbean as well as Europe, to find out about their potential for carrying out training and research in food and nutrition problems. I visited many countries in Africa either by myself or in groups which included some governmental technical assistance representatives. The universities where we found most potential for joint efforts were Ghana, Ibadan, Cameroon and Nairobi. The Nairobi programme progressed very fast as it gained the interest of German Technical Assistance, GTZ, who paid for the foundation of the programme. The Ghana programme took a while but it also got started before I left the UN University. I made an interesting visit to Trinidad and Tobago to look at the institution there, but I did not follow up on the activities as they did not come to fruition until after I had left.

As part of this activity too, there were several conferences and meetings discussing and debating the nutrition issues. One of the most important took place at the Massachusetts Institute of Technology to discuss how to tackle the nutrition problem. The group soon appeared to be divided between those who were tagged as wanting to "provide band aids" and those who were considered as the ones with the much broader approach. Strange as it may sound, it took quite a while for the parties to be brought together. I believe this was largely because the economists and a few nutritionists believed that the problem was still being viewed in terms of protein deficiency, a food intake issue, as

opposed to a calorie deficiency due to economic, production and distribution factors. In fact the divide was in some ways a continuation of the debates of the late 1960s when protein/energy malnutrition was dominant and many of us viewed the nutrition problem largely as one of protein deficiency. So strongly had this view been held that in about 1968 a panel, including Nevin Scrimshaw, Sol Chafkin, and myself from the United Nations Subcommittee on Nutrition of the Administrative Committee on Coordination (UNSCN/ACC), was invited to advise the UN Secretary General, U Thant, on how to avert the protein crisis. The report was received well by the United Nations, but it raised quite a storm in the international food and nutrition community. The disagreement about the most rational scientific way to approach the protein⊠energy malnutrition problem raged on for quite a long time

To me, what the protein advocates were saying was that there were children who were suffering clinical and subclinical malnutrition and who needed to be supported immediately with a protein-rich therapeutic approach. The others were talking more of national approaches requiring the production of calories, the improvement of economies and the equitable distribution of income so that people could feed their children and themselves better. In the end, some kind of harmonious position was arrived at.

For clarity of the nutrition advisory group for the United Nations system at the time I would like to quote a personal view of Scrimshaw's:

"The ACC is the Administrative Committee on Co-ordination, made up of heads of UN Agencies, who meet at least twice a year. It has established several sub-committees for coordination, among them the sub-committee on Nutrition (SCN), established in 1977 as a partial successor to the Protein Calorie Advisory Group (PAG) of the UN System. Through the SCN, the individuals responsible for nutrition programmes within their agencies meet once or twice a year. To maintain the independent advice formerly furnished by the PAG, the Advisory Group on Nutrition (AGN) was set up, with distinguished scientists, both biomedical and social, as its members. They are Mr. Sol Chafkin (Chairman), Dr. Fred Sai (Vice-Chairman), Pr. Priyani Soysa, Dr. Alberto Carvalho da Silva, Dr. Abraham Horwitz, Dr. Bede Okigbo, Dr. S Venkitaramanan, and Dr. Ratko Buzina." (Downloaded from www.un.edu/unupress/food/8F032e/8F032E06. htmwww.un.edu/unupress/food/8F032e/8F032E06.htm).

I served on this committee for several years, at one time being its chairman.

I did not stay too long with the UN University and left them after about three

years. From that time on, I was on my own as a consultant and I worked for a time with the Carnegie Corporation as an adviser to Jill Sheffield, who had then taken on the task of helping the Carnegie Corporation develop programmes dealing with adolescence and mothers. This started a friendship which has been partly responsible for my continuing as an international advocate for gender and reproductive health and rights.

Identifying and working on a suitable project for adolescents in Africa was not easy. The needs for education were obvious and huge. There was also a crying need in the reproductive health fields. We agonised about suggested projects for the assistance and reclamation, if one may use the word, of girls who had dropped out of school. The ethical questions raised by such a project were disturbing. If there are poor girls doing well and attending school but needing clothing shoes books etc., how should those who have got pregnant be given priority support? What happens to those doing well and "behaving themselves" as the society would have it.

I did not stay around too long, but Jill kept in contact and started thinking about breaking off on her own to deal with maternal health issues as her main focus was reproductive health work. These were the beginnings of Family Care International.

10 un international conference on population

I was in this state of taking on assignments wherever they came from, when the United Nations International Conference on Population in Mexico was considered. I had then become firm friends of the Ross and Abbott Nutrition Group. They had invited me to visit Columbus, Ohio and see their laboratories. Dr. McCoulloch, one of their chiefs, had become a particular friend since the days of the UNICEF/WHO Infant and Young Child Feeding Conference in Geneva in 1979. I went on the visit with my wife.

After the visit and with Population Crisis Committee support I decided to join the PrepCom for the proposed 1984 population conference in New York. This was in March 1983. Since Ghana had no delegates at the time, except some of the staff from the Mission in New York, I discussed the possibility of my joining the delegation with the Mission head. Mr. Victor Gbeho, then the ambassador to the United Nations, readily agreed and got me registered. This was fortunate, since I learnt later that the government of Ghana, at the time under Flt. Lt. J.J. Rawlings and with Mr. P.V. Obeng as the *de facto* Prime Minister, was not at all happy about my being among the Ghana delegates. Unfortunately for my country but fortunately for me, and perhaps the rest of the world, by the time the displeasure of the country could be disclosed, I had been elected to join the bureau as one of the vice-chairs handling the PrepCom. In this position, it became quite obvious that one was bringing great strength and depth to the discussions. The occasions on which I chaired the programme discussions made clear to all delegates how much progress could be made in very short time. This was to make the majority want to see me as the chair of the conference's main committee itself. In the end, quite a few clauses and recommendations remained in square brackets and were sent to the main conference in Mexico City for further debate.

For the main conference in Mexico, too, I was a member of the Ghana delegation, although Ghana did not pay for my being there. My fare and stay in Mexico were paid for by the Population Crisis Committee (PCC), now known as Population Action International (PAI), through an arrangement with their then chief executive, Fred Pinkham.

Fred had been a friend of mine for some time and we had already agreed that no matter what my country did, I was going to be in Mexico as one of PCC's representatives.

Chair of the Main Committee

I arrived in Mexico City on a Friday and on Saturday there was a small Africa regional group meeting to elect the chair of the main committee as the conference had decided that the chair should come from the Africa sub-region. Unfortunately, at the time, the sub-region thought that the chair should come from eastern Africa and therefore wanted Mr. Mwai Kibaki, the current President of Kenya but then minister in charge of population issues for Kenya, to be the chair. When we met in the group, I made it clear to them that chairing the main committee was completely unlike chairing ordinary committees in the United Nations conferences. This one required the individual really to be confident about the subject, to be able to point out if things were not accurate and, was most importantly, the chair was likely to spend most evenings not at the conference socials but actually working with a small group, including the secretariat, on getting the documents prepared and finalized. Nigeria supported my position. Also, having already chaired the PrepCom and being well versed in what had happened, people felt that I should be the one to chair the main committee and the Africans finally elected unanimously me to be the chair for the main committee.

The US Delegation and the Mexico City Policy

The 1984 conference started on a bad note because the US had previously announced what came finally to be called the Mexico City Policy. This stated that the US would "no longer contribute to any non-government organization which performs or actively promotes abortion as a method of family planning in other nations". This really cast a shadow over the whole conference. It was made even worse when we realised who were representing the US at the conference.

At the PrepCom, Ambassador Richard Benedick had led the US delegation ably and had agreed with the majority of the conference participants on most of the important recommendations. For the conference itself, the US came with political representatives – Senator James Buckley (Republican, New York), a known conservative, was the leader of the delegation and he was assisted by Dr. Allan Keyes, who had previously been one of the younger assistants of Jean Kirkpatrick when she was the US ambassador to the

United Nations. This man turned out to be a most terrible representative as far as I was concerned. He did not endear himself to anyone. He was opinionated and was so convinced about what was right and what was wrong that he was hardly ready to compromise on even the smallest change of wording which could help advance any discussion. Keyes remains the only person with whom I ever had a face off while chairing a United Nations meeting. He tried to accuse me of partiality in the speaking order and not allowing his delegation to speak at the proper time. This was not correct. Anyway, it was very difficult for me to handle the position of the US, but we managed to wade through the total programme.

Of the issues that created most problems, one remembers the introduction of the Israel-Arab border problems, which the Arabs insisted were also population issues and therefore had to be dealt with by the conference. Fortunately for me, at this time, it was possible for the conference to decide on how to handle such an issue with a simple voice vote. I proposed that we should form a special open committee of the whole, to handle the issue of the Israel-Arab conflict. This was ably chaired by Leon Tabah, an internationally respected demographer, who was leading the French delegation and who had only recently left the position of Chief of the Population Division of the United Nations and who therefore knew everything about UN operations in this field. It took quite a long while to get the special committee to finish its work and submit its recommendations. By this stroke I have no doubt that the main committee was able to make time and get the conference recommendations and the Programme of Action document ready on schedule.

At the conference, the question of women was also given quite a lot of prominence. Bernard Lisse of WHO was able to get one of Zimbabwe's representatives Dr. Esther Boohene, twin sister of Mrs. Sally Mugabe, to give some very good comments on the importance of maternal mortality and morbidity and the relationship of abortion and other easily preventable conditions to these. But, of course, the conference did not take any real decisions on the abortion issue, except to state that abortion "in no way should be promoted as a method of family planning". This was inserted at the insistence, as one can imagine, of the Vatican and a small group of country representatives. To my knowledge no family planning programme was promoting abortion as a method of family planning and I said so openly.

As the one who handled this main committee as well as the one ten years later, looking back, this was a much more difficult assignment than the one in Cairo. It was

difficult, largely because positions which were rather peripheral to the population issues were injected and the Mexico City Policy of the United States made the US stand out in a position of not being at all helpful. The big clout of the United States, threatening a veto from time to time, occupied several group meetings and small consultations which took up a lot of time of the secretariat. In the end, though, we were able to come out with a good programme of action. However, after all its efforts to get changes made to the wording of the document in some important areas, the Vatican maintained the stand of not supporting any family planning by "non-natural methods" to the end, and declined to sign up to the final declaration.

Achievements

Jyoti Singh, in a few sentences in the publication *An Agenda for People*, edited by Nafis Sadik, writes succinctly about what happened in Mexico City. He rightly states that the United States, which had been a long standing supporter of family planning, had changed its position with its government and representation at the conference claiming to see population as "a neutral issue", opposing all discussion of abortion and playing down the importance of family planning". He went on also to talk about the Mexico City Policy. On abortion, he states, "the US announced that it was cutting off all funding to IPPF and other NGOs that would not support the new US policy on abortion, irrespective of whether they use US funds in supporting programmes that performed or promoted abortion or not". Subsequently UNFPA was also stripped of funding by the US because of their support for family planning in China; the US claiming that "the China programmes were coercive". He goes on to point out that a most interesting reversal from Bucharest took place in that China now supported measures to slow rapid population growth. Other states, the developing countries particularly, also made a near universal acceptance of the importance of family planning in development. Practically all of them endorsed Article 14(f) of Bucharest which states, "all couples and individuals have the right to decide freely and responsibly the number and spacing of their children and to have the education, information and means to do so".

More importantly, whereas Bucharest had been convened mainly at the request of the development partners, Mexico turned out to have been convened largely at the request of the developing countries and several regions had held regional meetings before coming to Mexico. Some of these had actually come out with declarations of some consequence. In Africa's case, the countries had met in Arusha, Tanzania in

January 1984 and adopted the Kilimanjaro Programme of Action, which provided the framework for the formulation and implementation of population policies and programmes in Africa. The Programme of Action was still strongly linked to the socio-economic development of the region, but it increasingly recognized the importance of family planning services. Recommendations concerning family planning included:

- governments should acknowledge that family planning and child spacing strengthen the stability of the family;
- countries should incorporate family planning services into maternal and child health-care services;
- governments should ensure the availability and accessibility of family planning services to all couples or individuals seeking them and should offer services free or at subsidized prices;
- governmental national family planning programmes should make available a variety of methods to allow choice to all users.

Essentially this declaration also maintained that family planning and development were sides of the same coin and one could not take place without reference to the other.

Senior Population Adviser, World Bank

One of the most unexpected but very welcome personal benefits of my chairing of the Main Committee of the International Population Conference in Mexico City in 1984 was an invitation to join the World Bank as its Senior Population Adviser. Though I knew the World Bank was looking for someone to fill the post, I thought I was too old to apply. At one of the sittings of the main committee I noticed Mr. A. W. Clausen, President of the World Bank, enter with some of his staff. He left before the sitting ended. But later in the day one of his staff, I believe it was Barbara Herz, informed me that I would be invited to apply for the position at the World Bank. She claimed that the World Bank President had come to the Committee Meeting to assess my performance for himself; and that he had agreed to my being approached. Interviews were arranged for me after the conference and I was appointed to the position from 1st January 1985, for three-years. This was later extended to June 1990.

I left for Washington after Christmas 1984 and had a most generous offer from Dr. Fred Pinkham, then President of the Population Crisis Committee (now PAI) to stay with him and his wife Helen till I found a more permanent home. Florence joined me

about a month later and we quickly moved into an apartment while we searched for a suitable family accommodation. This proved relatively easy with the help of the World Bank staff and resources. We settled on Caderock Springs, an area which was described as a World Bank/IMF ghetto because of the large number of staff from the Bretton Woods institutions who lived there.

It proved to be a most congenial area and when the family joined us they really enjoyed the club swimming pool and other facilities. It turned out, too, that my immediate administrative supervisor, Mr. John North. who had left the Nigerian Colonial Service at the time of independence, also lived there. John, his wife Jane, Florence and I became good friends. Out of the blue another staff person called Roberto Cuca turned up to welcome us and he offered to help with my transportation to work. We drove in his car to Glen Echo and took the bus to the bank for all the time I was in the Bank. A wonderful gesture.

My immediate colleagues in the Department were Alan Berg with whom I had worked on the SCN, was the Nutrition Adviser and Dr. Anthony Measham was the Health Adviser. We grew into quite a harmonious working team. My only immediate staff was a secretary and I recruited Ms. Sonia Ainsworth from Jamaica. She stayed with me till I left the Bank and sadly died a few years later.

About a year into my stay, I made the case for a research associate and recruited a charming English woman, Janet Nassim, wife of an Internatioanl Finance Corporation staff member. She also stayed with me till I left the Bank.

I found my role as Senior Population Adviser fairly complex and multifaceted. (see paper by Fred T. Sai and Lauren A. Chester for a description). Briefly the Senior Adviser was to provide "leadership in discussing the whole range of policy and strategy issues of interest to the Bank in the population field; he provides technical and professional guidance to Bank staff to ensure that the Bank's research and project activities in population respond to the needs of member countries; he acts as a link at the highest possible levels between the Bank and other organizations in the population field. The adviser also interacts with senior officials of member countries to discuss population policy".

When I took up my appointment there were at least two major debates in the population field. The National Academy of Sciences had issued a report which did not find any real adverse economic consequences of rapid population growth, maintaining that in terms of the economy population was at best "a neutral". As can be expected this was taken by those against all efforts to curb population growth as a reason for

stopping family planning support and programmes. My stand was to emphasise the health rationale for family planning. For Africa, in particular, my approach was also to stress the region's own aspirations for its people and the difficulty of achieving those goals if the demand side of the equation were to be allowed to grow so rapidly.

The other major debate had been between those who felt the world's resources were finite and therefore there should be a limit to growth and those who felt technology would always help provide for more and therefore human numbers did not count. Julian Simon represented the latter and Paul Ehrlich the former. No matter how the arguments went, the crash of fuel prices in the mid-eighties and other technological developments led the Simonites to claim victory. I wish he were alive now. Like it or not, I had to play a role in many debates and discussions explaining and defending the World Bank's role in population and family planning.

Within the Bank I was involved actively in seeing that opportunities for including population and family planning in national development discourse and plans were not ignored. I assisted in the development of the component in national projects. I see no point in writing much about all the projects in which I was involved since those interested can access these through the World Bank. I will just highlight a couple which illustrate success and failure.

An on-going project which claimed much of my attention was that of Bangladesh. In 1985 there were quite a few criticisms of the Bangladesh population project. A couple of deaths from post-sterilisation infections had led to questions of quality. The incentives of pieces of cloth for clients and money for transportation were seen by some as coercive for the very poor. I was involved in answering these among other concerns. A visit to Bangladesh assured me that concerns about coercion were exaggerated.

My stand was that anything which made it possible for the poor to implement their own unpressurised, informed choice could not be unethical. If a poor person wanted family planning and could not access it because s/he could not afford the transport cost I did not see providing that cost amounted to coercion. Nor did I see the provision of a three yard piece of cloth as such. What I found worrisome was the payment, per case referred, made to those in the villages who referred cases.

The issue of quality had been tackled in another way. An international consultant was posted to supervise and report on the programme. Secondly a team of external and internal consultants visited and did an audit once or twice a year. I was on these teams several times and in the end I was very satisfied with the progress of the programme.

The Bangladesh population activities had many different partners, both local and international, bilateral organizations and non-governmental organizations. It grew so large that a co-coordinating body was formed, led by the World Bank. The courage of the government in confronting its population realities was most admirable. It was Bangladesh that decided to accept menstrual regulation as a family planning method and made uterine evacuation prior to diagnosis of pregnancy a respectable medical procedure. It was the position of the government that since a diagnosis of pregnancy had to be established before prosecution for the crime of causing an abortion, a procedure performed without such diagnosis could not be considered liable. By the time I left the Bank in 1990 Bangladesh was recognized as one of the Bank's successful efforts in population

I wish I could say the same for my efforts in Nigeria. I was involved in a population project in Nigeria almost from scratch. Discussions with the highest levels of government, the ministries of health, finance local government agriculture and others were open on population policy and programmes. After several years effort we managed to have a policy developed. Prof. Olikoye Ransome-Kuti, then director of medical services and later minister of health, was an invaluable proponent of family planning as a health and human rights issue. He wanted this recognized in his plans for decentralization of the health services to the local authorities and his decentralization efforts should be a classic lesson for all African authorities. The policy was finally launched in 1988. Its rather long title was National Policy on Population for Development, Unity, Progress and Self Reliance. Stated goals were

a: to improve standards of living and quality of life;

b: to promote health and welfare, especially that of mothers and children;

c: to achieve lower population growth rates;

d: to achieve a more even distribution of the population between urban and rural areas. Whilst aiming at reducing the Total Fertility Rates (TFR) it nevertheless stressed voluntariness.

Getting a project developed was another matter altogether. The late Dave Radel and I worked very hard at this. In the end we managed to get what might be called a project fund agreed soon after I left my full time position. If I remember correctly, the sum of US$87 million was made available for activities which could be supported. Nigerian individuals and organizations could develop sub-projects, based on the suggested

activities, for funding. Unfortunately, even before proposals had been made, an accounting officer had paid some of the first tranche into a personal bank account and taken out the interest up front. The bank had collapsed and the amount was lost, but the government of Nigeria had to refund it. By the time the project really got going, I was no longer involved. But according to information I later received, it was so unsuccessful that it had to be cancelled.

During my interview for the Bank position I brought up my concern that the Bank should be working closely with non-governmental organizations (NGOs) who have a good record in the family planning and population field with Mr. Ernie Stern, Senior Vice President,. He had maintained that the Bank's rules and methods of operation did not permit direct working with NGOs, but I leant that governments could on-lend as they wished. I was determined to make Bank/NGO collaboration much stronger. One approach was to encourage local NGOs to get involved in all Bank discussions with their governments and try and show how they could be of value in projects. This happened in Kenya and Ghana and, in the end, NGOs had Bank support from national project funds.

The second approach was to get international NGOs directly supported from Bank funds. It turned out that one of the problems was the small size of NGO projects. The second was that they would normally receive grants, not loans or credits. After much discussion and trying, I was allowed access to some funds for NGO grants. These were not to take too much Bank staff time so we had to have an intermediary. IPPF performed this role in the early days of the grant programme: later the programme was expanded and a small committee of Bank staff evaluated proposals and made grants directly.

Before the existence of such grants we had been able to co-sponsor a conference with what may be described as an NGO. With Parliamentarians for Global Action (PGA) the Bank sponsored an all African Parliamentarians Conference for Population and Development in Harare. This was well prepared and attended by parliamentarians from 29 African Countries. The conference which was also attended by UNFPA's chief executive and Mr. Jaycox, Vice President for the Africa Region of the World Bank, came out with a bold declaration of the importance of population in development. It stressed the role of parliamentarians and called for the establishment of an African Population Council and the development of population caucuses by all parliaments.

After leaving the Bank I consulted for the PGA for some time and helped with the establishment and strengthening of several parliamentary population and development caucuses in Africa. To me, the later founding of The Forum for African

and Arab Parliamentarians for Population and Development, with its headquarters in Dakar, Senegal has some of its origins in the Harare conference. Another major conference which the Population Health and Nutrition Department of the World Bank co-sponsored was the Safe Motherhood Initiative. (see page 186) (see *Preventing the Tragedy of Maternal Deaths, A Report on the International Safe Motherhood Conference,* February 1987.) The Bank's commitment to reducing maternal mortality led to the creation of a Safe Motherhood grant programme, modelled on the successful population NGOs programme. Family Care International (FCI), an NGO with which we had been working on the Safe Motherhood Initiative, had proved its capacity and willingness and was our chief intermediary for channelling grants to organizations working to build the initiative.

My period at the Bank coincided with the explosion of the AIDS epidemic. I personally heard of the problem of HIV in 1985 and then heard in 1986 that Ghana had identified its first cases. I attended the 1986 AIDS Conference in Washington DC and was very concerned about the health and demographic importance of the new disease. Anthony Measham and I found out as much about the problem as we could and started holding small seminars on it. I learnt of the work being done in Ghana by Konotey-Ahulu, J. K. Quartey and others and asked them to send me copies of a video they had made.

A point in this video which still remains with me is the need to be careful in transmitting information. A female commercial sex worker had been plying her trade in Abidjan and had come home to Ghana sick. But she did not accept that she was suffering from AIDS because "you get that disease when you go on the boats". Even with her sailor friend she had never had sex on a boat, so how could she be suffering from that disease.

Country work began in earnest; policy dialogue and research activities exploded and within a few years and soon after I had left the Bank it became one of the foremost supporters of HIV/AIDS programmes worldwide. It is also a co-sponsor of UNAIDS.

My work at the World Bank proved most satisfying. The atmosphere there was the closest one could get to an operational university. There were staff who had been teachers in universities, others who held dual appointments. Research work of substance was respected; field work was rigorously examined. The Bank had some of the most attractive personnel policies in my view. One we enjoyed to the fullest was spouse travel. After two hundred or more nights away from home the staff could go on

any following work trip accompanied by their spouse. The travel fare was covered. If the time spent away exceeded three hundred nights then every approved expenditure involved in the trip was covered. As I travelled extensively for my work, Florence and I had several trips together and once even did a round-the-world trip, first class.

Before leaving the employment of the Bank I recommended the establishment of regional population positions so that country officers could have ready access to population advice. The senior population adviser is too far removed from those with access to the funds. Actually I also made this call at a farewell party Mrs. Hamilton, my director after the departure of John North, arranged for me. Unfortunately owing to bad wiring, the speech which should have been made available for posterity went unrecorded.

11 ippf presidency

During the discussion of the 1977 study on the IPPF and its future, a major concern was the governance of the organization, specifically structural issues related to governance. The policy-making body, with the final authority, was to be the Central Council. It also had a small executive, which was to be involved in, as it were, day-to-day work in relation to the secretariat. The head of the Central Council was the Chairman of Council and this was to be the position which had direct responsibility for all executive IPPF activities and therefore, was the only one that, officially, had to be in communication with the Secretary-General.

There was also to be a Members' Assembly, which was to meet once every three years. Although the Members' Assembly, to be made up of representatives from all the member family planning associations, had no executive authority or power to change anything done by the Central Council, it could make recommendations but unless the Central Council found the recommendations acceptable, these would go nowhere.

Apart from the Chairman of the Central Council, there was to be a President of IPPF. This was to be purely honorific and it had very limited roles – one of them being chairing the consultative Members Assembly every three years. It also had the responsibility for chairing the search for a Secretary-General, if the occasion arose.

I had the pleasure of being involved in two Members' Assemblies and meetings. The first was in 1992, when we celebrated IPPF's 40th anniversary. This was held in New Delhi and instead of simply having the assembly, it was decided that there should be a conference – Meeting Challenges, Promoting Choices – to go over family planning developments and the hopes for the future. Special papers were presented, workshops and plenaries were held and the publication that came out of the conference was edited by Dr. Pramilla Senanayake and Dr. Ronald Kleinman. By 1992 Ronald Kleinman had become medical editor for the Federation and was directly in everything published by the Federation for twenty or more years. I chose on this occasion to present a version

of my paper linking the ethical issues involved in sexuality and family planning, particularly in Africa.

A year or two before the assembly, the Secretary General, Dr. Halfdan Mahler, had led a study of what should be the mission and the vision of the IPPF for the future. Where should the organisation be concentrating its efforts? Once again the leadership for the study included Nuray Fincancioglu. In the end, the study recommendations became known as *Vision 2000*. A draft version was submitted to the Members Assembly for endorsement. It was then that IPPF produced what I consider one of its best contributions to the population and family planning field. There were six challenges in *Vision 2000*: unmet needs; youth; sexual and reproductive health; unsafe abortion; quality of care; and women.

As the president of the organization and the chair, I had to help navigate some very interesting waters. I remember clearly one or two of the FPAs expressing their discomfort with what was being said about unsafe abortion, particularly the recommendation that whenever possible family planning associations should help to educate their countries about the problems of unsafe abortion, the role that restrictive laws played in unsafe abortions and thus their being partly responsible for quite large proportions of maternal mortality in many countries. Once more, the place of youth sexuality was discussed extensively and again, the question of service for youth was a point of contention. In the end, though, it was agreed by all that all the challenges had to be met by the organization. For the first time since I joined the IPPF, it had produced a document that could be considered its strategic plan. It was clear though that, as a federation of autonomous associations, these could only be indicative of directions. To get full support for implementation extra funds would be made available.

For once, at the end of the meeting, it looked as if practically all the family planning associations were enthused with the spirit of the conference and they would start making major efforts in this. It was unfortunate that when Mahler left, the new Secretary General Dr. Ingar Brueggemann became quite, quite cool on the unsafe abortion issue and, in fact, did not provide the leadership for IPPF in this field which her predecessor had started and that I had hoped she would continue.

At the next Members' Assembly, held in Manila in 1995, the *Charter on Sexual and Reproductive Rights*, and the *Clients' Charter* were approved. Although a lot of groundwork had been done by Karen Newman and the Europe Region Executive to have lawyers and experts from every region involved in the preparation and clearing of

the charter, it still required some manoeuvring and reasonable chairing to get leaders to educate their regions and let them buy into the rights charter.

The IPPF *Charter on Sexual and Reproductive Rights* was a comprehensive document which took quite a while to develop. Karen Newman, the leader in the development of the Charter, was working from the European office of IPPF, but she took care to carry those concerned with these topics from all of the regions with her. To me, the production and passage of this charter was one of the most public spirited activities undertaken by IPPF and it showed how the Federation was prepared, at that time, to take leadership among non-governmental organizations, making governments and the whole world realize how important sexual and reproductive health were in human development.

The rights, literally, were derived from consensuses, charters and even treaties, which had been agreed by governments within the United Nations systems or in other internationally recognized bodies. The 12 rights recognized were :

1 the right to life;
2 the right to liberty and security of the person;
3 the right to equality and to be free from all forms of discrimination;
4 the right to privacy;
5 the right to freedom of thought;
6 the right to information and education;
7 the right to chose whether or not to marry and to found and plan a family;
8 the right to decide whether or when to have children;
9 the right to health care and health protection;
10 the right to the benefits of scientific progress;
11 the right to freedom of assembly and political party participation;
12 the right to be free from torture and ill treatment.

These, as is obvious, are rights that can be translated into different fields of activity but in this instance, the presentation related the rights to the reproductive health issues, services that are provided for reproductive health and how both clients and the service personnel have the right to protection of their activities and support.

Based on these rights, too, the clients' rights were also developed and these also were presented as a charter of what rights a client should expect from service providers and the services in the field of reproductive health.

These Rights are defined as the:
1 right to information;
2 right to access;
3 right of choice;
4 right to safety;
5 right to privacy;
6 right to confidentiality;
7 right to dignity;
8 right to comfort;
9 right of continuity;
10 right of opinion.

I found the IPPF governance at this time, rather cumbersome. The important areas which disturbed me were the powers to block that seemed to have been given to the regions. These powers, in my view, were not being exercised reasonably, particularly by the Africa Region, and I said so. In keeping with good administrative practice, it looked as if this subsidiarity theory had been accepted wholesale – whether or not a region and its secretariat were in reasonable shape, they still had the authority. I found this difficult but try as I would, I never got anywhere in getting the problem resolved.

Another problem which I found disturbing was volunteer/staff relations. Again, many of the volunteers of the IPPF, harking back to history, could not separate their roles as volunteers and policy makers from executive action and, at the FPA level, at the regional level and even at the central level, there were situations where unnecessary conflicts between volunteers and staff were plaguing the organization. In fact, in some instances senior volunteers became 'godfathers' to some staff and interfered in no small ways with the progress of the organization.

Finding a new Secretary General

In or around the middle of 1994, Halfdan Mahler, the Secretary General of IPPF, made it clear that he would not seek a renewal of his contract. It therefore became necessary for the IPPF to search for a replacement. One of the more concrete and responsible activities allocated to the President of IPPF at that time was the headship of the team searching for a Secretary General. I was therefore charged, with the Chairman of Council and the Vice Presidents of the regions, to form the team to look

for a replacement for Halfdan. This was not be an easy task as the Secretary General had really taken the IPPF to new international heights.

I could not help casting my mind back to around ten years before this, when I had tried to be considered for the Secretary General's position. It was when Carl Wahren was leaving. I spoke to Avabai Wadia who was then the President of the IPPF, asking her whether she thought I would be eligible to contest the secretary generalship. She spoke to me in enthusiastic terms and claimed that I was very suitable and I should certainly apply. I was very surprised, therefore, that the search committee then did not even have the courtesy to tell me I was ineligible, or, I could not even get on the shortlist. Anyway, this reflection led me to making sure that nobody who wanted to apply would be treated shabbily, that everybody who wanted to be considered would either be considered or would be told they were not being considered.

One of the first things we did was to get a search organization to undertake the preliminary work of advertising and sifting through candidates. It turned out, back then, that IPPF was quite attractive and we had candidates from all over the world including high level politicians from Europe and the United States, non-governmental organization leaders from Asia and Africa and, in a couple of cases, well-known academics.

We went through and shortlisted from a list which the head-hunters had produced and decided to do the interviewing ourselves. We interviewed thoroughly around eight or ten individuals. I remember very well that one of the senior level politicians who had applied had made quite a name in the international field. It turned out, however, that the individual knew hardly anything about international family planning nor the non-governmental organization set up, so they had to be ruled out. Others from the political arena were considered, but they were found to be lacking the kind of managerial expertise or ambition that was needed for the position.

There were one or two in whose cases I, as chairman of the committee, could not really find the reason why my committee did not want to consider them, even for a second round. One such person had, at my request, written a major text for us on what the secretary general's position should involve and how a secretary general could help shape the future of the organization. All on the committee thought this was a wonderful contribution to IPPF's progress in future. This particular paper, together with advice on what the position entailed or should entail in the future were major guiding instructions to the committee.

In the end, we were almost at the time when Dr. Mahler was going to leave and

still had not come to closure on who should be his replacement. So, it was decided to re-advertise or ask the search committee to source some more people. One person who came up top was Ingar Brueggemann from Germany. Ingar had been with WHO and, before coming to us, she had been involved closely with the WHO/UNICEF Conference on Primary Health Care – the Alma Ata conference, which produced the Health for All 2000 recommendations. She had also been in the European Union headquarters as a representative of the Director General of WHO, dealing with inter-governmental and non-governmental organizations, dealing with the United Nations – at the time she applied, she was serving as Director of the WHO office in the United Nations.

I had known Dr. Brueggemann very well, knew that she could speak on health issues well, but I had not known her to be of managerial material. Unfortunately, at this time, we were really hard pressed. What was more important, the rumour mill was suggesting that the committee was being pushed to the wall, so that one of the committee members, in fact, the Chairman of Council, could have the opportunity to run the organization.

It must be stated at this point that, before we started the search, we asked for any member of staff or any of the volunteers who were concerned with the search to declare whether they had a personal interest, either in the outcome or in being considered for the position. If such declaration was made, we would have asked the individual to excuse themselves from participation in any of the deliberations but none of our people had so declared. So I was able to I dismiss the rumour.

Unfortunately, in one or two instances, I could not help feeling that the reasons why individuals were not being seriously considered was not be because of their position or whatever, but for reasons which had more to do with either religious or quasi-ethnic biases of some kind. I don't think I am doing any member of the committee an injustice if I say that, in one or two instances, it was quite obvious that members were committed for or against an individual for reasons not really based on their suitability.

In the end, as was to be expected, as somebody who had worked closely with Dr. Mahler and had been in the health field for such a long time, Ingar Brueggemann convinced the committee by her handling of questions on the family planning field, non-governmental organizations and our relationships with the United Nations and other international bodies, the international consensuses and everything that concerned the family planning and population field at that time. She was, therefore, appointed.

I must say that, without my expressly saying I was in disagreement, I made it

quite clear that I was not particularly happy with the appointment. This was indeed carried to her and she later confronted me with the statement that she was not the candidate of my choice. I told her that I definitely did not feel she was my number one candidate. I gave her the name of my number one candidate and whether or not she disagreed, it was never clear.

She was very gracious, I must concede, and she worked as closely with me as possible. She sought my advice, we had several meals together when we discussed IPPF. Indeed, when she was in difficulties with volunteers and other members of the Federation, long after I had left office of president and was simply working as a volunteer, she consulted me extensively.

It was a pity though, that she could not follow the leadership that Halfdan Mahler had introduced and implanted in the minds of the Federation and the world through *Vision 2000*. She did very little to advance the cause of unsafe abortion – in fact, she was noted for her very deep silence on the subject. I was sad to see how her relationship with the major volunteers deteriorated in the last few years of her stewardship. A few things she achieve for the Federation were converting the title of Secretary General of the Federation to Director General, reorganizing and making some of the positions of the secretariat even more important than they seemed.

IMAP, on the other hand, continued under the able leadership of Pramilla Senanayake and Carlos Huezo. Carlos had been employed soon after the formation of IMAP as an assistant to the Medical Director. He came from Latin America, had been an epidemiologist with the CDC in Atlanta and he was definitely on his way up. Within the IPPF he blossomed and he took on a lot of the leadership in IPPF's technical relationship with WHO.

12 meetings and conferences that made a difference

I have moderated, chaired or been one of the principal officers for many international meetings, some of which I cannot remember at all. But I can think of four of the meetings that made a difference to our way of handling issues or thinking about issues of concern. One has been described already in the International Conference on Population held in Mexico City in 1984.

The other four are the:

- WHO/UNICEF Infant and Young Child Feeding Meeting, which was held in Geneva in October 1979;
- Family Planning in the 1980s Conference, which was held in Jakarta, Indonesia, in April 1981;
- Safe Motherhood Conference, which was held in Nairobi in 1987; and
- International Conference on Population and Development, which took place in Cairo in 1994.

Infant and Young Child Feeding

The WHO/UNICEF meeting on Infant and Young Child Feeding took place amidst a major controversy over the infant formula industry and their advertising practices. A brief history would recall that as long ago as 1966, Dick Jelliffe, in an article on child nutrition in developing countries, had produced a brochure for the United States and expressed concern about dangers of breast milk substitutes in developing countries. I must say that this concern, although expressed by Dick Jelliffe, had been troubling many of us who were working in infant, clinical and child nutrition during that period. We were making it clear that because of two major reasons. Firstly, in an unhealthy environment and particularly in the absence of good potable water for mixing the milk, the milk substitutes given to the children were frequently bacteriologically contaminated. Secondly, and perhaps even more importantly, because mothers were so poor, they tried to make the powdered milk go so far that, in the end, the children

were not receiving enough nourishment. Five years after Jelliffe's brochure, a United Nations meeting in Bogotá also expressed the same concern. But there were disagreements among the experts.

In 1972, the light was turned onto the marketing practices of the infant formula manufacturers. The international explosion followed a publication by the New Internationalist in 1973 entitled *The Baby Food Tragedy*. There was also an exposé of Nestlé in an article, *Milk and Murder*. Nestlé invited journalists to Vevey, Switzerland for a discussion. Then in 1974 when Mike Muller of War on Want published a pamphlet entitled *The Baby Killer*. To stoke the fires even further, Third World Action Group (TWAG) published a German translation of the article under the title *Nestlé tötet Babys* which in English is *Nestlé kills babies*. Naturally, Nestlé could not sit back and watch this and a legal battle ensued, which was joined by the World Council of Churches among others, and the infant food companies formed a council, ICIFI, to develop a code of ethics for self regulation of the market place.

In July 1976, the Nestlé case was decided and TWAG was found guilty and fined a paltry 300 Swiss francs, a pyrrhic victory as Nestlé was not spared in the judgement. It was advised to alter its advertising practices, particularly in developing countries. This stoked the fires yet further and a boycott of Nestlé's products was instituted worldwide, led by INFACT of the United States. In 1978 the US Senate held a hearing on the subject, chaired by Senator Edward Kennedy who, after the hearing, advised the Senate that WHO was to try and bring the parties together to get an international consensus on infant health and nutrition.

I got to know all of the above in only after I had became involved with the Conference in 1979. I had left my full time position at IPPF and had been working with the UN University since the middle of 1978, so was deeply involved in nutrition issues at the time. A call came to me from Geneva, followed by a letter inviting me to a meeting on Infant and Young Child Feeding. The participants were to include the baby-food industry leadership, the people who were carrying on the boycott of Nestlé, scientists who were concerned with infant and young child nutrition, country and regional representatives and non-governmental organization representatives with an interest in the subject.

Before I arrived in Geneva, I had a call from Dr. Moise Behar who was then the chief of nutrition of WHO. He asked me when I was arriving in Geneva so he could meet me at the airport. I found this request quite strange since it was not the normal

Above: The Safe Motherhood Conference, Colombo, March, 1990.

Below: With Nelson Mandela, November 1997.

Above: With (left to right) Jane Fonda, Dr. Pramilla Senanayake (IPPF), Florence and Dr. Indira Kapoor (IPPF) at a Nile cruise reception, Cairo, 1994.

Below: The board of Family Health International, April, 2002.

practice of the WHO divisional heads to meet invitees at the airport. Anyway, Behar and others met me at the airport and on the way to my hotel they asked me whether I would be able and willing to chair the meeting. They briefed me extensively on what it was about – their fears that the meeting might degenerate if it was not properly handled – and stated quite openly that they were looking to me not only to come out with reasonable conclusions on what to do so that we could all move forward, but also to see to it that the meeting did not degenerate into an open squabble, with accusations and counter accusations. According to WHO practice, of course, they could not put me up as their choice of chair so they had to lobby participants and they were trying to find out my view before they started. Fortunately for all of us, the group agreed readily and I duly took the chair of the meeting which lasted from 9-12 October, 1979.

The major groups there were the International Nestlé Boycott Committee (INBC) and the International Baby Food Action Network (IBFAN). The scientists, some of whom I remember as being very vocal and frank, included Jelliffe, Scrimshaw, Waterlow and Morley. Governments, representatives of the United Nations system, intergovernmental organizations and NGOs were also present. After very, very hot discussions and debates including issues like a call for the banning of all baby food advertising; banning of all gifts to doctors and health workers, irrespective of what their value was; non acceptance of gifts of milk foods from milk industry representatives and so on, the terrain was clarified somewhat. At the beginning, there was a lot about the actual science – what formula feeds were doing in the developing countries; their adverse influence on the growth rates of children and what happened to children who did not breast feed properly. These were very major issues that needed to be discussed. One area which was truly emphasized was that as breastfeeding alone, in practically all cases, could be sufficient for children between the ages of zero through six months; there was no need even for the addition of water. The majority of infants did not even need extra water whilst breastfeeding. In a very few cases, however, some children started either not gaining weight or actually losing weight round about the fourth to the sixth month.

Another thing which was established was that all countries should try to emphasise breastfeeding only, at least for the first six months. Then, after the first six months, most babies, if not all babies, would need some kind of supplementary feeding. This where a lot of difficulty arose because the infant food manufacturers thought that the scientifically determined commercial products for supplementary feeding were much

superior to traditional methods of supplementary feeding. Although this was contested vigorously, in the end a level of agreement was reached.

Successful and complete breastfeeding could conflict with the mother's development aspirations, her work or training activities. This led to a discussion of opportunity costs and the contribution of breastfeeding to the total national income; an area which had been largely ignored by researchers. Legal mandating of breastfeeding for the first six months would require reasonable periods of paid maternity leave. This could prove inimical to the further employment of women. A possible way of avoiding this was the social change of making babies welcome in the work place if at all possible. In the end, the advice was for countries to try and ensure that adequate paid maternity leave and/or baby friendly work environments were provided for women.

The major conclusion of the conference was that there should be a discussion under WHO auspices to develop a code of marketing of infant foods generally, the role of breast milk substitutes and other infant foods.

Over the next year or two, several meetings were held in Geneva and elsewhere, to develop the code of marketing. This was finally placed before the WHO Assembly and adopted in 1981. Nestlé formed a coordinating centre for nutrition and an infant formula audit committee, which was known as the Muskie Committee, to monitor compliance of what the baby food manufacturers were doing. The infant food manufacturers tried all kinds of ways to come together to look after their interests as well as to promote good practices in their advertising. Many times, I was consulted by one food manufacturer or another until I went into the World Bank. And at the time I was leaving the Bank, I was invited to be the secretary of a group that was being formed to audit and oversee the marketing practices.

Among the outcomes of the 1979 meeting, apart from the international code of marketing, were the committees that I have mentioned. Another was the establishment of baby-friendly hospitals; the ending of gratuitous baby formula donations to hospitals and health facilities, and in many countries including Ghana, the enactment of laws which controlled the marketing of baby foods and regulated conditions under which supplementary feeding was to be undertaken. The major points in the International Code of Marketing of Baby Foods are:

Companies may NOT:

1 give free supplies of milk to hospitals;

2 *promote products to the public or to health workers;*

3 *use baby pictures on baby milk, bottle or teat labels;*

4 *give gifts to mothers or health workers;*

5 *give free samples to parents; and*

6 *promote baby foods or drinks for children under six months of age.*

In addition to these, companies were advised or expected to use labels on their products in languages understood by mothers and other users and to include in these languages warningss of the adverse health consequences of not using the products according to the agreed principles. Whilst many developing countries have been making an effort to abide by these principles, I have noticed breaches in advertising in several advanced countries, but I suppose it does not matter much. There was certainly an arrest or reversal of the decline in breastfeeding in the majority of countries after the conference.

Family planning in the 1980s Conference

For some strange reason, this conference has not made the waves that it deserves. It has been overshadowed by the major UN conferences. It is not clear whether this is because the Family Planning in the 80s Conference, unlike those sponsored by the United Nations, was not inter-governmental. Nevertheless, this conference, which took place in Jakarta from 26-30 April – actually ending on 1 May, 1981 with the consideration of the final Jakarta Declaration and Recommendations, should be classed as one of the major landmarks in the population and family planning field. It must be remembered that during the 1974 United Nations Population Conference in Bucharest, family planning and population really came in for quite a bashing. It will be recalled that the then Indian Minister of Health even coined the phrase which became almost a theme song of the Conference, 'development is the best contraceptive'.

In the end, however, the population and family planning field breathed a sigh of relief because they managed to get the Bucharest conference to emphasise and accept the inherent rights of couples and individuals, particularly of individuals to have the information and means to plan their own reproductive activities. Nonetheless, after the 1974 Bucharest conference there was a certain amount of gloom within the family planning community and I recall several meetings between various agencies and individuals trying to find out what we could do to carry forward the momentum, which had built up during the late 60s and early 70s.

It was agreed that we needed a conference, which would bring together leading programme, policy and technical heads of family planning activities around the world, to look at what family planning had indeed achieved, and to see to it that some impetus was given to the field for the 80s. It took a little but in the end, the United Nations Fund for Population Activities, as it then was called, the Population Council and IPPF came together as joint sponsoring agencies for a conference devoted specifically to family planning.

It was realized that since the Geneva Conference of 1965 there had not been a conference specifically devoted to family planning in the world, so the time was considered opportune. It took at least two years to do the actual organization and the planning for the conference. This lengthy gestation period proved more than worthwhile because the conference was a resounding success, and I personally believe that some of the strategies and approaches mapped out in that conference remain relevant to our work, even today.

For the preparation, there was a steering committee based at the Population Council, chaired by Dr. George Brown. This committee had the overall charge of seeing to all of the preparatory activities that had to be undertaken. Two technical committees were formed, working with and to this steering committee. The first was the Family Planning Consultative Group, which was I chaired, and then the Policy and Resource Group, which was chaired by Ms. Billie Miller, then Minister of Health and later Deputy Prime Minister of Barbados.

The conference participants included a few ministers but were mainly technical and programmatic leaders from both developed and developing countries. In all, 133 people from 63 countries attended the meeting in Jakarta. I was elected the overall chairman of the conference. Indonesia had been chosen as the venue for the conference for one very good reason and that was because of the remarkable progress it had achieved in its family planning programme in a very short time. The Indonesian programme had demonstrated how, with the involvement and coordination of government and the BKKBN or the National Family Planning Board, family planning information and services could be brought to villagers and to diverse communities without any coercion and in ways that they readily accepted.

The Indonesian Government organized visits after the conference to allow participants to see actual family planning activities in operation. Dr. Haryono Suyono, then the head of the BKKBN, was very instrumental in making this a very major conference indeed.

The conference report, which was printed under the auspices of the Population Council entitled *Family Planning in the 1980s: Challenges and Opportunities*, is probably out of print but it should be a most useful second-time read for people who are interested in family planning and seeing how strategies and technical discussions should be undertaken. For new entrants and those who criticise the movement as coercive,e a careful study of this document will help them appreciate how wrong they have been

The objectives of the meeting, as stated in the publication were: "*to review the accomplishments of family planning over the past decade, access the challenges and opportunities for the 1980s, and identify means to strengthen commitment to family planning as an essential component of development.*" This was strictly adhered to.

A major background document was prepared with an annex, which went into greater detail of the technical and financial aspects of the family planning programmes. This, and other conference documents, were distributed to participants ahead of the meeting so it was possible for the meeting to get into business from day one.

Many major speeches were made. His Excellency President Suharto, himself, gave the opening address, followed by his Minister of Health and Chairman of the National Family Planning Coordinating Board who was made the President of the Conference, Dr. Suwajono Sunamigrat. The late Dr. Raphael M. Salas, Executive Director of UNFPA also made a resounding statement and Carl Wahren and George Zeidenstein made statements representing the IPPF and the Population Council respectively.

I had the honour of giving a keynote address and as I consider this one of the most important statements on my personal beliefs and views on population and family programmes and how they should be pursued, I have produced a summary of it below.

The meeting decided that there were four strategic issues that should guide family planning programmes. The first is the users' perspective. This came to be considered one of the most important points to consider when providing family planning services during the 80s and even today. It was believed that too many of our family planning programmes were being unnecessarily medicalised and what the actual clients wanted, how they wanted to be served and where they wanted to be served was not being given enough consideration. The users' perspective, therefore, required that family planning programmes should give their clients a voice in the selection of contraceptive methods and how these methods should be delivered.

Then there was the requirement to develop workable techniques for identifying local people's needs, problems and preferences and incorporating this directly into the

design and operation of the programmes. And lastly, we needed to launch new training programmes to enable family planning managers and staff at all operational levels to respond more effectively to the needs of the people and communities they serve.

The second strategic issue which arises directly from the above is community participation – family planning should, as much as possible, be made a concern of total communities, and something for them to internalize within the community.

The third area was the integration of the services. Stand alone family planning services were often considered unsatisfactory and unsuccessful. To a certain extent, one can even say they can be insensitive to other needs except where circumstances were absolutely against integration. The committee's recommendation was that family planning should, as much as possible, be integrated into other services that were to individuals and communities.

The actions recommended by the conference included:

1 offer family planning services as one component of care for the entire family and incorporate family planning as an essential service in primary health care programmes;

2 facilitate the incorporation of care and other social services into existing family planning programmes where these other services are not currently available; and

3 extend the range of family planning services by building upon other development activities such as education, agricultural extension, cooperatives, women's organizations, etc.

The status of women was emphasised as another strategic issue and that family planning programmes should both advocate for the improvement of women's status as well as make women subjects in the planning and implementation of family planning activities, not merely objects for services. Within the conference thinking, the status of women could not be separated from men's participation and the extent to which men had been ignored was examined and found to be completely at odds with proper programming. The following actions were recommended:

1 promote improvements in the status of women by seeking changes in laws, customs and practices that discriminate against them;

2 assist women to improve their lives by supporting special women's developing programmes in education, health, nutrition, income

generation and other areas;

3 design family planning services to address inequities between men and women. To do this programme, need to greatly increase the participation of women not only in provision of services but also in management, policy making and programme design; and finally

4 improve information and services including development of acceptable and effective methods of contraception to meet the needs of men and to enable them to assume a greater role in contraceptive decision making and practice.

A final strategic issue was the commitment of resources and on this the conference recommended that on average, "US$1 billion or less than US$0.05 per person is [made] available annually for family planning services in developing countries. Another US$500 million is provided through the national development assistances; however, the demand for family planning information and services far outstrip the available funds and the gap is growing". So a long list of actions were being advocated, one of which was to increase overall national and international expenditure for population and family planning programmes to US$3 billion annually, as rapidly as possible. Of course, as it turned out later the amount was far too small.

It is my hope that either the Population Council, IPPF or perhaps the UNFPA find a way to bringing the recommendations made at this far-reaching conference to the public once more. To me, two major issues that were emphasised in Jakarta, and have continued through all of our subsequent discussions and debates on family planning, relate to the users' perspective on the quality of care and the women's status and participation in family planning programmes.

Many in different parts of the world would like to copy what is happening in Western Europe and North America and insist that family planning programmes be based on doctors and the medical system. Where such systems are comprehensive, sufficient and are really the major ways of providing health care to a large proportion of the population, I would not disagree that the medical system should include family planning. But for many in the rural areas of developing countries another system of delivery for information and services often is required, to complement the medical system or even to take leadership in providing services to these unfortunate people. There is a problem when family planning alone is supported financially with a lot of

resources and through incentives and disincentives of various sorts. Then, family planning appears to have bene made the programme which will help resolve all other problems. This was not what the conference advocated. The conference was advocating that family planners should be aware of all of the needs of the communities they serve. With the communities, plan an attack on how to resolve to meet those needs to the extent possible. That family planning within either a component or if need be, a leadership programme, for helping communities to access resources and activities, that will help them meet some, if not all of these needs.

For the individual, a woman in most cases, who is a family planning client, the quality of care or client's perspective would mean that the social and geographic gap between them and the providers and areas for providing the services – where the individual wishes to be served and where they are most likely to be most comfortable – should be as short and as harmonized as possible.

I would advocate that it would be better to have a system where, within a village, women who are either educated or enlightened are brought into a programme and made its leaders, given supplies of various contraceptives and taught what the side effects are likely to be, how to handle them and when to refer such side effects. I believe that this would be a much more user-friendly way of handling contraceptives than to make women pay for transportation, come to bigger villages or health centres, have a perfunctory examination then go home where, if there is a problem, nobody knows how to handle it.

Of course, there is always the question of handling women whose only contact with the health service is when they are in need. In such cases, the kinds of health services that should be developed are those which go to where the women are likely to be before they find themselves ill or even pregnant. It must always be remembered that there is such a thing as the ratio of risks. What is a more serious risk, unplanned pregnancy, a side-effect from abortion, or a side-effect from a contraceptive? I personally believe that we should allow ourselves to be moved by compassion and make it easy for our clients to receive all of our services.

The International Safe Motherhood Conference

I had joined the World Bank in January 1985 and attended the Nairobi Conference on the Decade of Women in the same year. At the conference, a couple of things came out. One was a question about the neglect of women as mothers, as well as, as mothers to be. The other was an emphasis on the adverse effects of the unequal status of women

in the world generally. It came as a bombshell to the conference when the WHO representative, Dr. Angela Petros-Barvazian who was in charge of maternal and child health, quoted findings from research conducted by Dr. Robert Cooke. It indicated that half a million women were dying around the world each year from pregnancy and childbirth-related causes.

Since very few countries actually had reliable maternal mortality statistics, questions were raised about the validity of this, but even those who were most sceptical were prepared to accept that something not good was happening to pregnant women. To bolster this situation, in the same year, Allan Rosenfield and Deborah Maine, published a paper in *The Lancet* entitled *Where is the M in MCH?* This stimulated a lot of debate and discussion because its major thrust was quite clear. By combining maternal health issues within the programme of so-called maternal and child health, mothers lost out. This was because child health was technologically responsive and also had a strong emotional appeal. Additionally, rightly or wrongly, most maternal and child health activities concentrated on the promotion of the child's health than that of the mother. In many, many countries women received little more than perfunctory weighing at antenatal clinics and open hospitals or open clinics for those women who wanted to deliver in them. That left the majority of women in most developing countries, especially in Africa, delivering outside and without trained birth assistance.

These two findings stimulated a lot of discussions in health circles and the World Bank took up the issue. I remember Barbara Herz, who headed the Women in Development division, Tony Measham who was the health adviser and I, among others, took the question very seriously. Then the recently-formed Family Care International (FCI), led by Jill Sheffield, also became very interested and there was much to-ing and fro-ing about what the world should do. In the end, it was decided that a major conference should be held in one of the developing countries to attempt to analyse why the women were dying and what was to be done about it.

The conference, held in Nairobi in February 1987, was jointly organised by the World Bank, UNFPA, and WHO. The Administrator of the United Nations Development Programme (UNDP) and the Secretary-General of IPPF were present, and Family Care International was assigned the responsibility for much of organisation. Several papers were provided and invitations went out to WHO, ministers and programme planners, obstetricians, gynæcologists, health workers and the development partners. President Moi graced the opening with a speech. I was assigned the

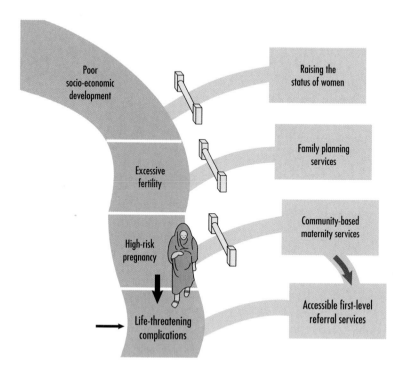

Maternal death road

responsibility of moderating the overall conference. It was challenging but the conference went well. It soon established the kinds of problems that women faced from infancy till death, through childbirth and so on, which made their lives, to use the words of the 17th century English philosopher, Thomas Hobbes, "solitary, poor, nasty, brutish, and short".

A most outstanding presentation, which kept the whole conference in perspective, was made by Professor Mahmoud Fathalla of WHO and Assiut University in Egypt. He styled his presentation *Why did Mrs. X Die?* It showed the challenges faced by a female child, from lack of maternal and family care, even before her birth, through her malnutrition or discriminatory nutrition, and child rearing practices as far as the female child is concerned, through discriminatory education attendance, to being given out to marriage early, or being put out to work too early, and not being cared for during pregnancy properly and there not being proper maternity care when she had to deliver and she dies during delivery or immediately thereafter.

At every stage, Dr. Fathalla pointed out exit avenues that, if we did something better for women even before they got pregnant and then did not discriminate against the girl child but gave the her a good nutritional foundation that would prepare her for the future; if we gave the girl child a good education it would ensure her economic strength and her ability to make choices for herself; if she were not pushed into marriage too early, if she were allowed to have family planning practice when she started having sex and continuing into marriage or child bearing so she could plan her children. Many of these things could have been avoided until the final days of *ante* natal and *intra* natal care. A fascinating document, which became a most sought after video teaching material.

The conference itself had ministers including the late Prof. Ransome-Kuti of Nigeria and the WHO Africa Regional Representative of the time, Dr. Lobé Monekosso making very powerful statements. They mainly emphasised why the whole world should feel ashamed that such bad treatment of girls and women was leading to so much suffering and premature death. There was a general feeling of outrage and of humble acceptance that what was happening to girls and women, because of the disproportionate biological burden placed on them by their natural role of replacing the human resource, should be an affront to humanity and our technological development. In all, 140 experts from 30 countries were present at the conference.

The outcome of the meeting was a declaration on what to do for achieving safer motherhood. The history of the evolution of this declaration is interesting. Right at the beginning of the conference, I appointed a group to help track our recommendations and findings and help put them together as a declaration at the end of the conference. It was not too long before I was informed that the group was completely divided over some issues which had been aired on the floor of the conference. Apparently, some of the donor representatives felt that one aim of the conference was to advocate the establishment of a United Nations agency for women if not for maternal health by itself. If such an advocacy group existed, I was not made aware of it – but then I had only relatively recently joined the World Bank, so I did not know where the World Bank stood on an issue like this.

It became obvious to me the day before the conference was scheduled to end that the group had been so completely engrossed in arguments that they had not kept abreast of what the conference's conclusions and recommendations were. I therefore had to improvise my own conclusions, which I presented verbally the evening before the closure of the conference. Ms. Ann Starrs of FCI took careful notes of my oral

presentation and helped write it in a final form. This became the conference declaration which was endorsed with practically no change by the conference the next morning.

Apart from the declaration, which became the basis for the International Safe Motherhood Initiative, an outcome of the conference was the formation of the Safe Motherhood Inter-Agency Group, which included the three sponsors of the conference plus UNICEF and UNDP, as well as IPPF and the Population Council. This group, I must say, kept safe motherhood on the front burner of both agencies and countries for a long time and if the Initiative did not achieve success in the ten or twenty years which followed, one cannot say that it was the fault of the Inter Agency Group. I do not think any group I have worked with has shown so much enthusiasm and so much application for its major role.

The declaration de-emphasised the dependence on traditional birth attendants. It emphasized access to both professional and emergency obstetrics care. It also laid emphasis on a comprehensive approach to women's health care and this has been criticized by many medical people and observers as having misled the field into spending money on areas which did not make an immediate impact on maternal health or maternal mortality. I do not think those of us who were at the conference need to feel any remorse or regret at this, because the holistic approach to health care is what is being practised and advocating an holistic approach did not exclude concentration on areas which required specialised care.

Below are the major points in the declaration which I read out:

- we need to generate the political commitment to reallocate resources to implement the available strategies that can reduce maternal mortality by an estimated 50 percent in one decade;
- we need to remember that the industrialized countries faced this challenge in the past. For some the change has taken place in our lifetime, through dedication and the reallocation of priorities;
- we need an integrated approach to maternal health care that makes ita priority within the context of primary health care services and overall development policy;
- we need to reach decision makers in family and government to change laws and attitudes, and to improve the legal and health status of women generally, especially in areas such as adolescent marriage and restrictions on health care delivery;

- we need to mobilize and involve the community, and particularly women themselves, in planning and implementing policies, programmes and projects, so that their needs and preferences are explicitly taken into account;
- we need to utilize a range of information, education, and communication activities to reach communities, women, men, boys and policymakers through the media and all culturally appropriate channels;
- we need to carry out additional studies to gain better country- and locale-specific information on maternal mortality – its immediate causes, which we know, and its root causes, some of which either we do not know or we ignore;
- we need to have ongoing operational research and evaluation activities to assess the effectiveness of various programmes;
- we need to expand family planning and family life education programmes, particularly for young people, and make services for planning families socially, culturally, financially and geographically accessible;
- we need to use appropriate technologies at all levels so that women have better care at lower costs;
- we need to strengthen community-based maternal health care delivery systems, upgrade existing facilities, and create relevant new ones if necessary;
- we need to ensure that pregnant women are screened by supervised and trained non-physician health workers where appropriate, with relevant technology including pantographs for monitoring the progress of labour as needed, to identify those at risk and to provide pre-natal care and care during delivery as expeditiously as possible;
- we need to strengthen referral facilities – hospitals as well as health centres – and locate them appropriately. They need to be equipped to handle emergency situations effectively and efficiently;
- we need to implement an alarm and transport system that ensures that women in need of emergency care reach the referral facilities in time to be helped.

These activities need to be seen within a comprehensive, multisectoral approach, although they do not have to wait for all sectors to achieve improvement simultaneously. These

activities need to involve governments as well as take advantage of the flexibility, responsiveness and creativity of non-governmental organizations. They need to stimulate and support input from the communities themselves.

Perhaps the most important contribution of this Safe Motherhood Initiative will be to call attention to the problems related to it, and to create an awareness that something can, should – indeed must – be done, starting with the commitment of heads of states and governments.

A philosopher from my country – Ghana – once looked at a map of Africa and said, "It is asking the question 'why?'". Today the women of developing countries, like mother Africa, are asking "Why are you letting us die?". The answer is in your hands.

Again, a criticism was made that if we were to save mothers from death, then what was necessary was a very clear-cut clinical approach to the problem and we should be sure that emergency obstetric care had full government support and was made accessible to practically every woman who became pregnant.

Ten years after the initiative was launched, there was a meeting held in Colombo, Sri Lanka, to try and assess what had been achieved and what was to be done in the next decade. This meeting agreed to a large extent, that TBA, should not stand for "traditional birth attendant", but rather "trained birth attendant". The trained birth attendant could be a medical person or a nurse/midwife trained in obstetrics, who would know where the dangers were and would be able to refer to the next level if necessary. The service, it was agreed, should be developed and should not depend solely on pre-delivery identification of risk groups, since the majority of women who had problems were women in whom no previous risks could be identified. So the best approach, we felt, was for the trained birth attendants and families to be able to identify risk signals and move to the next level as quickly as practicable. The need for transport, well developed and equipped facilities and professionals with the skill to handle things rapidly preventing unnecessary, but all too frequent, delays were all emphasized at the ten year re-visit of the Safe Motherhood Initiative.

One area not emphasized at all in 1987, which for some reason even I myself omitted, was unsafe abortion. Many have quite rightly pointed to this as a failure on our part. On reflection we must have been skirting away from the possible influence of the US Mexico City Policy. There was at the time an effort to be all inclusive and focus on the areas on which we could agree. I have since made my personal position much clearer in papers and in public speeches. Unsafe abortion is, in many

developing countries, the number one or two cause of maternal mortality. Eliminating it as a cause should be a priority in programmes.

Twenty years later, the initiative blossomed at its review at the Women Deliver Conference in London, which also was so very well attended and led to many, many changes which I shall discuss later.

The Safe Motherhood Initiative, apart from the declaration, apart from getting governments to shape the rhetoric right and apart from getting medical scientists to do the necessary research for the evidence on which programmes could be based, led to the clamour for the inclusion of maternal health and the reduction of maternal mortality in the Millennium Development Goals (MDGs). Unfortunately, these goals did not include the other reproductive health goals, but at the review of the MDGs in 2005, universal access to reproductive health services and education was added under the maternal health goal as a target and now the concentration and the evidence-based approach to safer motherhood is reasonably well established.

13 the cairo conference, september 1994

Of all the conferences in which I played a major role, perhaps none has been of such international significance as the International Conference on Population and Development (ICPD), which took place in Cairo in September 1994. It was the sequel to the Mexico International Population Conference, which had taken place ten years earlier – the assumption had always been that these conferences would be held at ten yearly intervals.

In 1989, five years after the Mexico City conference, the Economic and Social Council (ECOSOC) of the United Nations approved that a Conference on Population and Development should be held in 1994. Dr. Nafis Sadik, the UNFPA Executive Director, was appointed Secretary General and the Chief of the Population Division of the United Nations was appointed as her deputy. This combined appointment, I suppose, ensured that the two agencies most directly involved with population issues in the United Nations system should take on the leadership of the conference, unlike the very first conference, Bucharest 1974, which was led by a former minister. The early decision ensured that there would be time enough to prepare thoroughly for the conference.

The preparations for the Conference were detailed and very intense. They consisted of expert group meetings, regional group meetings and then preparatory committee meetings which took place yearly for the three years before the conference itself was held. The expert group meetings included:

1 Population Environment and Development, held in New York in January 1992;

2 Population Policies and Programmes, held in Cairo in April 1992;

3 Population and Women, held in Gaborone in June 1992;

4 Family Planning, Health and Family Well-being, held in Bangalore in October 1992;

5 Population Growth and Demographic Structure, held in Paris in November 1992;

6 Population Distribution and Migration, held in Santa Cruz in
January 1993.

I was only able to attend the meeting in Bangalore, which took place at a time when
the International Planned Parenthood Federation (IPPF) was holding its annual
meeting in India. It was a very fruitful, coming out with very far-reaching declarations
and conclusions emphasizing really the importance of family planning and the need
to combine family planning with more holistic care of women and children.

I was also involved in the Africa Regional Meeting which was held under the
aegis of UNFPA and the Economic Commission for Africa in the N'gor Hotel in
Dakar, in December 1992. By then I was chairman of the Ghana National Population
Council and I was therefore attending in my capacity as a national delegate.

I found this regional meeting most intriguing and quite a contrast with
previous Africa regional meetings where the subject of family planning and the need
to moderate population growth rate had been challenged on the pretext that as Africa
had a large land mass, was under populated, and that Africa's problem was one of
development and not population growth.

At this meeting, whilst it was accepted that, purely on numbers per square
kilometre, Africa did not have a high-density population. Nevertheless, when
considered in terms of the growth potential, the amount of arable land available for
Africans, the potential for water stress in different countries and regions in Africa,
Africa needed to look at her population growth rate in relation to her own development
needs and aspirations. Furthermore, the political realities of Africa demanded that the
population be looked at not for the continent as a whole but almost nation by nation.
It was made clear that Africa's population structure, particularly the youthfulness of
the population, posed problems for its fertility moderation and thereby its overall
population growth in relation to its resources. There was a need for serious attention
to planning for the needs of ever increasing populations. At the end of the conference
a draft declaration was issued which included the following points:

*"The draft declaration focused on the following areas: population, sustained
economic growth and sustainable development; family, fertility and family
planning; mortality, morbidity and AIDS; urbanization and migration;
refugees and distressed persons; women in development; children, data
collection and analysis information; dissemination, training and research;*

information, education and communication; the role of private and non-governmental organizations; the sub-regional and regional groupings; the World Bank and relevant organizations of the United Nations systems; and the international community...

"African countries, they declared, should integrate population policies so as to reduce population growth from the present rate of 3.0% per annum to 2.5 per cent by the year two thousand and to 2 per cent by the year 2010.

"Environmental Issues and Food Security were given special attention. The targets set on the contraceptive prevalence rate for Africa were to reach 20 per cent by the year 2000 and 40% by the year 2010. The following targets were to be attained by the year 2000. Life expectancy in Africa at least 55 years and infant mortality rates of less than 50 per thousand life births, childhood mortality rates of 70 or less, programmes to prevent AIDS were also stressed. The declaration called on UN organizations, the World Bank, the Organization of African Unity and the African Development Bank to implement the recommendations. The international community was requested to consider conversion of the African debt into grants to be used in the financing of population activities."

Even though I was one of the chief movers of some of these things, I was pleasantly surprised at the ease with which many of the numerical goals were accepted. That goals for population growth rates could be accepted in Africa in 1992 would have been difficult to forecast in 1974 or even in 1984 when the Arusha Meeting declared for family planning as a part of comprehensive development. In reviewing whether the low resistance to the inclusion of goals made for more vigorous and successful implementation, I must confess to much disappointment. I cannot say that the African countries have moved very rapidly towards attainment of the goals, except avery few countries that will be mentioned later.

The preparatory committees, known as PrepComs, started in earnest. I attended part of the second PrepCom and took the chair on occasion. I was heavily engaged as chairman for PrepCom III which met twice in 1993, and was supposed to be the final preparatory meeting to deal in detail with drafts for the Programme of Action.

For these United Nations conferences, because of their size, there is the need to have a draft of the principal document in advance. These drafts are agreed at the PrepComs which are committees of all of the countries belonging to the United Nations, plus those non-governmental organizations which have in consultancy status with the United Nations.

For ICPD, however, Dr Nafis Sadik decided that all non-governmental organizations, which were dealing with the subject of population, family planning and women's development in one way or another, could, if they wished, register with the United Nations and become participants in the conference. What was more important, the non-governmental organizations were given a right of involvement in the conference, including making plenary statements to the conference, which had not been done before.

During PrepCom III, the final preparatory meeting before Cairo, several issues became very contentious. These included adolescent sexual, reproductive health and rights; equity and equality of women; and abortion. Several country representatives did not appear to distinguish between sexuality and sex. For some, reproductive rights were simply equivalent to licentiousness and to others it was a dodge for abortion on demand. None of this was correct but much of the debate was like a dialogue between the deaf.

The issue of abortion, perhaps, became the most contentious thanks to the Vatican and a handful of countries. This group maintained that the inclusion of the phrase 'unsafe abortion' was not right, because abortion was deadly for the foetus irrespective of what happened to the mother to be or the pregnant woman, afterwards. There was also the insistence that once fertilization had taken place, the product was not only a potential life but an actual human and therefore the destruction of that life would be a major sin, one to be equated to murder. Of course, the majority of the world's participants did not agree; but the debate on how to put wording into the document which satisfied all sides was so prolonged and so intense that the final determination only took place in Cairo itself. Many other subjects went to Cairo for determination, too. These included gender equity and equality; sexual and reproductive health and rights; adolescent sexuality among others.

For some representatives from Islamic countries, gender equality in a strict sense would be against some tenets of their religion. The problem of sexual health and reproductive rights were related by and large to the sexual orientation that was implied in sexual health. Some groups maintained that this was giving rights to gays and lesbians,

which their religious teachings or cultures abhorred. Some countries or some cultures would not accept that women, and adolescent girls in particular, had rights outside their families or the protection of their males who should take responsibility for them.

To some extent, the divergent and sometimes extreme positions held inside and outside the United Nations building, instead of detracting from the conference, actually helped to keep the conference and its problems in the media. I am sure it did a lot to stimulate so much enthusiasm for the conference that, in the end, it resulted in far greater participation by heads of state, governments and top level delegations than at any other population conference.

The Vatican really mounted a major war on the conference document. At one stage during the PrepCom III the Vatican representative accused the draft document of being devoid of any ethical basis. I felt rather riled by this and retorted that the Vatican was not the absolute repository of ethics which had to be based on cultural social and legal realities of countries and communities. In a similar vein the Vatican had disseminated a critique of the draft document to all countries and states calling on them to reject the document because it was against many of the religious and ethical principles of Christianity. The Ghana copy was sent to me from the Castle, our seat of government, for a reply. I chose to advise that it be ignored.

The conference assembled in Cairo and I was again elected to chair the main committee – it was only in 2009 that Dr. Nafis Sadik informed me of how hard she had worked the telephones to get my government to send me to Cairo at all. Dr. Maher Mahran, the Minister of Population and Family Welfare of Egypt, was the Conference Vice-President; the President of Egypt was *de jure* President. ICPD turned out to be the biggest of the population conferences thus far – it had 11,000 participants from some 180 countries with around 4,000 attending a parallel non-governmental organization forum. The conference itself was opened by Hosni Mubarak, President of Egypt. There were many glowing stimulating and challenging statements from heads of states and governments. Some of these gave indications of the battles to come during the effort to come to closure on the draft programme of action. Of the truly challenging statements I recall those by the Secretary General of the United Nations, Boutros Boutros-Ghali. He set out a number of "vital questions" to help us meet our objectives:

- what are the links between population, sustained economic growth and sustainable development?

- what should our attitude be to population growth and structure?
- how can equality of the sexes and emancipation of women be ensured?
- what is the role to be played by the family?
- how can child and maternal mortality be reduced?
- how can we protect the dignity and well-being of the old?
- what is the best way of promoting population and family-planning policies?
- how can internal and international migratory movements be controlled?
- what should be the role of the non-governmental organizations in addressing these fundamental problems?

He went on:

> "...I should like to suggest to you, not a method of work, but what I should like to call 'principles of conduct'. These principles, which should set the tone of the Cairo Conference, can, it seems to me, be embodied in three essential words which I offer for your attention: rigour, tolerance and conscience."

While tolerance and conscience are immediately clear, rigour might need a little explanation. By rigour the Secretary General was asking the conference to examine the scientific evidence and give due respect to it as a basis for the recommendations. As the chairman of the main committee, responsible for finalizing the Programme of Action, I considered this a direct charge to me.

Norwegian Prime Minister Dr Gro Harlem Brundtland made some good points on religion, family planning and the importance of decriminalising abortion:

> "Sometimes religion is a major obstacle. This happens when family planning is made a moral issue. But morality cannot only be a question of controlling sexuality and protecting unborn life. Morality is also a question of giving individuals the opportunity of choice, of suppressing coercion of all kinds and abolishing the criminalization of individual tragedy. Morality becomes hypocrisy if it means accepting mothers' suffering or dying in connection with unwanted pregnancies and illegal abortions, and unwanted children living in misery.

> "None of us can disregard [the fact] that abortions occur, and that where they are illegal, or heavily restricted, the life and health of the woman is often at

risk. Decriminalizing abortions should therefore be a minimal response to this reality, and a necessary means of protecting the life and health of women."

Vice-President Al Gore emphasised that the United States was not seeking a new international right to abortion:

"I want to be clear about the United States position on abortion so that there is no misunderstanding. We believe that making available the highest quality family-planning and health-care services will simultaneously respect women's own desires to prevent unintended pregnancies, reduce population growth and the rate of abortion.

"The United States Constitution guarantees every woman within our borders a right to choose an abortion, subject to limited and specific exceptions. We are committed to that principle. But let us take a false issue off the table: the United States does not seek to establish a new international right to abortion, and we do not believe that abortion should be encouraged as a method of family planning."

Benazir Bhutto dealt extensively with the issue of gender. The courage of a woman from an Islamic state challenging long-held views such as gender equity and equality, whilst defending others, was most refreshing to me.

The statement from the United States was very encouraging, particularly to those of us with memories from Mexico, 10 years earlier. Whilst Al Gore defended the right of the American woman to abortion according the United States constitution, as stated by the Supreme Court in Roe v Wade, he also made it clear that the United States was not advocating an international right to abortion. At this time, the Clinton administration was in power and the leadership on the population issues had changed and so had the United States' position and behaviour. Their team was led by Tim Wirth, a wise and convivial character, who got on very well with practically everybody and who provided United States leadership in a very quiet and subtle way. He met with Europeans and others and made his country's position clear. He met with the secretariat and got to know where difficulties lay. I had meetings with him and I found him a most encouraging and engaging person. Because of his personal effort, much of the conference was made a success. His behaviour and that of the United States' delegation contrasted so sharply with the aggressive and intolerant behaviour of the US delegation in 1984.

This time, everybody felt that the United States was playing a leadership role worthy of the most powerful country in the world, a country which really and truly has done so much in putting money into the fields of population and family planning.

I decided to hand over certain sections of the document for discussion by committees. The vice-chair who handled the most difficult portions of the document, on sexual and reproductive health, was Nic Biegman, the Ambassador of the Netherlands to the United Nations. I took on the handling of the *Introduction to the Programme of Action* as practically the whole chapter was in square brackets, meaning it had to be completely re-negotiated. This was going to give the principles within which the programme was to be developed and be a guide to its implementation. I must state at this point that although the representative of the Vatican made his position quite firm when necessary, he was most understanding and provided some very helpful wording for some of the knotty sections of the *châpeau* and the preamble to the programme of action.

Ambassador Biegman did sterling work and I am eternally grateful for the way he handled the abortion issue and came out with Article 8.25 which has become perhaps the most often quoted article of the whole programme of action. It states:

> *"In no case should abortion be promoted as a method of family planning. All governments and relevant inter-governmental and non-governmental organizations are urged to strengthen their commitment to women's health, to deal with the health impact of unsafe abortion as a major public health concern and to reduce the recourse to abortion through expanded and improved family-planning services. Prevention of unwanted pregnancies must always be given the highest priority and every attempt should be made to eliminate the need for abortion. Women who have unwanted pregnancies should have ready access to reliable information and compassionate counselling. Any measures or changes related to abortion within the health system can only be determined at the national or local level according to the national legislative process. In circumstances where abortion is not against the law, such abortion should be safe. In all cases, women should have access to quality services for the management of complications arising from abortion. Post-abortion counselling, education and family-planning services should be offered promptly, which will also help to avoid repeat abortions."*

This, to me, was an excellent outcome after long hours of somewhat tedious debate.

I was particularly pleased with the statement about "where abortion is legal". Since abortion is completely illegal only in a tiny minority of countries, my understanding was that we could now handle legal abortions openly to the extent permitted by the law and its interpretation. In fact when the 21st Special Session of the United Nations General Assembly dealt with ICPD five years later, Article 8.25 received special attention. In the end a statement which made what to do "where abortion is legal" even clearer was agreed. Article 63iii of *Key actions for the further implementation of the PoA of ICPD* states :

> *"In recognizing and implementing the above, and in circumstances where abortion is not against the law, health systems should train and equip health-service providers and should take other measures to ensure that such abortion is safe and accessible. Additional measures should be taken to safeguard women's health."*

Some difficult issues which could have proved problematic in Cairo had been deftly handled quite early in the discussions in New York. One of these was how to handle population growth and environmental problems. Another was how to handle migration.

Population, the environment and pollution

First, population, the environment and pollution. Efforts by the west and others from the industrialized north to make it appear as if there was a linear relationship between population growth and environmental degradation, and particularly with pollution and climate change were quickly put to rest. It was made clear that there were different relationships depending on whether we were dealing with wealthy regions or with poor ones. The relationship was not entirely linear. Whereas the environmental degradation that accompanies development activities in the less developed areas could be attributed to poverty and the lack of capital, and maybe, also direct pressure on very few natural resources by increasing numbers, these did not cause as much major environmental pollution and other global problems as were caused by the more developed parts of the world, by way of their bad industrialization policies, bad disposal of waste policies and their excessive consumption and general greed. It was accepted that when all the factors that influenced the environment were put together the small numerical increase of the population in industrialized countries had much greater adverse impact on the global environment than the larger population increases of most developing countries.

The problem for the developing countries was mainly the poverty-driven environmental degradation, mostly involving biological degradation of their sources of water, erosion and the destruction of their forest support systems all of which help aggravate poverty. It was finally agreed that since environmental issues had had a hearing at the Earth Summit that was held two years earlier in Rio, there was no need to go into them again, and that numbers *qua* numbers could not be held as solely or largely responsible for all environmental problems. This helped us concentrate on the major objectives of the ICPD and prevented the possibly unending discordant debates on the importance of population growth rates on environmental degradation and climate change.

On the question of migration, it was decided very early on in the PrepCom process that as migration was such a huge issue, it was better left to another conference to be organized by the United Nations.

Of course, during and after the conference, there were quite a few who thought that the word 'development' had been attached to the end of ISCPD's name simply to make it "sexy"; and that neither at the PrepCom nor during the conference itself had there been any deep discussion of development. I cannot help but disagree with this. No conference can discuss everything related to development; so this conference on population and development chose to concentrate on those areas of development which had a very direct relationship with population, its growth or diminution and its structure. Areas of development such as health, education, and women empowerment were therefore the logical areas to be considered in detail and recorded in the document.

The document which came out was agreed to be setting some kind of programmes and goals to be achieved within two decades. This again was something which had not been done before.

There were some important points which came out in the Cairo Conference, which have remain points of contention, even today. A major one is that Cairo, by putting population into the context of the holistic development of individuals and families, and in putting actions to influence population growth rates, particularly family planning, into the context of sexual and reproductive health, it had moved people and institutions away from thinking of the demographic realities which should be of great importance in development programming. I beg to differ.

What Cairo tried to do was to point out that the strategies for attacking family planning or for trying to reduce population growth rates, which had been pursued by

many, strategies which one could describe as mono-purpose or monovalent, were not succeeding well in countries where development of women had been stifled for cultural, social or economic reasons. Secondly, the evidence was increasing that providing better health care for populations was a major way for making communities and individuals appreciate the need for keeping their population growth rates down.

Finally, education and socio-economic development go hand in hand. The evidence available at the time seemed to show that women's education, in particular, contributed to greatly enhancing the acceptance and implementation of family planning programmes by a community or family. It was thus necessary that proposals for undertaking fertility management of any kind should take account of this. And so it was that Cairo decided that people should now be looked upon not as simply biological individuals who could be coerced or advised to do something about their numbers, but that their whole life, particularly their education, their family circumstances, etc., needed to be considered. Hence the holistic approach that was taken by ICPD.

The ICPD therefore, went into this and, from my viewpoint which I expressed in a lecture sponsored by the MacArthur Foundation, given in Lagos a year after the ICPD:

> "... Cairo signalled an understanding that population is at last seen as part of the necessary investment in people, without which none of our development or environmental problems will be solved. Educating girls and making women truly equal partners in development, reducing infant and child mortality, promoting safe motherhood, giving access to quality family planning, tackling the problems of sexually transmitted diseases and providing clean water, are all connected with improving family health and reducing family size. Slowing population growth, in turn, will feed back its social, economic and environmental benefits."

I quote here also something of what I presented in Copenhagen at a seminar dealing with the follow-up to ICPD in 2005. I maintained:

> "... Cairo went far beyond population and family planning concerns and developed the Programme of Action on an holistic platform which made the role and status of women central to human development needs generally and those related to sexuality in particular."

I asked the question, "what did we agree in Cairo?" and the following were the four essential points that emerged from the ICPD processes to underpin its Programme of Action:

1 *It was accepted that population and development problems are not simply a relationship between numbers and development needs such as schools, health care and low savings and investments but also between numbers and development attainments. By this, I mean lifestyles and consumption practice, as stated elsewhere.*

2 *The need for poverty alleviation programmes between and within countries as an essential plank to all efforts to lower fertility and human numbers. This was taken forward at the Copenhagen World Summit on Social Development (WSSD) March 1995, which followed immediately after the ICPD.*

3 *It was accepted that population problems cannot be tackled from a purely macro numbers approach. Solutions must be found at the micro level. So much of what is to be done depends on a proper understanding of people as individuals, families and communities – the status and roles of women, their education, economic pursuits and the proper attention to their general health and reproductive health needs in particular.*

4 *Population and development are issues of concern to many sectors. They should therefore be shared issues, to be handled by many stakeholders severally and in coalitions.*

I then went on to say that based on these major principles, a 20-year Programme of Action was developed which included the following actions by countries:

1 *Ensure universal access to [high] quality and affordable reproductive health services including family planning and sexual health. Reproductive health services, including family planning, can save the lives and improve the health of women and children. A 1996 report by UNICEF concluded that the "the first and most obvious step towards reducing the toll of maternal mortality and morbidity is to make high quality family planning services available to all who need them." These services are also a key component in efforts to slow down population growth.*

2 *To enable couples make real choices about family size through a series of social investments.*

3 *Improve rates of child survival. No country in the developing world has experienced a sustained reduction in family size without first reducing*

*infant and child mortality. Couples must feel confident that their
children will survive before they are willing to have fewer children.*

4 *Expand educational opportunities, close the gender gap in education and
provide universal access to primary education. Educated women tend to want
smaller families and are better at looking after the children they do have.*

5 *Invest in women's development. When women can exercise their full legal
and social rights, they often have both the desire and ability to choose
smaller families.*

6 *Expand opportunities for young women. In the year 2000 some 400
million adolescent girls stood on the brink of adulthood. If many chose to
delay child bearing even for a few years, they will enhance their health,
education and employment prospects. In the year 2100 the developing
countries' population would be smaller by 1.1 billion if the average age
at bearing the first child is delayed by 5 years.*

But perhaps what will go down as one of the most remarkable achievements of Cairo
is also the area that is creating the most debate and outright dissent in some circles:
the concept of sexual and reproductive rights. The governments agreed that these
embrace certain human rights and include:

1 *The right of individuals and couples to decide freely and responsibly the
spacing of their children and to have the information and means to do so.*

2 *The right to attain the highest standard of reproductive and sexual health.*

3 *The right to make decisions free of discrimination, coercion or violence.*

Unfortunately, I believe that strategies to implement these programme ideas and how
to pay for them received very restricted discussion in Cairo. Even at the five year
review, that is the ICPD+5 in 1999, not much was done about them. Although the
programme of action ended with some ideas about how much money would be
required for paying for strategies and programmes, based on the actions
recommended, these did not receive any true endorsement or pledges of what to do.

For the world I believe the inclusion of so many of the ICPD goals in the
Millennium Development Goals (MDG) was a recognition of the importance of the
conference. Ideological and religious opposition and the deliberate misrepresentation
led to the omission of a goal on reproductive health, an omission later corrected by

the addition of a target under MDG 5 on maternal health. Better late than never.

Among the many activities that I have been pursuing since the ICPD none has been more rewarding than helping to implement the ICPD Programme of Action at the national, regional and international levels. This has taken the form of workshops, seminars and conferences. As the majority ended in declarations, summary reports or calls to action accessible easily, I would like to concentrate here on a few in which my participation was strong.

When it became clear to the international non-governmental organizations that there would be no United Nations sponsored 10-year follow up of ICPD, IPPF, jointly with FCI and PAI, decided to hold a conference in London at the end of September 2004. The conference – Countdown 2015 – aimed to evaluate what progress had been made in implementing the programme of action and to recommend what should be done to achieve the aims and objectives in the years to 2015. A small planning committee, on which I served, had met in Bellagio and worked hard to develop a programme. A magazine style brochure had been produced with a pullout section giving figures and data evaluating various parameters. I made what was a powerful plenary statement calling on reproductive health and rights advocates to be fearless, but also to listen and use language and approaches that made sense to the clients.

As a purely non-governmental organization sponsored meeting, with some 700 participants from 109 countries, it had none of the restrictions of the United Nations ones. It was able to discuss all areas freely and the questions of unsafe abortion and youth sexual and reproductive health received good attention; the latter through very active youth participation. The former area benefited from an Ipas-sponsored workshop. The conclusions and the recommendations have been widely disseminated so I would like to mention only three important statements:

- "... sexual and reproductive rights are human rights – universal, inter -dependent and indivisible";
- "... make safe legal abortion accessible and available to every woman who chooses it, free from the threat of violence or coercion",

and perhaps the most challenging, was the expression of a vision for the world as follows;

- "a world where all who need them have access to health, education and social services, and where spending on books replaces spending on missiles and warplanes".

It must be remembered that these statements were being made during an American election campaign for Mr. Bush's second term when the American right was being its most vicious self against reproductive health and rights.

Women Deliver

The year 2007 was to be the 20th anniversary of the Safe Motherhood Initiative and we started discussing what to do soon after Countdown 2015. Another international conference was the suggestion, but with a different title and it would have deal with more than just safe motherhood, perhaps girls, women and mothers in a comprehensive way. Jill Sheffield suggested to me that the conference be termed *Women Deliver*, with a full title of *Women Deliver – Invest in women, it pays*. It rang well with me and obviously to practically everyone who heard it. The conference was very well prepared by a large working group in which I was involved. FCI was the lead organization and this time United Nations agencies were readily involved. While the planning committee decided on all aspects of the conference, the true leadership went to Jill Sheffield and Frances Kissling. The latter led in developing the content of the programme whilst the former was responsible for everything else, including fund-raising at which she amazed the entire committee.

The conference which took place at the new Excel Conference facility in London's Dockland in October 2007. It was attended by more than 2,000 people from some 109 countries. It consisted of plenaries, break-out sessions, a speaker's corner, a youth symposium, and exhibitions. But perhaps a most important item was the forum of ministers.

Originally we had wanted that to be for finance ministers and health ministers, but unfortunately the dates clashed with a World bank-IMF meeting so most finance ministers could not come to London. One or two did manage and with ministers of health, of women affairs and of welfare, a most successful forum took place chaired by Steven Sinding. The grand opening ceremony saw a video message from the British Prime Minister, Gordon Brown. After opening remarks on the history and objectives of the conference, Douglas Alexander, UK Secretary of State for International Development; the Deputy Secretary General of the United Nations, Ms. Asha-Rose Migiro; and Ms. Mary Robinson, a former president of Ireland, gave stimulating welcome addresses.

I then moderated an opening plenary based on a background document prepared

and delivered by Geeta Rao Gupta, President of the International Centre for Research on Women (ICRW). My high level panel consisted of Julio Frenk, former Minister of Health of Mexico, P Kamalan of the International Trade Union Confederation (ITUC) from Malaysia, Thoraya Obaid of the UNFPA, Peter Piot of the UNAIDS and Mary Robinson.

Practically everything that happened at this conference is now on the internet so I will only state how important the conference was and the fact that it has succeeded in raising awareness of the issues of women's sexual and reproductive health needs and their relationship to all of human development to a greater extent than expected. Several countries pledged financial assistance for safer motherhood, The MacArthur Foundation announced its funding for field research into the anti-shock garment and the minister's forum came out with a most important statement. My own closing statement emphasized the need for all to be involved. Perhaps our seriously unanticipated result was the call for *Women Deliver* to become a separate organization from the FCI so it could move the agenda for women even more forcefully. The organization is now up and running and will hold the next conference in Washington DC in June 2010.

Back to back with the *Women Deliver* conference Marie Stopes International (MSI) and Ipas held the *Global Safe Abortion* conference in the Queen Elizabeth Hall, London. Efforts by an opposition group to mount a demonstration were singularly unsuccessful and petered out after a day. Some 800 experts, human rights activists, women's activists, programme planners and legislators from all over the world took part in this conference which coincided with the 40 year anniversary of Britain liberalising its abortion laws, A report of this conference is available on the internet. I spoke at the opening plenary and after openly stating how my position on restricted abortion laws had developed I went on to call for all involved to interpret the ICPD statement on abortion "where legal" as widely as possible to benefit women. My anguish at the apartheid-type interpretation of the law led me to state: "... The implementation of restrictive abortion laws end in the worst form of apartheid, those who are rich get safe abortion whilst the poor die from unsafe abortion". A global call to action for women's access to safe abortion was agreed, stating among other things, that the participants would agree to work to:

- stop deaths and injuries from unsafe abortion;
- end the silence and hypocrisy that surround the issue of abortion;
- give voice to the voiceless women and girls who suffer most from this tragedy;
- ensure universal access to safe abortion care;

- erase the stigma that hinders progress on this issue;
- fight for social justice and for the health, well-being and equality of all women.

To me, the call to action emphasises the national and international need to have all concerned work to free women and girls from the burden that unsafe abortion places so unfairly on them. The question I ask myself, my government and all who are against abortion is how do we continue to fight against a public health problem so easy to solve?

14 the africa population advisory committee

In the middle of 1990, I left the World Bank and went back to Ghana. Before leaving, I managed to arrange for a position with the World Bank which was rather interesting – working as a consultant/adviser to Edward Jaycox, then Vice President for the Africa Region. Although I did not have regular duties, my pay was based within Jaycox's office and as such I could then be hired as a consultant to any part of Africa without the group inviting me having to pay from its budget. This proved a most satisfactory arrangement to many of the staff. It was in this capacity that I helped to deal with the development of a major project in Nigeria, devoted a great deal of time to the Agenda Programme of the Africa Population Advisory Committee and the several important contributions made to the programmes of the World Development Institute, the training arm of the World Bank.

While I was in the World Bank the question of how to make Africa population assistance more effective and how to get family planning programmes better accepted by our African populations became a hot topic. After a lot of discussion, I brought up the way I had started the Danfa Comprehensive Family Planning and Health Research Project in Ghana, as Professor of Community Health or Professor of Social and Preventive Medicine. It was based on the simple idea which has now become commonplace – listening to the people.

When we wanted to start the project in Danfa, we went to the people and asked them what they wanted. They told us the first thing was safe drinking water, the second was a health clinic and the third was a market. What we then did was to find some people, headed by my wife, who could deal with the ministries of Social Welfare and Community Development and the Water Department, to get water supplies to the village. We also started demarcating market areas in some villages – that took a long time. Meanwhile, we sat with them discussing how to get the clinic going. They agreed, plans for the building were drawn up, and agreements were reached as to who would be responsible for what. The villagers were to provide manual labour whilst the medical

school provided the materials for building the clinic. The rest of this is history and can be found in other documents and papers.

I told this story to many people in the World Bank. At the same time the World Bank also had a gentleman who had dealt with the same subject, listening to the people, in Latin American during an urban building project. It was agreed that we should try this on the African continent. Ishrat Hussein who was then in the Africa Region of the World Bank was very active in trying to get this organized from within her department. I provided support with some non-governmental organization allocations that remained unused. We hired Prof. George Benneh, of Ghana and Dr. John Oucho, from Kenya, as consultants to come and help us map out the directions in which we would go with this idea. They made far reaching recommendations, including getting universities, research institutions and programme personnel to undertake pilot studies which might be exemplars of how to get family planning efforts better understood and accepted. They also advised that the findings should be a basis for advising policy makers on how to approach family planning programme development in Africa.

It was agreed that we should form a committee, which would be the overall steering committee for the whole programme. It was to be called the African Population Advisory Committee (APAC). The committee as formed originally, consisted of 18 eminent people drawn from the fields of politics, including ministers of state; environment; economic development; law; and gender. It also had programme planners and some university research and evaluation experts and covered both the major geographic and linguistic divisions of the continent.

The first members of APAC were:

Hon. Patrick Balopi, Minister of Local Govt. and Lands, Gaberone, Botswana;

Prof. George Benneh, Dir. Pop Impact Project University of Ghana Legon, Accra, Ghana;

Citoyenne Chirwisa Chirhamolekwa, Dir. Project des Naissance Desirables MOH, Zaire;

M. Sidiki Coulibaly, President Union des Etudes sur la Population en Afrique, Senegal;

Prof. Samba Diarra, Prof. OBGYN, Abidjan Côte d'Ivoire;

Hon. Mersie Ejigu, Minister for Planning, Ethiopia;

Dr. Shimah K. Gyoh, Director General, Fed. MOH, Nigeria;

Mme. Gaudence Habimana, Director ONAPO, Rwanda;

Hon. Mwai Kibaki, Minister of Health, Kenya;

Hon. David J.M. Kwidini, MP, Min. for Sports, Secretary General, Africa Parliamentary Council on Population and Development, Zimbabwe;

Prof. Pauline Makinwa Adebusoye, Nigerian Institute of Social and Econconomic. Research, Nigeria;

Hon. Mah Tansah Michael, MP, Cameroun, Rep. of African Parliamentary Union;

Prof. H.W.O. Okoth-Ogendo, Director, Pop Studies and Research Inst. Nairobi, Kenya;

M. Nassour G. Ouaidou, Director CERPOD, Bamako, Mali;

Hon. Olikoye Ransome-Kuti, Fed. MOH, Lagos, Nigeria;

Mme Marie Angélique Savané, AFARD Dakar, Senegal.

As adviser I was a full member, as was Dr. Gyepi-Garbrah, the executive secretary. This committee was launched in Abidjan in 1989 at the African Development Bank.

APAC decided that the best approach to its work at the country level would be to set up teams with combinations of university researchers and programme planners, who would then lead a preliminary and rapid expedition to different parts of their countries, to find out why the people were not particularly interested in family planning and related activities. This was to determine what issues people were interested in and then to help them come to conclusion as to how to approach family planning through the issues that they themselves claimed to be interested in. This programme was developed and called the Agenda Programme. Ben Gyepi-Garbrah of Ghana, as the officer in charge, had his office with the Africa Region at the World Bank. Although I retired from the staff of the World Bank in 1990, I had a special relationship as an adviser with this programme and it is my opinion that much pioneering work was done through the Agenda Programme.

The Agenda Programme started operating in 1990 and a very active beginning it was. So active, in fact, that APAC was accepted as the population advisory committee to the Global Coalition for Africa when that was set up in 1990, chaired by the former president of Botswana, HE. Q.K.J Masire, and Robert McNamara, former President

of the World Bank. The programme was supported initially by the World Bank, UNFPA, IPPF, the governments of France, Germany, the Netherlands, Norway, Sweden, and the Rockefeller Foundation.

Findings Africa Region Number 77 of December 1996 carries a useful summary of the activities of the Agenda Programme. It states:

> "... *the Agenda process begins with the selection of a coordinator – generally an academic with strong interest in community work – who in turn selects a team of people with interest in social issues from academic and other institutions, Community facilitators are then selected, trained and deployed in consultation with local agencies and community leaders. Facilitators should speak the local language, understand the local culture, and be prepared to serve as change agents during the implementation of community actions. Using focus group techniques, the facilitators initiate discussion in communities around four themes*
> * *the main concerns of the community and households;*
> * *links, if any, between family size and community concerns;*
> * *suggestions for addressing these concerns; and*
> * *actions which the communities are prepared to undertake to solve the problems."*

[www.worldbank.org/afr/findings/english/find77.htm]

I participated actively in quite a few of the national activities of the Agenda as we called it. The process got going at full strength in 1992, by the end of 1996 some 90 or so community projects scattered around different parts of Africa, covering the linguistic and sub-regional groups were being underway. I was actively involved in many of these and took great interest in the durbars or comprehensive discussions which took place when the Agenda group interacted with the communities. We took care that at such meetings the heads of both the local government and the district political administration were present as were representatives of line agencies and ministries who would help provide the financial and human resource needs for implementation. The paper referenced above describes several of the projects. Though involved in the initiation of many of these projects I came to be most closely associated with the projects in Ghana, Nigeria and Kenya.

The publication cited above describes the Moree, Ghana project in which I participated actively. Moree is a traditional Fanti fishing community with a population

of about 30,000 in which literacy levels were low, school attendance erratic and large families the rule. Environmental degradation was serious with trees hardly able to mature before being cut down for firewood. In fact the people believed strongly that big trees provided resting places for witches and so should not be allowed. The Agenda team, headed by combined leaders from the Universities of Cape Coast and Ghana Legon, gained the trust of the people and the support of all levels and types including political, religious and youth leaders. An effort at educating the community in home and environmental sanitation was initiated – community toilet building was one effort which took some time.

Education on the importance of tree planting and the sustainable use of firewood was embarked upon and in a couple of years this started to yield results. A massive education campaign, including training workshops for the leadership, film shows and house-to-house campaigns helped greatly with the spread of the family planning message. By this time HIV/AIDS was also gaining importance, so messages on HIV prevention were emphasized. I visited the project area in 1993 and 1995 and noticed tremendous changes – trees were growing, family planning knowledge was increasing and the uptake of contraceptives by the women had increased.

In Kenya, the process in which I was involved was based on getting the district population officers to know their work and get themselves accepted in their communities, and to establish good links between them and the district administration. In Nigeria, I was an active participant in the durbars when the Agenda team presented their community assessment. The interaction between the women of the community and the government representatives was vigorous and ended in local council representatives agreeing to provide the women with money for their small trading efforts.

After some time in the Bank, some of the supporters, particularly the bilateral agencies led by the Netherlands, which had supported the APAC Agenda process throughout, decided that APAC should be seen, not as an institution within the World Bank, but an African institution in its own right. Legal advice was sought and it was agreed that the best way for doing this was to set APAC up as a non-governmental organization operating in one of the African countries. In the end, APAC was located in Nairobi and it has been there ever since.

15 my involvement in the political field

Dabbling in politics had been a hobby of mine for a long time. When I returned home from the World Bank in August 1990, partisan politics were not permitted in Ghana. Flt. Lt. J. J. Rawlings was ruling supreme, and anything smacking of partisan politics was done in secret. I knew that there were groups meeting as clubs and it was not till 1992 that partisan politics was permitted. I quickly wrote to B. J. da Rocha to try and join the newly formed New Patriotic Party (NPP) but it took a long while before I found my way clear to becoming a founding member. Later I managed to get involved as a member of the central executive and as one of the elders. In this capacity, I did quite a few things for the party that had some impact.

During the period 1996-1997, after Mr. Kufuor's first attempt to fight for the presidency failed, there was a major squabble between him and Peter Ala Adjetey, the then chairman, as to who was the leader of the party. The party's constitution, as I read it, implied that anytime the party went to a congress and chose a person for as flag bearer, the flag bearer had precedence over the chairman of the party. But once the elections over, in purely party terms, the flag bearer no longer took precedence.

Unfortunately, the outside world was not to know this and on a particular occasion after Mr. Kufuor had become well known, letters had come in which bore his name as leader of the NPP. On another occasion, it looked as if he had accepted an outside invitation without telling Mr. Ala Adjetey. This led to a confrontation which proved unpleasant and threatening to the party. I was asked to chair a committee which went into this, and although we tried hard, in the end, a serious debacle ensued. It is only recently that I learnt how the matter had finally been resolved: Ms. Ama Busia told me she had invited the two men to a dinner and brought them together after hours of discussion.

I also got involved in the affairs of the party elders Again, it looked to me as if they had no proper standing within the organizational structure of the NPP. With a committee, we were able to make recommendations, which, when accepted, would have given the elders a much better role within the NPP.

The committee felt the Council of Elders should be able to:

- give guidance in the affairs of the party and help bring about unity of purpose, understanding, goodwill and compromise among the leadership of the party;
- to make recommendations and proposals for the consideration of the National Executive;
- to introduce improvement by agreeing to facilitate more active participation by members.

The Committee recommended that the Council of Elders should be more active in fund raising, that its membership be increased and attention paid to gender balance. It also recommended the representation of the Council of Elders on the National Executive Committee, the Steering Committee, the Vetting Committee and the Disciplinary Committee of the party. Some of the recommendations were accepted and implemented immediately. A few are being revisited.

In actual fact owing to happenings in the 2008 elections a more active role for the elders is now being advocated by many in the party, mainly the youth wing, and it is my view that the elders should play a much better role in the NPP. The whole idea of the party elders' recent passivity while 17 people campaigned and competed for the flag bearership of the party, right till the end, gave a very poor impression to the public at large, and, even if in a small way, must have contributed to the loss that the party suffered in the 2008 elections. The obscene demonstration of the importance of money in the campaign led many people to question from where the funds came. If a party cannot find a way of keeping down the number of people aspiring to be a flag bearer to fewer than four, I don't believe that it has really got itself properly organized for taking power. I believe this is a major area in which some of us have to give fault to the Party.

In 1998 Mr. Kufuor was nominated the flag bearer of the NPP. Efforts by some of us to make the party understand that it needed major restructuring and the strengthening of its grassroots organizations fell on deaf ears. In fact, my advocacy for the need to restructure the party before selecting a flag bearer sounded perhaps as if I did not want Mr. Kufuor to win and it put me bad dour with many of his followers for a long time. Many might be surprised, however, to learn that one of the things I did at the time was to advise another aspiring candidate, Nana Akufo Addo, to

withdraw and bide his time. In fact, the perception was so strong that efforts to get me elected as Chairman of the Party were derailed by followers of Mr. Kufuor.

It was only after Mr. Kufuor won the election of 2000 that I got myself rehabilitated to an extent; and this, despite all the effort I put in to collecting money, giving advice and helping in diverse ways during the campaign.

For the 1996 campaign of Mr. Kufuor, I had actually made a personal contribution to him and when he lost, he was gracious enough to come with his wife to my house to give me a bottle of cognac, thank me and express the hope that I would continue to support him, which I did in every way.

For the 2000 campaign, I, with encouragement of Hackman Owusu Agyemang, formed a group which we named the Diamond Club, with sub-divisions. This was simply to raise money and help finance the campaign in response to requests from the campaign manager, the flag bearer or from ourselves when we noticed there were areas in which we could help. The very first thing we did was to present Mr. Kufuor and his campaign team with six second-hand vehicles and it was my understanding that these vehicles were used for his very first major campaign in the Brong Ahafo and the Western Regions. Fortunately for us, the campaign of Mr. Kufuor went well and he won the election.

With the NPP in power, it was my hope that Mr. Kufuor, as the president, would be gracious enough to do what he did to me when he lost – come and meet the group with whom we had raised funds in support his campaign. I had told him his gift of cognac was waiting to be opened. But,up to the time he left office, Mr. Kufuor never found time to meet the members of the club and thank them for their efforts – or to have me open the cognac in his presence. This does not mean some of us were not recognized in one way or another. Probably this individual recognition was why, as president, he did not think it necessary to meet with and thank the group. He seemed not to realize that personal contact would outdo any other form of appreciation.

When Mr. Kufuor won, we were in trouble because no arrangements had been made for a transition to take place. In fact, it was the outgoing administration which sent a note to the incoming president saying we should meet to form a joint transition team to facilitate the hand-over of government. On 1st January, 2001, New Year's Day, when we were all busy enjoying our celebration, a meeting was called by Mr. Kufuor, as President-elect.

At this meeting, after short introductions and the reading of the invitation from

Above: My political supporters in 1969!
Below: Family support from Obodai and Shormeh.

Above: Welcoming President Kufuor to the Academy's dinner, November, 2002.

Below: The board of the Bank of Ghana, 2008.

the outgoing administration, Mr. Kufuor turned to me and said that I should lead the transition team for taking over the government. He went on to elaborate that Prof. Adzei Bekoe would head a group which would be in charge of the inauguration and J.H. Mensah would head the group which would be in charge of taking over the ministries. It was therefore not made clear, really, as to whether the team which was taking over the executive, headed by me, should be considered as heading the overall transition team for the president. Obetsebi Lamptey, taking a cue from this, also went ahead and elaborated on these teams and wrote long lists of all kinds of people who should be on them. The President-elect amended these considerably and the teams were formed much in his image. There was practically no briefing on what was to be done; we simply had to improvise.

Statements made by the media amongst others that the transition team pursued an agenda of witch hunting and displayed gross intolerance for the views of the out-going administration were and are very unfortunate. There were no briefings from the president-elect, party executives or anyone with authority around the campaign team as to how we were to handle the transition.

Actually we only had six days in which to effect the transition. Fortunately or unfortunately, the outgoing team had its own long list of what it wanted to see done. When we met at the Conference Centre to launch the transition arrangements Mr. Kufuor and Prof Mills were made joint chairmen of the Joint Transition Team, as it was called. This was just a formality. Sub-teams were formed for the actual tasks and all business meetings were chaired jointly. My group, which was to take over the executive, was chaired jointly by Totobi Quakyi, who had been the security minister for the outgoing government, and me. Ato Dadzie, who was Chief of Staff to President Rawlings, was a member of the group and the Secretary to the Cabinet, Bebaako-Mensah, now secretary to President Mills, was made the Secretary of the Committee. In view of later happenings I would like to emphasise that my team accepted Bebaako-Mensah who had been with the outgoing administration with the respect he deserved and still deserves as a principled public servant. None of the team members of the incoming government received any kind of allowance – I remember our having a tea service only once.

The meetings started very cordially. Both Totobi Quakyi and I made statements to the effect that we should remember that what we were doing had never been done in Ghana and we should be careful to set a good example for all subsequent transitions. This was accepted and it was agreed that minutes would be written of our meetings and

then confirmed before agreements were put into action unless the group had decided on immediate action because of the brevity of time. In the case of the Inaugural Committee there was no question that they should be given the mandate to do everything possible about the inauguration and see that it took place without too many problems. When I was free, I sat with Prof. Adzei Bekoe and saw how things were progressing for the inauguration. No matter how hard the committee worked and the efforts of State Protocol, much went wrong with the inauguration. The insistence that the swearing in be done in the environs of parliament as required by the constitution meant that the size of the crowd witnessing the actual swearing-in would be limited. It was therefore agreed that after the swearing in there would be a more public presentation of the president at the Independence Square. Then chaos! Getting the crowd and parliamentarians to the Square was a nightmare. Somehow even with changes, the problem of how to avoid traffic problems on such major state occasions still eludes us.

Parallel to the meetings of the transition team, I sought advice on what and how to go about the business of the transition. Out of my consultations came ideas which I transmitted to the president-elect. The most important to me were that:

- he should seek an invitation to meet with the out-going President before the change over;
- he should request permission to meet the service chiefs and the Chief Justice before the handing over; and
- in his speech after the changeover he should announce the award of the highest state honours to Ex-President J.J. Rawlings and Prof. E.A. Mills for their graciousness in handling the elections and handing over peacefully.

Whilst Mr. Kufuor agreed with the first two items he ignored the last completely and did not tell me why. Of course it was his prerogative to give or not to give me an explanation, but I could not help wondering if the subsequent deterioration in the relationship with the Ex-President Rawlings might have been prevented with this simple acknowledgement. In fact, when the offer of national awards to Ex-President Rawlings and Prof Mills in the last year of the Kufuor administration was rejected by the two, I felt convinced that it was the timing which made it possible for them to do so. The ifs of history – maybe things could have been quite different.

One area of discussion was what the constitution meant by the takeover being on 7th January. The 7th January would normally start immediately after midnight on

January 6th and therefore we sought counsel from the military and they told us that when they say they are taking over at a certain time, what happened was the takeover started from one minute to the time and ends one minute after the time. Hence, in our case, it was to start one minute to midnight on the 6th and end one minute after, on the 7th. This handing over ceremony would take place in the Castle or in the military headquarters since the military was changing its commanders-in-chief.

The question which arose from this was, with this agreement and yet without the swearing in, what should happen in case any trouble brewed after the midnight handover of the executive. Nobody could answer this question, but on reflection from what I know of the American situation, it should have posed no problems whatsoever, since once the time for handing over is over, the president-elect has become the president of the country, swearing-in or no swearing-in. Whether our constitution is as clear on this as the United States' constitution, I am not sure.

The meetings continued and an issue which produced the greatest difficulty for us, and which led to the ultimate disintegration of the committee and the whole transition idea, was that of state assets. It is unfortunate that at the start of the transition, I did not know of the existence of the Greenstreet Committee Report. Nobody ever brought it out as one of the background items of information that we needed to consider. It turned out that Prof. Miranda Greenstreet had headed a committee that had recommended severance pay, gratuities and remuneration of various kinds for the outgoing political office holders as stipulated in the constitution under Article 71. The recommendations had been discussed by parliament, approved in secrecy and the executive had also discussed recommendations for Parliament and approved them in secrecy. The public, at large, had no true knowledge of what was what.

It seemed to me really ridiculous and dangerous that, in a country which had become democratic, the pay for its political leaders and their remunerations should have been handled in this way. It is to be hoped that what happened then and what seems to have happened during the 2009 handover, will be the last, and that the pay of the executive, parliament and everybody else which is drawn from the consolidated fund of the national exchequer should be transparent. There is no way that any discussion of this, together with the remuneration itself, should be taken away from the general public.

The constitutional stipulation that a sitting president should organize a committee to determine these issues is also wrong. I strongly recommend that this cease forthwith. This way, the normal constitutional protocol that changes in a

constitution or in any standing law should not be made by an occupant of the seat for changing that law, to inure, first and foremost, themselves. Such an understanding together with full and open discussion of remuneration and benefits will avoid getting the public so upset that they seriously challenge what is happening.

In my situation, I was presented with a long list of vehicles that were with the outgoing president and what he required. The outgoing ministers also said they should be treated like the civil servants who, it had already been agreed, could buy the vehicles which they had used if were two years old or more after a proper valuation by the chief transport officer. When I looked at the recommendations from Greenstreet, some of these were not in keeping with the requests that were being made on behalf of the outgoing President and I stated this quite clearly. I made it clear that we should go strictly by the Greenstreet recommendations, which had already been agreed, then discuss any other issues. So we did and appropriately allocated the numbers of vehicles that were to be given to the outgoing President. President Rawlings was asked what accommodation he wanted and he made it known that he would be happy to stay in the home which had been occupied by his wife for quite a long time – just that another house next to it should be added. This was readily agreed.

The houses in question are old colonial style bungalows with a lot of space but not with much sleeping accommodation. I therefore thought the request was even modest. Several of our press did not think so, but I thought they were ill-informed. The second house of the group, in my understanding, was to be an office. In view of the happenings of 2009, I would like to state categorically that the outgoing president had taken the decision on where he would like to live and the transition team was merely informed.

In my view, this was to be a temporary solution since nothing was available and Greenstreet had stated that the outgoing president should discuss a permanent abode with the sitting president. If there were any discussions about securing more permanent accommodation for the former president, I was not party to it.

Several things which the outgoing group put before us and which we rejected related to:

- the need for a research building for the outgoing president for his work on malaria;
- the need for a guest house to be allocated to him; and
- the need for transportation to be allocated to him for looking after guests who might come to visit him.

With respect to the research building, we stated that everybody who wanted to undertake research had a right to look for support and the outgoing president, like everybody else in research, should look for his own funding and rent accommodation accordingly. This was allowed to drop.

With respect to monetary emoluments, we found when we realized that *ex gratia* payments were to be made, that instead of the joint committee simply being faced with a request for the *ex-gratia* payments, it was presented with a *fait accompli*. Whilst we were told that *ex-gratia* payments were to be paid to members of the executive, it turned out that the monies for such payments had been withdrawn from the national exchequer before the end of the year and paid into a private bank. These had then been paid out, before the joint transition team knew anything about it. Of course, I felt betrayed. I felt that this was no way to be transparent and honest. I said so and I still stand by my view because it is really the incoming administration which should finally authorise any ex-gratia payments to outgoing public officers. They should be thanked by the incoming government, saying, as it were "you have handled things well on behalf of the country, and these are your benefits with thanks". I hope that this country will learn and take the handling of *ex-gratia* payments, cars, retirement homes and other benefits and facilities out of political hands and make them the concern of public service. A transition process is for taking over the government machinery and activities; it should not be for auditing, inquests, inquisitions or unbecoming squabbles over cars and bungalows.

Another area of difficulty was over bungalows. People who live in politically assigned bungalows in other countries left practically the day after the declaration of election results or, at the latest, on the hand-over. What happens normally is for temporary accommodation to be made available for people who are likely to be, as it were, thrown out of government accommodation. We have no such temporary accommodation available; and therefore, we tried to determine what was best.

First of all, there were people who clearly should not be in government bungalows. The secretary of a political party has no business being assigned a government bungalow with the utilities paid by government. This is wrong. It was wrong in President Rawlings' period and if it happens in anybody else's period, it is wrong. There is a difference between people who working for the state and who people work for a party. So we insisted that those who were not working for the state but for the party should leave as soon as possible. We tried to get a list of who was occupying the bungalows and we ticked off those who should leave immediately as it were.

It was agreed that, since the civil service permitted three months for leaving a bungalow, those who had proper public service appointments, such as ministers and deputy ministers, could also have three months within which to leave. In the specific case of Vice President Prof. Mills it will be recalled that the incoming Vice President had to stay in other house for a very long time. At the time, Prof. Mills requested President Kufuor to give consideration to the fact that he, Prof. Mills, had no accommodation ready as he had not finished his own building. It must be remembered that Greenstreet had stated vice presidents should not be entitled to any accommodation or anything like the remuneration that was given to outgoing presidents, because the vice president had every right to fight for the presidency, as indeed has happened; and Prof. Mills, after two attempts, did indeed win the presidency.

To come back to the transition. President Kufuor informed me of Prof. Mills' request, with the instruction that we should not give Prof. Mills any time limit. He was to stay in the vice-president's accommodation until he found an alternative and he could move at his leisure. This was communicated to the joint committee and I personally was very happy that the president took the decision. It is a pity though that, whenever others spoke of people being turned out of accommodation during the 2001 hand-over, nobody mentions this very gracious act of the President Kufuor and the transition team. What is mentioned is the mistake that some over enthusiastic officers made. They went to see how many cars were in the vice presidency whilst Mrs. Mills was there and created a furore for which the were punished and an apology rendered. I am not sure that this should have been made such a major campaign issue without mentioning the fact that while the new government's vice president was staying in a guest house which was not an accommodation for a Vice-President, the Prof. Mills remained in the vice president's accommodation well beyond the three months. In fact taking into consideration the time needed for renovations, the new vice president, Alhaji Aliu Mahama, took almost a year to be settled. I believe that if Ghanaians want to criticize, they have to do so from factual knowledge.

And then there were the issues over cars. We had agreed that saloon cars which had been in the possession and use of public officers for two years or more were to be valued and the officers, if they agreed, would pay that value and make the cars their private property. This was accepted by the committee. When the minutes were written and brought to me, I noticed that a phrase had been inserted stating that "4x4 vehicles

in exceptional circumstances, might also be permitted". This had not been agreed so I called Totobi Quakyi to tell him that this had not been agreed. He said he would look into it but never came back to me on this and from that time on, when I called him, I never got a response.

What happened was that a government transport officer, by name Allotey, valued the cars. Mr. Allotey informed me that after the valuation was given to Ato Dadzie, the transport officer had been called to Mr. Dadzie's office and, in front of others, been had browbeaten to lower the valuations. Of course, I had been given a copy of the first valuation so when the second valuation came, I was appalled and I said so and, after the transport officer had given me a written statement of what had actually taken place, I told the president. Since this was beginning to look as if we were anxious to deprive the outgoing executives of vehicles which the law permitted them to buy at a certain price, we had to go on radio and TV and explain the position. Finally, the president decided that the original valuation of the transport officer should stand and there was to be no question about that.

The lesson that I drew from this is that these asset issues should be removed from the office of the chief of staff. A chief of staff has so many very important things to deal with in the handing over process that the least should be the prices and the buying and selling of cars. I think a public office should be available to look after all of these assets, audited appropriately yearly and valued yearly so that when it comes to separation, all concerned would know where things stood. In fact I wonder if we should not try to pay public and civil servants well enough for them to own their transport and accommodation.

Meanwhile I think Ghana has developed long enough for the transition law, which I have advocated for over eight years now and which is only now being considered, to include the separation of the assets registry, assets audit, etc from the office of the chief of staff. It has saddened me greatly to see what happened during the transition of 2009. We should have done better. Following my experience of 2001, I wrote a memo and had an article published, calling for a transition law. Early in 2004 I addressed a memo to the President again calling for a transition law. In this instance I went on to suggest that the probability that he would be returned to power was the more reason why the law should be enacted and tested in the calm climate. No action was taken. I hope the current dismay at the way the transition went will not die without a serious effort to pass such a law starting with the IEA draft which was being

discussed before the 2008 elections. I personally do not think the draft I have seen is comprehensive enough.

Two officers for whom there should be immediate temporary accommodation after the elections are the out-going president and his vice-president. A fully equipped transition office should always be available, together with a decent budget. And most importantly, the timing of the elections has to be re-considered so as to make ample time available for transition. It must be accepted by all that the transition is mainly to hand over, not to carry out police and audit work. Those should be on-going and separate.

16 promoting medical education and training

My interest in medical education helped me become involved in the international medical field quite early in my career. In the mid-1960s, the Rockefeller Foundation decided to study medical education in the developing countries and to give advice and help on the establishment of new medical schools and the directions in which they might go. A committee was formed to help examine this issue, chaired by Dr. Walsh McDermott who was also chair of the Council of Cornell University. On the committee were Dr. Loeb, the famous physician and co-editor of Cecil and Loeb's *Textbook of Medicine*, the recent revisions of which had been undertaken by Drs. McDermott and Beeson. Others whom I remember as being on the Commission were Dr. J.Z. Bowers of the Macy Foundation and Dr. Bob Glazer of Stanford University.

I found myself on this august body and we held our first meeting in the beautiful surroundings of Bellagio, the Rockefeller Foundation's Italian conference centre near Milan. The study itself was to be undertaken by a group that was later joined Dr. J.H. Bryant. It was from his observations during the study that he wrote *Medical Education for the Developing World*.

A major problem which exercised both the steering committee and the study group was how to produce enough doctors and other health personnel in a relatively short time for the growing populations of the developing world. Emphasis, naturally, was on Africa, where the situation really was dire. The conversion of medical assistants into fully qualified doctors had been undertaken for the Congo, now the Democratic Republic of Congo, where, under Belgian colonial rule, no indigenous qualified doctors at all had been trained. Work on this committee gave me a great insight and experience in what was happening in medical education in Africa as well as some of the developing countries in Asia.

A major issue, which we termed the quantity versus quality debate in African medical practice, related to how enough doctors could be trained to handle the workload that we were seeing in the hospitals and clinics. In many instances the illnesses which had brought patients to hospitals could have been handled more

213

peripherally had a system been developed to handle such a situation. If enough medical doctors could not be trained rapidly enough to handle the entire load, what other approaches were available to us?

Medical assistants

Of course, some had argued that the training of large numbers of medical assistants would be one way of resolving the issue. Most countries that we visited refused to accept the possibility that their medical assistants could be considered members of the health team. This, to me, largely arose from the lack of a clear definition of what we meant by medical assistants.

Of course, if first class students who could easily qualify for medical schools to train as doctors were taken and, because they are to practise in developing countries, given less than adequate medical training and then made medical assistants, their natural inclination would be to try and get themselves fully qualified as doctors. Further, if this were a temporary arrangement, then the question of who supervises whom arises when there are reasonable numbers of newly qualified doctors without the experience which some of the assistants are likely, by then, to have accumulated.

The committee finally decided that there were roles for both fully trained doctors and medical assistants in many developing countries. Indeed, the situation existing in even quite advanced countries where some medical work was deliberately delegated to specially trained nurses or assistants, lightening the load of the medically qualified doctor, was cited – particularly the nurse pædiatric practitioner and the dental hygienist. But in the end, practically all the African countries decided only to train full fledged medical doctors.

To me, this rather short-sighted decision has come back to haunt us. As we try to provide medical care for all of our people, we now find that simply depending on medically trained doctors cannot help us achieve our aims. As we see our hospital and clinic outpatient departments overflow with a mixture of the severely ill and the not so ill, it is now quite clear that some kind of less than fully-trained doctor needs to be involved in the delivery of medical services. In fact, some countries have already progressed so far that physician assistants are already working in the fields of anæsthesia and even obstetrics.

In my own country, Ghana, there was a time when anæsthesia was handled almost exclusively by nurses who had been given special training. This needs to be expanded but unfortunately there is a professional problem when we create a different profession from an existing one – are the nurse anæsthetists to be considered as nurses

all of their lives or are they will they be viewed as some other sort of professional. A similar situation was created in dentistry, where dental care practitioners can be nurses. I personally believe that the best way to handle this is to create the assistant fraternity as medical and dental technologists, put them in a technology category and if they have to form a union, let them form the union and be considered as such.

My involvement also extended to consultancy services to the newly developing medical schools in Africa, including Nairobi and Makerere. In Nairobi, I remember working with Dr. Frank Schofield on the establishment of a field station in the Machakos District. This became a very famous research ground similar to our Danfa Project in the late 60s and early 70s.

It was during this period also that I had the opportunity to do some external examining in public health, preventive and social medicine, and community health in the University of Nairobi Medical School, Makerere, Lagos and Dar es Salaam. When I examined in Nairobi I was fascinated by the high level of training in community health that the first graduating class had been given. Then the programme called for the class to be examined in community health one whole year before their final graduation. That arrangement actually meant that students devoted a great deal more attention to public health than would have been the case had the subject been examined with the clinical subjects at the end of the course. Although it is not generally the practice, it is a good practice worth looking into.

What I remember most about this particular period examining in Nairobi was the overwhelming excellence of Dr. Miriam Were, as she is now. This young lady, at the time of the examination, was nursing a broken leg. She had also written a novel and she did so brilliantly in the exam that I gave her a distinction. Her work since graduating has fully justified the judgement that her tutors and I made at the time.

Examining with John Bennett in Makerele was a joy. The charming host that he was, he arranged to give me quite a tour of Uganda. The terracing that I saw in Kigezi remains a fascination, even today.

I was also an examiner for Maurice King in the University of Dar-es-Salaam in 1966. I remember 1966 because I had just completed this examination when it was announced that Dr. Kwame Nkrumah had been overthrown in Ghana.

Involvement in the Ghana School of Public Health

A year or so after coming home from the World Bank, Prof. George Benneh, then

the Vice Chancellor of the University of Ghana, invited me to join a team from the university to discuss the establishment of a school of public health in the University of Ghana, at Legon. Prof. John Nabilla, who was, with Prof. Benneh, in the department of geography and with whom I had established quite a close contact because of our involvement in the population field, chaired this committee. Both John Nabilla and George Benneh had been very active in a major population and family planning seminar that had been held with USAID support in 1986. On my recommendation USAID had sponsored a short fellowship for Prof. Benneh to prepare him to head a major population initiative in Legon. This heralded the birth of the IMPACT project in the University of Ghana, Legon, which set out to educate policy makers on the importance of population in national development.

It was recalled during the meetings of the committee that efforts had been made in the mid to late 1980s to start a post-graduate course in community health or public health within the University of Ghana Medical School, in Korle Bu. The efforts had been led by Prof. Samuel Ofosu-Amaah, who was then in charge of the department in the medical school. He had actually been able to produce several MPH graduates but this had come to a stop mainly for what would appear today as a small misunderstanding, though of course at the time it was important enough. It was for no other reason than that the earlier efforts were being largely supported by USAID and the United Kingdom's Overseas Development Administration (ODA), now Department for International Development (DFID). Later on DFID gave the support for students to be taken for training at the Universities of London, Liverpool and Leeds. I could not find any good reason for the change.

It turned out that in one year, when Prof. Gilford Ashitey was in charge of the department, efforts to get the ministry of health to release medical officers to undertake the post graduate course produced a conflict. This was mainly due to the fact that for entry into the medical school's programme, an examination was required. In this particular year, those who passed the exam were enrolled in the medical school locally and some who did not pass the exam were given scholarships and sent overseas for training. Of course, since every Ghanaian wanted to have some overseas credentials or at least to gain some experience overseas, the ones who passed the exam were furious and complained to the then Chief Medical Officer, Dr. Moses Adibo. Finally, Adibo decided and managed to get support for those who had been eligible to undertake the course in the school to be taken out and sent overseas too. So the course came to an abrupt end.

Well, in the early 1990s the Rockefeller Foundation was advocating the establishment of what was described as "Schools of Public Health Without Walls", simply meaning that we did not need to have full buildings allocated to a school before undertaking training in public health. Therefore the committee's assignment was to help establish a school "without walls". In fact, we thought our mandate went well beyond this simple physical expression and included having a school of public health which had a rather small core staff of its own and which would depend for teaching, tutoring and mentoring on staff from other departments and faculties of the university as well as working doctors of the ministry of health and even those in private practice.

Much time was spent discussing the duration of the course, eligibility for qualification, type of qualification to be obtained and the curriculum itself. It was decided that the curriculum should be as practical as possible, should include operational research foundation, computer literacy and competence and also, if at all possible, have a period of field work in which the students had the chance to observe exactly what was happening in rural communities day and night.

It was agreed that the course, instead of being one academic year or two years as was happening in Zimbabwe, would run for a full calendar year, that it would have a research base, that it would have modules and that it would have an elective for which the students would write a proposal and a long essay on completion. It was definitely going to have field observations, which would be based on the Danfa area as well as on other parts of the country.

It was felt by some of the people on the committee that I should be invited to be the head of the school when it was founded. At the time, I was fully involved with an open-ended consultancy at the World Bank and I could not immediately see how I could undertake such an assignment. Actually, that was only part of the reason. The major part was that in my friend Prof. Samuel Ofosu-Amaah I personally felt that Ghana had somebody who could handle this task much, much better academically and with much better diplomatic skills than I could ever possibly command.

I therefore mentioned this to the committee and the chairman and the vice-chancellor agreed that I should approach Prof. Ofosu-Amaah and find out whether he would be willing to undertake the task. Fortunately for me and for Ghana, Prof. Ofosu-Amaah, who was then leaving his position at UNICEF, agreed. After a series of discussions with Dr. Seth Beckley, then heading the health department of the Rockefeller Foundation, there was an agreement that the foundation would provide

the support for the head's position for an initial period. I am not sure how long that turned out to be. but after a lot of problems with the university's proposal, writing, presentation, etc., things were finalised and in 1994 the Ghana School of Public Health opened in the University in Legon with Prof. Ofosu-Amaah as its head.

Prof. Ofosu-Amaah, who at my invitation had also joined the Medical School's Department of Preventive and Social Medicine earlier in his career. did a wonderful job of establishing the school. He kindly invited me in the first couple of years or so to give a major seminar. I chose as my subject, *Ethical Issues in Primary Health Care* and I thought these seminars were well attended and enjoyed by all of the students.

One of the benefits to Ghana of Dr. Kwame Nkrumah's relationship with President John Kennedy which is not well known was the discussion that ended in the establishment of a US-Ghana Research Collaboration.

In April of 1962, Dr. John Edgecomb of the Cancer Institute of the United States National Institute of Health was designated head of the joint US-Ghanaian Medical Research Programme. The research was to start in Ghana. This was the result of quite a lengthy discussion, which had gone on between the presidents and between the technical institutions. After the break-up of the West African Medical Research collaboration, Nkrumah wanted Ghana to have research activities and personnel which would be equal to none in black Africa, if it was at all possible. It was agreed that we would establish a National Institute of Health and Medical Research (NIHMR) here and it was this Institute which was to be linked to the United States National Institute of Health.

The collaborative arrangements started on 2 April, 1962 and the leadership started to arrive. The United States Team was headed by Dr. John Edgecomb, a white American, with his deputy, Dr. George Lythcott, a black American. The team was quite large and they covered extensive health areas.

One of the main points of the agreement was that, as much as possible, each research person from the United States would have a co-research partner from the Ghanaian side. I was lucky since I was at the time looking after fevers in the Fevers Unit of Korle Bu. I was assigned to work together with a young epidemiologist. Dr. Richard (Dick) Morrow who arrived with his wife and a child. Whilst here, he produced another couple of children and had them named with Dr. Silas Dodu's Ghanaian family names. He was and is an enthusiastic researcher, currently working in the Johns Hopkins School of Public Health.

Dick Morrow and I developed not only the research partnership which yielded

some very concrete results but a friendship which still continues, enduring many of the difficulties in the US-Ghana partnership as well as separations across Africa and the United States.

I was very interested in what we called PUO, pyrexia of unknown origin, and which the Americans at the time called fevers of unknown origin. One of these was fever with jaundice. Morrow was interested in finding something about infective hepatitis in the Accra region, so I teamed up with him and we undertook all the clinical and other work required for looking after people who arrived with the diagnosis of jaundice or infective hepatitis, then a major cause of jaundice in Accra.

The research duration was from November 1962 through November 1963. We had some 136 patients gathered from all parts of the hospital, particularly referred by Dr. Dodu and Dr. Albert Hawe. Three research papers were written from this project and the findings proved very interesting and impressive (Morrow, Sai, *et al.*). We concluded that larger concentrations of hepatitis A were to be found in the *bidonvilles* of Accra, the Nima areas and others which did not have good sanitation. It was also found that death rates were much higher in people who had recently migrated into these areas and in women who were pregnant or had had a recent miscarriage. The clinical and epidemiological findings at the time led us to think in terms of jaundice following injections as many patients were found to have what was then called Australian Antigen which later turned out to be hepatitis B.

Unfortunately, Dr. Joe Gillman, Director of the Institute of Health, almost inevitably, created problems for the relationships and rightly or wrongly fed the authorities with information that the group included CIA operatives. In the end, with the break-up of the medical school negotiations in 1963, the research collaboration also petered out. With this and the earlier disbandment of the West African Medical Research Council, Ghana lost much of the impetus and organizational base for health research.

Fortunately the Japanese government had been negotiating an agreement for a monument to Hideyo Noguchi who, while a member of the Rockefeller Yellow Fever Research project, had died of yellow fever in Accra. The shrine was built but negotiations continued for assistance with the medical school building. In the end the Japanese agreed to help with a whole medical research institute as a memorial to Noguchi. This was built at Legon.

AIDS control in Ghana

I became involved in the HIV/AIDS problem from 1986, whilst working as

population adviser at the World Bank. In the next four or so years, the controversy and problems around the issue of HIV and AIDS ranged widely. It was during this period also, that I got to realize how devastating the AIDS epidemic was becoming in many parts of Sub-Saharan Africa. I must confess to being particularly anxious about what would happen if HIV/AIDS got a true hold in my country, based on what I knew about the sexual habits and sexual orientation of my people.

Before coming back home, I got in touch with the late Prof. Quartey who, with Dr. Konotey-Ahulu and others, was then examining the problem of HIV/AIDS in the Krobo Region of Ghana. They even managed to send me videos of some of their activities. A scene in one of the videos gave all who cared the vivid message "be sure when trying to be decorous in the education programmes; the message may be misunderstood" A girl in the scene was in the last throes of AIDS. She refused to accept that she had AIDS because she had not been on board a boat. Her Italian boyfriend had always been with her on shore. She had been told that you contracted HIV and AIDS only if you went on the boats for sex. Pitiful. She died soon after the film was made. This was at a time when Ghana had no access to any antiretroviral.

An area in which Dr. Quartey and his colleagues were involved at the time was trying to get some kind of treatment for HIV. A concoction they found that seemed to work turned out, on more critical analysis, to have value in controlling some of the troublesome symptoms,immune suppressed, so it was not a cure. This continued and it was from their work that I learnt that HIV had landed in Ghana in 1986, from a couple from Germany. The response was fear but this fear did not lead to any real action to try and prevent further spread. Truth to tell, nobody knew what to do. With the WHO's help, a committee was set up under the ministry of health to work out how to handle the HIV problem. This National AIDS Control Committee was under the chairmanship of the late Dr. Harold Philips, a very good general practitioner who had been teaching physiology in the medical school. In fact he was at one time Dean of the University of Ghana Medical School.

The goat serum

Soon after the turn of the century I heard of a treatment using goat serum. Unfortunately for me I did not pay much attention to the claim. A year or so after the START programme, during the second administration of President Kufuor, I had a call from the presidency asking me to meet with a group from the United States which

had invented a cure for AIDS goat serum. They came to see me at home and I was surprised to find that the group was led by a minister of religion. A Ghanaian doctor, whom I respected very much at the time, was with them. Their story was that one doctor, Gary Davis from the United States, had invented a completely novel and safe approach to the treatment of AIDS. He had injected the virus into goats and had extracted from the goats, after a few weeks, a serum which completely cleared the HIV virus from the blood of patients.

Although this method had proved its worth, according to the presenter, in the treatment of some sufferers in the United States, Canada, South Africa, Côte d'Ivoire and other countries, the US Food and Drug Administration (FDA) had not approved it for use. The representatives claimed that the main reason was the fear of competition from the major drug companies. They stood to lose their monopoly and thereby huge profits that they were making. Just thinly veiled also was the implication that they were afraid of crediting a black man with such a wonderful discovery. The Ghanaian doctor was oozing with enthusiasm and all but admitted that she had not observed the wonder drug in use.

The group wanted permission to produce and use the serum to treat patients in Ghana. I asked for evidence of the scientific basis of the claim, meaning the basic scientific findings and the clinical trials. I was given evidence of the first permission by the FDA for a phase one trial and the withdrawal of the permit. This looked odd to me. The group also had what purported to be photocopies of clinical trials undertaken in the Côte d'Ivoire. Frankly, if they had come via another channel, I would have terminated the interview. But coming from the presidency I wanted to be quite sure that I was not missing any important scientific finding justifying their claim. To a question as to whether they had contacted the FDA of Ghana, they claimed they were in the process of doing so. In actual fact they were applying for what amounted to a traditional medicine licence.

Finally I informed the group that we could not permit them to start clinical trials on the evidence they had provided. The basic science needed to be established so I arranged for them to work with the Noguchi Memorial Institute to establish that goats infected with HIV produced a serum which reacted with HIV. After that was proven then it should be established if such serum was free of any kind of toxicity. It would be only after such scientific tests had proved satisfactory that there could be an application for human trials. Dr. Davis and his group were be responsible for all costs of the exercise.

An agreement was drawn up between Dr. Davis's group and Noguchi and the work

was assigned to the department of virology. It took awhile to get started. Some months later I heard through the grapevine that the goats had produced reactive serum but only against HIV2 which were, at the time, was about 5 per cent of all infections or fewer. After a while a newspaper article appeared claiming that Dr. Davis's goat serum had proved effective against HIV and asking for government financial input to build a factory to produce the serum. The CEO of Noguchi informed me that he had asked the officer in charge of the research to write a scientific paper on the findings for a peer review publication. I was shown a copy of a draft. The paper had not been published when the head of the department convened a press meeting and discussed the findings. The major newspaper of Ghana, through one of its lead reporters, shrilly demanded government support; it also advocated the building of a factory. The whole report was slanted towards the GAC trying to suppress the introduction of a good treatment because those in charge were benefiting in some way from the drug industry. Normally I would have ignored such remarks but when I learnt from an internet search that Dr. Davis and his colleagues were injecting Ghanaian patients with the serum I was appalled and livid.

We convened a press conference to state the facts but, unfortunately, as all too often with AIDS treatments, the press mostly took the side of the serum pushers and would not listen to the science. We reported all this to the GAC and they agreed that the ministry of interior should have the situation investigated. There was evidence of criminality in the use of an unapproved drug and of a physician not registered in Ghana practicing medicine here. Meanwhile the heads of Noguchi, the GAC and I were being subjected to some highly vituperative attacks in the national media. Deeply unfortunate, too, was the involvement of the then head of virology of Noguchi who used such offensive language that the chairman of the council of state was moved to ask for a full briefing about the controversy. I gave him the story and some of the pictures from the internet. I also gave the full facts to one of Ghana's best investigative journalists and after he made these known, the problem sort of vanished. I was to learn later how the Ghanaian lady doctor was gearing up to produce the serum in her own laboratory.

I have chosen to narrate this controversy over the goat serum issue extensively for various reasons. First, it shows how much deviousness was involved in claims for HIV cures. Second, our papers, for some unknown reason, still do not seem to have any knowledge or trust in the scientific approach to medicine. The stages that a drug has to go through before approval for use are easily ignored. The introduction of race and the profit motive colours all reasoning in this field. Finally, the approaches to START, under

Dr. Peter Lamptey, and the handling of the traditional treatment by Profs. Konotey Ahulu and J.K.M. Quartey are in stark contrast to the handling of the goat serum. These latter had no financial interest, nor were they anxious to win a race for producing a safe cure while in the case of goat serum all involved were to some extent looking at the money to be made or greatness to be achieved.

The Ghana Aids Commission

In keeping with the worldwide understanding of how to approach the epidemic at the time, the committee was wholly under the ministry of health, although there were members from other sectors. Unfortunately it did not perform too well but did manage to get the ministry to organize a national AIDS control programme under the supervision of Dr. Kweku Yeboah, who did a good job of helping to track the epidemic – developing what has now become a very good mechanism for HIV/AIDS surveillance for prevention and management in Ghana, the Annual HIV Sentinel Survey. Currently, it is under the leadership of Dr. Nii Akwei Addo.

In 1999, as President of the Ghana Academy of Arts and Sciences, I devoted my annual address to the subject of HIV/AIDS. The presentation was entitled *Why is Africa losing the battle against AIDS?* (Proceedings of the Ghana Academy of Arts and Science, 1999). This paper excited the nation sufficiently for it to be published in one of the major national dailies. Soon, it was followed up by the government of the day who became interested in developing a national and a more multi-sectoral approach to the handling of HIV/AIDS in Ghana. Of course, by this time also, the international community had altered its views and had decided that the International HIV/AIDS Control Programme, located within the WHO, should now be an independent organization, sponsored by several of the United Nations agencies, including UNHCR, UNICEF, WFP, UNDP, UNFPA, UNODC, ILO, UNESCO, WHO and the World Bank.

By September 2000, the government of Ghana, under President Jerry Rawlings, had decided that it was time the government had a multi-sectoral and multi-agency AIDS commission. This was launched in Akosombo but to practically no national excitement whatsoever. Fortunately, though, the preliminary work for the commission had been done by a secretariat of Mrs. Bridget Katsiriku as administrator, Dr. Kweku Yeboah as a technical person and an additional person from the ministry of information. This group really helped to get HIV/AIDS control and prevention work started. With the assistance of Ms. Cynthia Eledu, the UNAIDS representative in

Ghana at the time, they had support from the USAID, DFID and GTZ to establish a secretariat for the programme.

I have to admit that these three, plus the UNAIDS representative, did a very good job in getting the basics of a secretariat established and helped develop the National AIDS Commission developed. Unfortunately, in the December after its inauguration, if it can be described as an inauguration, the elections were held and NDC government defeated. With it also went the commission, though to my knowledge no one actually asked for it to be disbanded.

During my handling of the transition on behalf of the incoming Kufuor administration, one of my tasks was to look at the various commissions and committees, particularly those relating to the health field. In fact, after the hand-over was complete, I asked the president for a mandate to help assess and renew the commissions dealing with matters related to health and population. Among these, the ones which I found needed most immediate attention were the National Population Council and the Ghana AIDS Commission (GAC). The council was quickly set up, but the AIDS commission had to wait for the manning of all of the ministries and this took some time. However, this gave us enough leeway to start developing the basics of a national strategic framework within which the AIDS Commission was to be established. Finally the AIDS Commission was set up with the help of Cynthia Eledu.

The next thing was to revamp the secretariat. World Bank finance had been obtained for operationalising the fund to the tune of, I believe, US$25 million covering a period of 2001 to 2005, including the full manning of the secretariat.

I undertook this personally and liaised with the Public Service Commission over all aspects of the recruitment for the secretariat. It was not difficult getting the first three or four candidates for manning the directors' positions – the director of finance and the director of policy positions were quickly filled. The director general's position became difficult because, although several doctors applied and they were good, the issue of their managerial expertise and competence remained a little questionable.

The only one who applied and who could have fitted the bill was Dr. Kweku Yeboah. Unfortunately, in my view, it would have been a wrong appointment since he was in charge of the National Aids Control Programme, located within the ministry of health, the technical programme which was driving AIDS activities at the time. If he were brought to the GAC, the ministry of health's programme, which was to be the flagship of the AIDS commission, would probably go down. Such an appointment

might easily have create bad blood between the nascent GAC and the ministry. Rightly or wrongly therefore, I called him personally and gave him the reasons why I did not think the time was ripe for him to move from his current job and join the AIDS Commission. Little did I know then that in another few months he would leave the Ghana completely and go overseas – had I known, I probably would have given him the job, though whether that would have made him stay is another matter.

The search for director general took quite a while but finally, Fiifi Hesse, a member of the Public Services Commission, alerted us to the fact that Prof. S.A. Amoa, who was then an Associate Professor in Management in the Ghana Institute of Management and Public Administration (GIMPA), could be persuaded to apply. This also was transmitted to me from the presidency through D.K. Osei. I contacted Prof. Amoa and had a chat with him. He agreed to apply and at the interview we found that he was very suitable managerial material to handle the programme. He was recruited and with his recruitment the World Bank gave the go-ahead for disbursement of funds.

I was then free to decide how the GAC would relate to the presidency and where it should be located. Based on experience of what was happening elsewhere, I thought the best place for it was in the presidency itself – that the president should appear as the *de jure* chairman of the Commission and he could assign *de facto* chairing to any of his ministers.

I discussed this with President Kufuor. At one stage he thought it should be assigned to the Ministry of Health. I managed to let him appreciate why this would just be a continuation of the over-medicalisation of the programme. He agreed and wondered about the newly-established Ministry of Women and Children's Affairs. Again, although that Ministry could be very useful in the programme itself, if the total programme were to be located there, in a new ministry which had not really established its credentials among others in Ghana, there might be a problem.

Finally, the president and I agreed that the GAC would be assigned as a special responsibility to the vice president of Ghana. So, His Excellency Alhaji Aliu Mahama was made the *de facto* chairman of the GAC. I must say at this stage that he tackled the job with enthusiasm and he saw to it that meetings were well organised. He tried to be involved in the development of agenda for meetings and, to the extent possible, he attended commission meetings. In the eight years of the commission's existence and the 19 meetings that were held, Vice President Aliu Mahama was absent only on three occasions. The first two occasions, he had to be called for an urgent national duty, the

last one was when he was busy campaigning to be the New Patriotic Party's (NPP) flag bearer for President of the Republic of Ghana.

The commission was made deliberately large to include as many stakeholders as possible. It was meant to create excitement for a national response, encouraging everyone to play their part The 45 members included. 14 government ministers, two representatives of parliament, representatives of non-governmental organizations including religious bodies, the Trade Union Congress, medical research institutions, associations of people living with HIV, the National Union of Students, and individuals with the knowledge and special interest in the subject. By law it was to meet quarterly. Its corporate profile states *"The Ghana AIDS Commission is a supra ministerial and multi-sectoral body established under the Chairmanship of H.E. the President of the Republic of Ghana... Its mandate is to provide leadership in the management and coordination of the national response to the HIV/epidemic in Ghana"*. Its main functions are therefore to:

> *"... formulate policies, strategies and programme priorities, provide high level advocacy for HIV/AIDS control; mobilize and manage resources for HIV/AIDS programmes; foster linkages among all stakeholders; promote, gather and disseminate information and documentation on HIV/AIDS; and monitor and evaluate all HIV/AIDS activities in the country"*.

[Quotes are from the GAC Diary2009]

I asked the president for permission to look after the Commission on a day-to-day basis on behalf of the presidency. He agreed, and I took on the title of Presidential Adviser on Reproductive Health and HIV/AIDS, a role I performed until the elections of 2008 put paid to my remaining an adviser. With President Agyekum Kufuor gone, I went too. If the NPP had won, maybe the new president would have invited me back; but with the National Democratic Congress (NDC) now in power, I thought this would be the end of my major role in the HIV/AIDS arena in Ghana. During the first couple of years I did this work *pro bono*, although later I received a small honorarium agreed by the commission. For some strange reason the administration did not register me even as one of the many aides to the presidency

Among the first activities we undertook were translating the strategic framework into programmes of action for the next five years and trying to get the legal basis of the GAC completely established. The Ghana AIDS Commission Act, Act 613 which

was enacted in 2002, immediately following that for the Bank of Ghana, Act 612, another area in which I found myself doing some high level national work.

After nominating his members for the Council of State, President Kufuor nominated members for the Bank of Ghana Board and for some strange reason, he asked me to become a member. When I complained and told him that my having worked in the World Bank did not give me have any real credentials in banking, he said he was not sending me to the Bank of Ghana to be among the bankers. He wanted me there to ask them the questions which the ordinary people of Ghana would ask and be sure that, in all its dealings, the Bank kept the ordinary people of Ghana in mind.

I believe my tenure at the Bank of Ghana enlarged my knowledge and experience enormously, and I had to learn some new language altogether. Experiences which I had gathered from the international boards on which I had served came in handy when I was made chairman of the audit committee of the bank. Under my chairmanship, a cleaning exercise helped to clear years of reconciliation issues which had been ignored. When the NPP lost the elections the in-coming government simply made a radio announcement dissolving all boards. The bank's board was to meet the day after the announcement and I fully expected the governor to go by the Bank's Act and convene the meeting but to my surprise, and that of all my colleagues, he had the secretary cancel it. This dissolution of the bank's board contrary to the law created a problem which at the time of writing have not been solved. One of the members of the old board, Sam Okudzeto, had gone to court to challenge the legality of the government's action and to place an injunction on the appointment of a new one. So for almost a year now the Bank of Ghana has operated without a board of governors.

The relationship between the AIDS commission and the various ministries, especially the line agencies, started off very well indeed. Many ministries even complained that they had a lot to offer and had been omitted from its membership. In the beginning, ministers themselves started came meetings and made valuable contributions. But gradually, as often happens in Africa, the ministers started giving the job over to the lower level personnel. This alerted us to the fact that if we did not take particularly stringent legal action, the commission might find itself in the same position as other inter-ministerial councils and commissions in the past, including the Nutrition Council, National Population Council, where things started with the ministers attending, then their deputies, then directors-general and finally assistant directors or assistant secretaries – people who had absolutely no mandate for taking decisions.

To ensure that this did not happen, we briefed the Attorney General's office to advise that no ministry, department or agency, was to be represented at a level lower than a deputy minister. If the representation was below that level, the person could be an observer, not a full participant of the particular meeting be it a full commission meeting or that of a standing committee, unless a different arrangement had been made. This worked for several years but in the second term of the NPP, unfortunately, several of the ministers stopped coming and in one or two cases, they did not even allocate the responsibility to their deputy ministers: in fact, some of them hardly turned up at all.

This was a shame, because during the first Kufuor administration, the attorney general, for example, attended practically all meetings himself. Yet towards the end of the administration's second term, the commission had to be very persistent with Attorney General and his office to get them even to send one of their principal legal advisers to a meeting.

If the GAC is to operate as expected, ministers will have to take a much more responsible position than they had been taking in the last three or so years. Non-governmental organization representatives who are on the commission are not permitted even to send anybody less than their chief officer. Individuals, who are on the Commission on their own strength, are very high level professional people and they feel disappointed if they attended meetings and cannot interact with the policy makers themselves. I would like to put it on record that if the AIDS Commission is to operate as expected, then ministers have to be much more involved than they have been in the past three or so years.

One of the major problems that confronted and still confronts the National Aids Commission is that of coordination – one of the principal activities for a commission of this nature. Its roles are to set policy, devise strategy, mobilise funds, promote and support programmes and then help with developing monitoring and evaluation methodology, in other words, what came to be known as the "three ones". The commission should evaluate the total programme, whether the individual activities are sponsored by itself or by other agencies they should know what is happening. This requires an awful lot of coordination, it requires a lot of moral persuasion as well as a lot of legally mandated authority. By legal authority I mean the need to be sure that the commission gets the strength of law and the support needed for the work. For coordination, the commission's periodic meetings are one avenue, but it has to have

much more than that. The first level of coordination is its steering committee that was formed to oversee the day to day activities of the secretariat. I had the privilege of chairing this committee, which was tasked as follows:

- to provide guidance to the GAC secretariat in implementation of the National HIV and AIDS Strategic Framework and the decisions of the commission;
- to review and recommend annual and project budgets for approval by the commission;
- to provide guidance to the GAC secretariat in the development and implementation of the national HIV, AIDS and STIs policy;
- to ensure that all processes and laid-down regulations are duly followed in the allocation of funds for project implementation;
- to review the performance of the GAC secretariat and make recommendations for improvement;
- to review the GAC secretariat's quarterly and annual reports and make recommendations for approval by the commission;
- to consider and approve matters in the management of the GAC secretariat that demand urgent attention.

Generally the steering committee exercises oversight management responsibility over the GAC secretariat. My own position as a presidential adviser was charged with the following functions:

- provide guidance to the GAC secretariat on the implementation of the National Strategic Framework and all decisions taken by the commission;
- provide guidance to the secretariat in the formulation and implementation of the National HIV/AIDS/STI and Strategic Framework;
- review and recommend annual and project budgets for GAC approval;
- ensure that all processes and regulations are duly followed in the allocation of funds for project/programme implementation;
- review the performance of GAC secretariat and make recommendations for improvement;
- review the secretariat's quarterly/annual reports and recommend them for GAC approval;
- consider and approve matters demanding urgent attention.

On an as-needed basis I performed many other tasks including the following:

- offered guidance on the development of the relevant project documents required for implementation of the national response by either leading the process as chairman or participating actively in the work (for example, the National HIV/AIDS Strategic Framework, National HIV/AIDS/STIs Policy, Joint Review of the National Response, Development of the National BCC/IEC Strategy);
- reviewed draft GAC Annual Reports and other statutorily required documents of the commission to ensure that they are professionally produced and circulated to create the appropriate corporate image;
- served as the link between the GAC management and the political leadership in matters relating to the national response;
- met with GAC management quarterly to review progress of work done during the quarter and guided the seeking of solutions to problems encountered and plans for the next quarter;
- participated regularly and actively in sessions of GAC management with missions of the development partners, most often on the request of GAC management;
- besides regular telephone communication with management, made frequent visits to the GAC secretariat to find out about any assistance that management needed;
- responded promptly to management's requests for assistance in addressing emergency issues, irrespective of time of day;
- reviewed draft minutes of all meetings of the GAC and all its technical committees to ensure appropriate presentation of coverage. It is to be noted that five or six such meetings were held every quarter and the management asked the presidential adviser to do this;
- reviewed draft speeches prepared by management for delivery by top government officials on special occasions, such as World AIDS Day;
- over the past three years I have personally and directly taken up the responsibility of searching for more suitable office premises for the commission on behalf of management, making the necessary contacts with the relevant authorities, prospective landlords, etc.;
- participated actively and taken personal concern to ensure the success

of every event that management organises including World AIDS Day, National HIV/AIDS Research conference, social functions, etc.;

- offered guidance to management on fruitful relationships with the development partners, for example, soliciting funds for the national response;
- personally defended the commission in matters that generate public concern or which could impugn GAC's corporate image, for example the goat serum issue, the prostitution debate, the alleged shortage of antiretrovirals, etc.

The GAC's steering committee met some 29 times during the eight years that it existed, tackling some very important issues on behalf of the Commission. Areas of controversy in which it found itself included dealing with commercial sex workers, men having sex with men and third party reporting of the status of HIV/AIDS. It dealt with the question of sustainability of the national response from all angles and recommended that financial sustainability would require the establishment of a special fund. insulated from the yearly government budget, devoted to the response. The government could make provision for putting money into this fund and it could work attract further donations from development partners, the private sector and individuals. The idea was considered favourably by our development partners but it was never considered by cabinet. The steering committee also remained in constant touch with United Nations groups and the development partners generally.

For coordination earlier on, the United Nations and the development partners had formed what they called the Theme Group – a group of the United Nations specialists or officers assigned to areas related to HIV/AIDS. To their meetings were invited the minister for health or his representative, the director general of the GAC or his representative and myself as the chairman of the steering committee. Although this Theme Group did a lot to harmonise the inputs of the United Nations system and the development partners, sometimes it would appear as if they were working against the GAS and the government, so it did not function and contribute as smoothly as one would expect.

When Cynthia Eledu left, she was replaced by Dr. Warren Namara who had long experience of AIDS commission work in Uganda. He brought this experience to bear on the situation in Ghana and quickly recommended that we needed two coordinating

mechanisms – one was a partnership forum which would include all of those working in the HIV and related fields and would bring together donors, development partners, GAC, the ministries that were involved, non-governmental organizations, and so on – in other words all those who had a contribution to make. These included the leadership of community-based and non-governmental organizations which might have come from a religious and traditional perspective as well as those with a technical perspective. The idea sounded good and we agreed to it. For four or five years now, we have been holding annual partnership fora where those doing AIDS work, including officially recognized HIV/AIDS work through the commission, would report what they were doing.

Unfortunately, after the first couple of years, the attendance at this partnership forum seemed to be getting less and less and I must put on record as a matter of regret, that the ones who are most negligent were representatives of the various ministries, departments and agencies of government that deal with the problem. Unfortunately, many of the commissioners also did not attend in the last few years. But despite this, it must be stated that the partnership fora have provided the impetus for getting AIDS messages across to people.

The business meeting, which generally followed the day after the fora, dealt exclusively with financial matters, the pledges that were to be made, what had been given and what donations had not been honoured, and so on. These also proved very good place for discussions of some of the difficulties in handling the support for the national AIDS programme. I firmly recommended that all these activities should be continued and, if possible, strengthened. Without them, the public at large will not know what AIDS work is going on.

The ultimate measure of the impact of a commission of this nature is what happens to the epidemic itself, meaning its prevalence and incidence, and the extent to which these change in the desired direction. In this regard it must be accepted that Ghana has held her own. After initial rapid rise in prevalence, a drop was registered and since then the prevalence has trended downwards over time. The national prevalence, as determined by anonymous survey tied to the DHS of 2003, gave a prevalence of 2.2% while in 2007 and 2008 prevalence levels have been 1.9% and 1.7% respectively. Naturally this cannot be attributed directly to the work of the commission, but in fairness its contribution must be recognized. The task of tracking the epidemic has been under the National AIDS Control Programme (NACPD) of the ministry of health since the virus arrived in the country.

The implementation of the national response must have contributed to
- a very high level of awareness of the HIV/AIDS epidemic;
- increased levels of advocacy;
- increased prevention, care and support services;
- high levels of community mobilization and participation;
- high commitment and participation of the private sector;
- rapidly increasing access to antiretroviral treatment for people living HIV/AIDS;
- increased levels of preventative mother to child transmission treatment;
- increased voluntary counselling and testing.

Key challenges include
- the need to give prevention a high priority within the response;
- the need to expand treatment and care rapidly;
- need to strengthen the people living HIV/AIDS associations and make them stronger partners in the response;
- need to improve human and institutional capacity development;
- need to change national laws and positions against commercial sex workers and men having sex with men;
- need to intensify stigma reduction campaigns;
- need for more sustainable resource mobilization;
- need for better mainstreaming of the whole response.

17 recognition

One of the wonderful things that can happen to one is to receive the recognition of colleagues, organizations or institutions and for one's work to be lauded, even to extent of being given money with which to carry on one's efforts. To spare my blushes, I will not list or describe all the honours awards and public recognition that I have been lucky enough to receive.

A public acclamation of my contributions came within IPPF in 1988 when I was given recognition as a co-founder of the Planned Parenthood Association of Ghana during their 21st anniversary celebrations and given a stool. In Ghana being given a stool means that one has arrived. I was given a stool as one of the elders. Another recognition of IPPF which I respect very much was to be considered a patron of the Africa Region. Surprisingly, though, the Region itself has been very reluctant in asking me to perform any task on its behalf and I have always felt closer to the central office of the federation. Even when I have had to help deal with a problem of the region the invitation came from the central office. I hope the regional volunteers remember that a patron is a resource to be used.

Perhaps the first true population recognition that I had was in 1984, when I was given the Hugh Moore Award for my contributions. The award ceremony took place in Freetown, Sierra Leone, where we had gone for an Africa regional seminar on population and development. It was at this seminar that my eyes were really opened to the difficulties that we were facing in the fields of family planning, reproductive health generally and particularly when dealing with the issues of unsafe abortion.

The Nigerian delegation was headed by the chairman of the Federation of Nigerian Women. The woman had great pleasure in telling us the story of their fights with the then Minister for Health, Prof. Olikoye Ransome-Kuti. It turned out that Prof. Ransome-Kuti had tried to put a paper to help to liberalise the abortion laws before cabinet, trying to take the onus away from the woman, make the abortee less of a criminal and also to try to expand the provisions beyond physical health to include mental health, rape, and incest.

This woman said that they, the women's federation, had threatened Prof. Ransome-Kuti that if the paper was put before cabinet and approved, they would march on the streets against him and his ministry. Of course, with such a threat, the Nigerian cabinet did not even consider the paper. Those of us at the meeting found this so difficult to accept that the majority received her information with boos. She quickly left the meeting and did not show her face again.

The award itself consisted of a sum of money and a shield. The shield had been made in the United States and carried over to me in Freetown by Phyllis Piotrow.

Another award which I found interesting was the one given me in Bandung, Indonesia, in 1991 by the International Association for Maternal and Neonatal Health (IAMANEH) formed by Dr. Hubert de Watteville who was also involved with the formation of International Federation of Gynecology and Obstetrics (FIGO). I am not sure if this organization still stands but the citation was for my work for mothers and children and again this carried a small sum of money. I found this useful for expanding some work which I was doing on adolescent health and sexuality through the Pediatric Pharmacy Advocacy Group (PPAG), then headed as executive director by I.K. Boateng. The money was for the work of a team to research both how much our adolescents knew about their body and its functions, as well as their knowledge and attitudes to sex and sexuality. I joined the team which conducted one-to-one and focus group interviews among adolescents in three regions in Ghana. These gave us many insights into adolescent sexuality and the understanding of adolescent reproductive health problems.

Some of the issues raised were quite revealing. There was no doubt that problems around menarche and the meaning of the menarche were uppermost in the minds of many of the adolescents. Among the stories around the menarche were the following.

- it was believed that if a girl started her periods and did not have sex soon thereafter she would have problems with her menstruation;
- if a girl has painful menstrual periods, they could only be cured by having sex; and
- if a girl goes through school or life generally without having sex until she gets married, the longer she had waited, the less likely she would be to have children when she finally wanted them.

These were major issues that we had to attempt to deal with. Fortunately, the PPAG was able to provide film coverage for these questions and also to provide educational

films which then were used to help approach solutions. Unfortunately, however, I do not believe there was ever any evaluation done of this.

FHI and the Support and Treatment for Antiretroviral Therapy, START Project

A major issue in the HIV/AIDS field, as soon as antiretroviral therapy (ART) proved its value in controlling the excesses of AIDS and in prolonging life, was how to make such therapy available to the millions suffering in the developing countries. The Family Health International (FHI) board had to face this issue squarely as Dr. David Barry, a board member who had been involved in the development of AZT as a treatment for AIDS, was a vocal advocate for doing everything possible to make the drugs available and accessible to sufferers in the least developed countries (LDCs).

The questions of the cost of the drugs, dependability of the health systems providing a sound basis for delivering drugs of such high toxicity and complex delivery requirements, plus patient compliance were thoroughly discussed. In the end the FHI board agreed to find some money from its own resources to undertake pilot projects in a few countries. Ghana was one of those selected and in 2002 a START project was launched in the Manya Krobo area of the Eastern Province. Not only was I a board member but, as the national adviser on HIV/AIDS and reproductive health, I was intimately involved in the discussion of the project, the selection of the site and some of the politico-social issues.

The project was launched at a grand durbar in Krobo Odumase and the Nene, or Paramount Chief, Sackitey II graced the occasion and received the party involved in his palace.

The START project in Ghana removed all doubts about the deliverability and patient compliance in a developing country. An approach, similar to the direct observed short course treatment, DOTS, for tuberculosis was adopted. The eligible client had to select a relation or friend who would ensure that the patient complied completely with the treatment regime. The success of this project, undertaken with the support of both the national AIDS control programme of the ministry of health and the GAC, formed part of the basis for a more comprehensive treatment of AIDS in the country. A national treatment guide was developed which has naturally undergone several revisions.

Before, during and since the START programme we have had many claims of successful treatment for AIDS, none of which has stood any scientific test. Frequently such claims were brought to my notice by members of the clergy or through the media. This was not peculiar to Ghana. Those in the HIV/AIDS field have had to deal with

myriads of claims of cures, the majority of which have proved false. Sometimes it is easy to dismiss a claim out of hand, for example when a claimant informed a research meeting that he could see the viruses in urine and was able to make them disappear. At other times a lot more investigation was necessary.

Fellowship of the Ghana Academy

The Ghana Academy of Learning was established in November 1959 by *Osagyefo* Dr. Kwame Nkrumah, with the following aims and objectives:

a to promote the study, extension and dissemination of knowledge of all the sciences and of learning;

b to establish and maintain proper standards of endeavour in all fields of science and learning in Ghana; and

c to recognize outstanding contributions to the advancement of the sciences and learning in Ghana.

The foundation fellows included the following;

Osagyefo Dr. Kwame Nkrumah, E.A. Boateng, Mr. Justice W.B. Van Lare, Lady Barbara Jackson, Sir Arku Korsah, Dr. J.B. Danquah, Dr. R. H. Stoughton, Dr. F.G. Torto, K. Twum-Barima, Dr. R.W.H. Wright, Geoffrey Bing, Dr. Silas Dodu, Dr. W.E. Duncanson, Dr. J.A.K. Quartey, Dr. J. Lamb, Dr. Susan Ofori-Atta, Dr. A.A. Kwapong, Dr. D.A. Chapman, Dr. C.A. Ackah and J.H. Nketia.

Of the 20, eight were scientists. The heads of the two university institutions and of Achimota, then the number one secondary school, were included. The inclusion of several non-Ghanaians working with or for the Government was noteworthy. On the whole most of the Ghanaians were at an early stage of their academic development and their inclusion was more a challenge to them to excel. Needless to say all of them did just that.

I was privileged to be elected to join the Academy in 1961. Others elected in the same year were Rev. C.G. Baeta, Dr. R.P. Baffour, Dr. R.H. Bannerman, Dr. C.O. Easmon, and Prof. L.H. Ofosu-Appiah and Prof. J.C. de Graft Johnson. Academy meetings were exciting and in many instances the chairman, then prime minister, attended personally. Anniversary celebrations of the academy were a national event to which many ministers and high government officials made the effort to attend. Sadly

top-level Ghanaian leadership has not made any effort to identify with the academy's activities to any great extent since the entry into the 4th Republic.

The academy changed its mode of operations in 1963 and became fused to an extent with the Council for Scientific and Industrial Research. This pattern was similar to the academies of the Soviet Union and Eastern Europe where their academicians had responsibility for the supervision and leadership of research programmes. As if to emphasise the Eastern European style the executive authority of the academy was vested in a præsidium to which I was elected when it was formed in 1963. The fusion did not sit too well and in my view it resulted in much friction between the fellows and some top scientists. After the 1966 coup there was a clamour for change. A committee under the chairmanship of Sir John Cockroft of the United Kingdom was appointed to advise on the structure, roles and responsibilities of the academy.

The committee advised that the academy should be separated from the research institutions and revert to its original purposes. It was to be named the Ghana Academy of Arts and Sciences. This was accepted and in 1968 the separation was legalized. I was honorary secretary of the academy during part of the period, 1967-1969, and the Vice President for the Sciences Section for 1971-1972. Dr. Letitia Obeng's *The Ghana Academy of Sciences: A Historical Perspective* published to coincide with the 50th anniversary of the academy is an informative source for those interested.

From the *Proceedings of the Academy* anyone interested may find my contributions but I would like to refer to three in particular. In 1966, as a fresh professor of social and preventive medicine of the medical school I gave a lecture on *Making the Community Healthy* in which I laid out my philosophy for providing health to the total community. In 1976, I gave the Danquah Memorial Lectures as the first scientist to do so since its inception in 1968. In my lectures, *Humanising Science and Technology for National Development*, I dwelt on Ghana's and Africa's population and food problems as part of the general development needs. I had been taken very much by Schumacher's *Small is beautiful*. My main thesis was that technology, whether developed or imported, should fit the social and cultural environments in which it is to be applied. And I advocated the selection of both hard and soft technologies as appropriate, rather than having preconceived notions of what is good technology. Needless to say I used examples from both the family planning and nutrition fields and warned of the need to balance our rates of population growth with that of our resources and needs for education and health care. The lectures were very well received by packed audiences.

Above: Being congratulated on receiving the United Nations Population Award, 1993.

Below: Receiving my doctorate from the University of Ghana, Legon, 1995.

Above: Fellows of the Royal College of Obstetricians and Gynæcologists, 2004.

Below: Receiving the Better World Award, 1986.

In 1999, as the new president of the academy, I gave a presidential address on the subject *Why is Africa Losing the Battle against AIDS?* In this lecture, which was also very well received, I called for the establishment of a national AIDS commission amongst other recommendations. I am sure the lecture and the fact that it was carried in the leading national daily newspaper contributed to the establishment of the national AIDS commission the following year. My two-term presidency lasted from 1999-2002. I tried during this period to get government to show more interest in the academy by supporting it at a higher financial level, by members of government attending academy functions and by the president himself sponsoring the Academy's anniversary celebrations. Apart from President Kufuor attending the Academy dinner in my last year and in sponsoring the anniversary dinner of 2003 in the Castle, my efforts were singularly unsuccessful. Getting members of the government to attend Academy functions remains a major challenge.

United Nations Population Award

In 1993, I had the honour of receiving the United Nations Population Award. The ceremony took place in the United Nations Building in New York and this is a recognition which gives the recipient a chance to say a few words in accepting the award. I believe the statement I made was filled with enough passion for it to be reproduced here. Again my wife, one of my daughters and her daughter were the people who were able to accompany me to this particular function. I am afraid I would like to record a note which I consider rather sad on this occasion.

I arrived in New York and expected that I would have some recognition from my own country's mission to the United Nations. There was absolutely nothing. Not even a note. I was aware that the UNFPA had informed the Ghana Mission of the award and of my coming to New York to receive it. Unlike what happened later in Bangkok, with Vice Admiral Dzang, no official recognition was given to my presence or of the fact that a Ghanaian had received the award for the very first time. It was the UNFPA that actually sent a car to take me from my hotel to the ceremony. Meanwhile, the Japanese winner of the Institutional Award had been taken to the Secretary General's office by his ambassador and it was with the Secretary General that he came down for the ceremony to begin. Anyway, once the ceremony began it became quite grand and was followed by as huge a reception as the United Nation is capable of mounting.

After the reception, Dr. Hernan Sanhueza, Director of the Western Hemisphere Region of IPPF, organised a sumptuous dinner attended by some 20 or so friends and

colleagues. It was great fun with both speeches in praise of my contributions and some considerable lampooning.

The Prince Mahidol Prize

Sometime in 1995, I received an urgent telephone call from Thailand, from the Prince Mahidol Foundation, inviting me to submit my *curriculum vitæ* because I had been nominated for the Prince Mahidol Prize for my contributions to the gender issue, to sexual and reproductive health including nutrition and family planning and particularly, for my activities during the PrepComs and the Cairo International Conference on Population and Development (ICPD). I was very surprised and elated, firstly because I had not even heard of the Prince Mahidol Foundation and secondly when I found out about it, it was considered one of the very highest honours given in the fields of health at the time.

I sent my CV and photographs as requested, and the next thing I knew was an invitation to Thailand for the award ceremony in 1996. Everything was paid for by the foundation including first class travel with my wife. We arrived in Thailand early one morning, and we were received into the VVIP Lounge of the airport. From there, without our having to even check our luggage out, we were taken in a Mercedes Benz of the king's fleet and driven through town with a dispatch rider so we had no hold-up at all on the streets of Bangkok. We were put up very comfortably in the Hotel Oriental.

Unfortunately, the King's mother had died a little earlier and she had not even been buried, so the royal household was in mourning. We had been asked to dress appropriately. Since the function was a black tie one this was no problem for the men, but for the women it meant wearing mourning dress but suitably made to be elegant.

The 1995 prize recipients included Prof. Carl Djerassi of the United States and Prof. Egon Diczfalusy of Sweden. These two received a joint award for their scientific work on contraception and contraceptives. Dr. Nafis Sadik of Pakistan and I received the joint prize for the public service of family planning and gender advocacy.

During the ceremony, I was pleased to have at least one member of my extended family, Mrs. Cynthia Omaboe in Bangkok, who attended. The Ghana government was represented at the ceremony by the Ambassador to Japan, who looked after both Japan and Thailand, Rear Admiral Dzang. I felt good having him standing behind me when I was given the prize. He was very pleased with the ceremony and he made me feel

extremely good and remained on friendly terms for a very long time. His involvement contrasted so sharply with what had happened at the United Nations Population Award in 1994 that I would like to say of him "there was a true a Ghanaian patriot". I felt so sad when he died recently.

After considering what to do with my prize money for a little while I felt it would be best to use it in pursuing some of the areas Nafis and I advocated in the Programme of Action of the ICPD. Women's education appealed to me. I recalled that one area of difficulty stressed by many was the low level of uptake of studying science by girls. So I decided to establish a fund out of which girls pursuing science in the University of Ghana at Legon might receive some help. The fund has supported over seventy girls since its establishment and it has grown quite a bit. In the past few years it received substantial donations from the UNFPA.

A few years after this, I had a letter from Dr. John Sciarra, who had been President of the American College of Obstetricians and Gynecologists, stating that he wanted to recommend me for the Honorary Fellowship of the College and that he would like to have my CV. I sent it but then I did not hear anything further for a couple of years. Suddenly a letter arrived stating that I had been accepted for the recognition of an honorary fellow of the American College of Obstetricians and Gynecologists. The ceremony would take place in San Francisco in May 2000. So it was, that in May of the millennium year, I received what I considered one of the highest honours that an internal medicine physician could receive, the recognition of a sister college to that of his, but in another discipline particularly the discipline of obstetrics and gynæcology.

As if this was not enough, in 2004 I received information that I was to be recognized with the Fellowship of the Royal College of Obstetricians and Gynæcologists in London. This ceremony was a major one, held in the college's grounds and followed by a very interesting dinner. Both my wife and my eldest daughter were able to attend.

University honours

I have had a couple of University honours. In 1989 Tufts University in the United States honoured me with a doctorate of human letters for my contributions to nutrition awareness in Africa and elsewhere. I found myself in some very high academic and exciting company – the world famous scientist Stephen Hawking was one of us. To see him make conversation through computer-based equipment because of the limitations placed on him by the uncompromising nervous disease was at once

saddening and ennobling. Pérez de Cuéllar, former United Nations Secretary General was another of us and he made the Convocation oration. I was assigned to make a speech to the medical faculty and give out the certificates to the graduating doctors. I reminded them of the global nature of many important diseases and the need for them to understand international public health and the role of international health agencies.

The University of Ghana honoured me with its honorary Doctor of Science for my contributions to nutrition, university education and gender advocacy. The award ceremony took place in 1995. In 1994 I had delivered the Aggrey/Fraser Guggisberg Memorial Lectures to large audiences. I had chosen as topic, *Adam and Eve and the Serpent*. I had tried to link the low status of women, particularly African women, to their biological bondage; how nature's sexism in making the female carry such a heavy portion of the biological task of human reproduction is a basis for social and cultural discrimination and suppression of women. I suggested many approaches to helping change the situation. I had given the lectures before the pro-vice chancellor of the university who informed me that the university awarded doctorates to those who delivered these lectures.

In 1998 I received the Harvard School of Public Health Alumni Award of Merit citation of which states it is "*the highest honour the School can bestow on a graduate. Presented annually, usually to three graduates, the award recognizes professional excellence, leadership, and commitment to the field of public health. Winners are selected by committee from nominations submitted by alumni worldwide*".

On 9th April 2005 I was privileged to be one of the first recipients of the newly established Lifetime Achievement Award of the Medical and Dental Council of Ghana. The citation read "*To Professor Frederick Torgbor Sai (Distinguished Public Health Physician, Expert in Nutrition and Population Issues, National and International Civil Servant, Medical Teacher, Academician and Humanitarian) In recognition of High Standards in the Practice of Medicine in Ghana.*"

The final honour that I would like to mention is the membership of the Star of Ghana. This was bestowed on me by J.A. Kufuor, the President of the Republic of Ghana, during the award ceremony for the year 2006. This award, which carried a sash and various other things, was for my contributions both to the public services of Ghana and for health, nutrition and services to HIV and AIDS and for my international recognition and making Ghana's name better known.

I have had public recognition from several organizations with which I have been involved one way or another. These have taken the form of receptions, lectures

and trophies of various kinds. Perhaps I should mention the acknowledgement of Ipas in Nairobi, in Addis Ababa and then in front of a large number of colleagues during the 2009 FIGO conference in Cape Town, when Dr Eunice Brookman Amissah, Vice President of Ipas introduced me. To my family and friends however, nothing betters the recognition given me by FHI in Accra early in 2009. The recognition ceremony, under the chairmanship of Dr. A Siemens, CEO of FHI, took the form of a brilliant lecture by Dr. Ward Cates, tributes from overseas colleagues – Dr. Pramilla Senanayake from Sri Lanka and Dr. Halida Hanum Akhter from Bangladesh – Prof. Gilford Ashitey of the Medical School and Alfred Teddy Konu, the Registrar of the University of Ghana, Legon. To be honoured by outsiders in your home was to me the very best.

18 my family

Writing an ending to these reflections on my past has proved more difficult than I expected. Commenting on some of today's burning issues in Africa could get me into a great deal of trouble. Looking into the future is always a dangerous exercise as things may turn out to be horribly different. Perhaps a combination of the two without being too dogmatic on the expectations might be the way to go. Whatever be the case, perhaps I should start by presenting my family as finally formed.

All families have triumphs and tragedies, the latter, sometimes, leading to disintegration. But handled properly, tragedies can lead to a strengthening of family ties or the building of new families.

My biological family was completed in 1962. Oboshie arrived in 1953, Adai in 1955, Obodai, the only male, in 1958, and Shormeh in 1962. The older two girls had practically all their basic education in Ghana apart from a year's primary and kindergarten in Brookline during my year at Harvard. They attended the Ridge Church School, Aburi Secondary Girls School for O levels, Achimota for A levels and then Legon where Oboshie read sociology and Adai zoology. Adai then undertook veterinary medicine in Nairobi.

I do not think the two girls ever really forgave us for sending them to Aburi Girls' School rather than to Achimota College, nearer home and better equipped, for which they had qualified. Apparently the water and sanitation situation in Aburi School proved to be very testing. They had to fetch water for bathing from a deep well and pit latrines had to be confronted by my children who, from birth, had only known full water systems. Our major reason for sending them to Aburi was to make them face another type of reality. When Florence and I went to Achimota we were moving upwards socially as it were: we had slept on mats on the floor and used the public toilet systems, our children slept on internal sprung mattresses locally called "Vono" from birth and had no idea of the pressures of environmental sanitation. Both girls finished their secondary education by spending a couple of years for their A levels in Achimota College.

By the time I moved to London both older girls were in the University of Ghana at Legon so they chose to stay at home. Obodai and Shormeh chose to continue their education in Britain and we got them into Culford, a boarding school in Suffolk, England. It had a religious bias and we thought they would be able to settle down. Indeed they seemed to enjoy their first couple of years very much and did well.

Obodai had inherited, in a worse form than mine, a familial ataxia which made for sudden and uncontrolled shaking of the hands. He had a lot of help, both medical and at school. For his O level it was agreed that he would have a scribe who would write to his dictation and this worked well, as he obtained very good results. He started on his A levels.

But then Shormeh started to feel uncomfortable in the School. She could no longer take the ragging by other girls. Suddenly, she was confronted with the nastiness that youngsters can provide over the issue of colour – she hated being compared to a golliwog. And I suppose she also missed her mother. So we decided to bring her back to Ghana to Achimota.

Her brother found it difficult to settle down after the sister's departure. He was now the only black boy in the school. Study suffered and his behaviour changed. So we brought him back home for a year to try and get him re-adjusted. Just a few weeks before his return to London the worst of a parent's tragic fears came true.

Obodai died in an unnecessary accident in Accra. He, Shormeh and a friend had gone to the cinema and were returning home fairly late at night, just before midnight. They had gone past the Accra Girls' School, heading straight towards Achimota. They had the right of way, but a driver who wanted to turn left chose to ignore all the rules of driving by trying to cut across them on the hypotenuse. He smashed into the side of the little car. Apparently Obodai had claimed to be unwell and had extended the front seat fully into a bed and was lying down. Normally he would be wearing a seat belt, whether driving or as passenger. Why he chose not to put the seat belt on whilst lying down no one knows; he had no chance whatsoever.

This accident is one of the commoner forms of bad driving in Ghana. Instead of those turning left at a junction knowing that they had to wait and do a rectangular turn, they will rush and cut across those with the right of way. The accident was handled very poorly. First of all the driver fled the scene and his employers did not produce him for quite awhile. It took the police a year to inform me they were taking that man to court. The charge – careless driving. In the United States, this would have

been manslaughter by negligence or negligently causing death. I think unless Ghana tightens its laws of the road and properly enforces them, the unnecessary slaughter on our roads will continue.

Less than a year after Obodai's death I returned to Ghana as a consultant to the IPPF and the United Nations University. The family healed slowly. Help came in different forms. Two of Florence's sisters sent their young sons to live with us. One in particular, Kwablah Ewusie, stayed throughout his secondary school years till he went to college to study medicine. He has done extremely well as a military doctor and an ophthalmologist with the rank of Lt. Colonel. He also received a national honour, the Grand Medal, for his services in the Democratic Republic of the Congo.

One fight that I had with him quite early on, which I hope he will not mind my recounting for the assistance of others who may be interpreting some of the Bible wrongly, was his reading of it day and night to the exclusion of everything else. I told him he should to read the Bible only for a short period during the day and then study his other subjects. He acquiesced and his progress was almost immediate.

I had hardly settled in Washington in January 1985 when I suffered another tragedy. I had a call from home informing me that my younger sister, Mrs. Charlotte Palm, had died. I was stunned and momentarily lost. She had been unwell for most of the four or more years since her husband's death but I did not think she had anything life-threatening. What was more upsetting, the couple of weeks before I left home I had tried to see her only to be told by an elderly relative that she had gone to Accra. As she was trading in all sorts of small items I thought she was OK. It was only after her death that I was told she had been taken to a prayer home for treatment. As a doctor I felt betrayed but there was nothing to do but to come home and see to the funeral. After the funeral the question of what would happen to her children was a major item for decision by the paternal family.

The family wanted the three children to be divided up and given to the surviving brothers. They were quite firm that the two boys, at least, should go to the brothers. I was very uncomfortable with this suggestion. What happened to my older sister as a result of the customary dividing of children among relations had always bugged me. Secondly, as a doctor I was very worried about the family history of my late brother-in-law. His father had died of a cardio-vascular accident at around 50, his mother had died relatively young, too, and my late brother in law had died of suddenly of a heart condition.

I suggested that I should be allowed to be the principal care-taker of the children

With Florence, 1990.

Our family, children and grandchildren, on Florence's 80th birthday, 2009.

since I had been assisting my sister since the death of their father. Any of their uncles and aunts could help. That way they would grow up and be close together as a family. My having a job with the World Bank in Washington would be of help since they would benefit greatly. The paternal house elder accepted my reasoning. So it happened that I became the official father to my sister's children.

Of course I had not put them on my application to the World Bank as my dependents so when I presented a request for their recognition, the authorities were doubtful. The argument that this had happened after the completion of my application was not acceptable. As proper certificate of their adoption was required, I went back to Ghana to see the paternal elder of the family who readily agreed. The poor man was given quite a tongue lashing by some members of his family as official adoption was not part of our culture. To us, the children were to be inherited by their father's brothers. But with the proper documentation, the World Bank accepted the Palms as Sai-Palms and Rita, Billy and Dunny officially became Sai children. Sad to relate the paternal uncles, like their brother, died relatively young and suddenly too.

What I find interesting about the final composition of my family is how it has fitted perfectly with what my wife had wanted at the time we married. She said she wanted six children while I had wanted two. In the end we had four biological children, but ended up with six after two family tragedies and the inheriting of a trio. The ages of the adopted children followed the biological ones perfectly; and the six have merged seamlessly into a close and happy set of siblings.

18 concluding thoughts

Recently I told an audience that I find it difficult to hold my head up high when I review the field of nutrition, reproductive health generally and family planning in Africa. The progress has been so slow and in some cases so miniscule as to be almost invisible. Sub-Saharan Africa seems to be lagging behind practically all other regions; in some instances even going backward. In numerical terms there are more malnourished children in Sub-Saharan Africa now than when I started, thanks to our propensity for rapidly reproducing ourselves. Although there has been some progress in family planning, the figures are poor by comparison with where we should be or when compared with countries at the same stage as us when I started the field. Some progress has been recorded with women's education but other aspects of the improvement in the status of women remain daunting. Women's representation at policy making levels is still very small. Of course some countries can be proud of the fact that they have equal pay for equal work though the proportions of men to women might be seriously skewed.

In all of this it is Ghana which makes me saddest. The independence of Ghana, led by a charismatic and purposeful pan-Africanist, Kwame Nkrumah, instilled pride, hope and the can-do spirit in us young professionals. Of course history turned out differently. The international struggles between East and West, the emphasis of the colonial legacy endorsing a Balkanized situation, poor governance including strong-man rule or misrule, life-presidencies, detention without trial and other forms of human rights abuses all combined to make Sub-Saharan Africa unable to fulfil the hopes and aspirations of its people.

Recently things appeared to be taking a turn for the better. Democracy seems to be taking root. Ghana, after several military interventions, has taken the democratic path in the last two decades. But even here, the democracy is extremely fragile. Consensus governance has been thrown overboard, while government by exclusion seems to be the order of the day. What the Americans call the "the permanent campaign" is taking root. Governments have spokespersons or even ministers and deputy ministers whose major

role is to extol the achievements and intentions of government, no matter what – and, to the extent possible, denigrate anything done before by others This is partly sponsored by media which is emerging from suppression and, rather than taking leadership in public education, finds partisan politics an easy area for public interest. Of particular concern should be the lack of civility in public discourse. Language can incite. This situation, in my view, is partly responsible for little or no attention being paid to subjects like family planning and reproductive health when advocating social development programmes.

The introduction of the National Health Insurance Scheme in Ghana by the Kufuor administration and the concomitant proclamation of free maternity care services, supported by a British government grant, gave many of us in Ghana hope that things would change for the better in the health and reproductive health field. Unfortunately the policies completely excluded free family planning supplies. This omission alone makes me wonder if our leaders understand the role of family planning in development, especially in the gender area and even specifically in the reduction of maternal mortality and morbidity. An effort, under my guidance, and with Pathfinder support, to reposition family planning in Ghana was held up by the ministry of health for some two years. When it was finally launched, the then minister almost succeeded in convincing the audience of the non-importance of family planning and population. Neither the current economic development argument nor the established facts of the relationships between family planning and maternal health would convince him.

Ghana is not alone in not giving family planning and reproductive health the priority they deserve. There are countries in Africa today whose leaders still want to withhold family planning so that their populations can grow even more rapidly. Such leaders make one wonder if they belong to the group that thinks that power is knowledge rather than the other way round. The population projections for Africa should be frightening to our leaders if they really wish to see rapid development rather than large numbers of uneducated and easily swayed votes. Quite rightly our leaders have been party to many international consensuses and agreements on fundamental and basic human rights. These include the right to education, the right to health and the right to reproductive health education and care, among others. My question to our leaders is, why do you not see how family planning helps you in trying to fulfil these promises? The right to good health should not mean simply the right to care when sick. It should mean also the right to prevent disease and ill health and the right to sexual and reproductive health education and services – as agreed by consensus in Bucharest, Mexico and Cairo.

Many countries do their annual economic development assessments without considering their population growth. A growth of GNP of 5 per cent translates really into 2.5 per cent if the population is growing at 2.5 per cent. When a country's population is growing at 2.5 per cent, per year, that country stands to double its population in 28 years or so. How many Sub-Saharan African countries can double all of their services and infrastructure in such a short time? And yet at the basic level that is what is needed simply to stand still.

These facts and many more have been given out at international conferences and non-governmental organization meetings of various kinds. As an advocate of these causes, I have been involved in many which have given me a platform from which to speak or to guide national or international discourse. Some have questioned the usefulness or the cost benefit of these conferences and meetings, but I believe they have been of great value. They afford an opportunity to examine the scientific findings and test them rigorously, and out of such examination to arrive at soundly based recommendations. It is such foundations also that give courage to our leaders to speak out on sensitive subjects.

Of course at times, even when the science is clear, the international howl of the minority might make some leaders unwilling to speak. In the international arena, the years from 2001-2008 lost to family planning and other reproductive health activities is illustrative of how the minority can cow the majority, despite the science. Even if the major meetings do not themselves enable funds to flow, their conclusions can be used for bilateral negotiations for funding. Perhaps one of the most important outcomes to these major meetings is the strength they give non-governmental organizations to advocate activities at the national levels and evaluate governmental action in specific areas. But far and away the most important outcomes of these meetings are to keep important development issues on the international agenda for research and action.

In conclusion I would like to humbly call on the African Union (AU) to lead the continent actively and aggressively, not only in politics but also in the fulfilment of the human rights of our people. From my own perspectives the AU must be more aggressive in its agenda for women, especially in the protection and promotion of their rights. Fundamental to the enjoyment of all rights is the right to life. Should not the AU declare the next decade as the women's rights decade? Ten years in which equality and equity will be achieved, in which women have free and comprehensive access to all their health needs and in which no woman dies from making her natural contribution to the human resource-base of Africa? To me the success of African leadership in the decade should be judged first and foremost by the progress made in the lives of our women and girls.

appendix

Your Holiness

On this World Population Day there are many concerns which unite men and women of goodwill. People of all faiths recognize the need to renew the Earth as, what Father Thomas Berry has called, "a bio-spiritual planet".

Most agree, as the Brundtland Commission on Environment and Development did, that rapidly increasing human numbers allied to our consumption habits and damaging technologies, are creating an interlinked crisis which threatens any sustainable future for Man on Earth.

The Catholic Church has helped to add a human and a spiritual dimension to the debate on these issues. The Church has rightly stressed the need for economic justice in and between nations, it has supported human rights in many settings, it has sided with the poor and campaigned for transitions to democracy. It has joined in efforts to alleviate the load on those afflicted by disaster and denied their social rights. Above all, perhaps, it has attributed value to individual human beings in an inhuman era.

For 40 years the International Planned Parenthood Federation has stood for similar values. Its driving force has been concern for the health and welfare of women, their children and their families. It has sought to empower women to make choices about their reproductive and productive lives and to make such choices available to the poor and neglected in the villages and shanty towns of the developing world as well as to those in countries such as Romania where choice was for so long forbidden by a heartless state.

It is sad, therefore, that in this one aspect of human rights and human development, the contemporary Catholic Church has chosen to be an obstacle rather than an ally. The opposition of the Church to contraception (other than periodic abstinence) and the vehemence with which this opposition has been expressed, unfortunately overshadows so much on which we can agree.

Recent statements attributed to the Catholic Church likening legal abortion to the Nazi holocaust, and claiming that the Pill and other forms of contraception have

not liberated women but enslaved them, show the deepest misunderstanding of the family planning movement.

One of the saddest tragedies of our times, I believe, is the hidden sorrow and suffering of women afflicted by unplanned pregnancies. Half a million women every year die from causes related to pregnancy – 5 million every decade. Millions more live lives blighted by chronic anaemia and ill health.

Ninety-nine per cent of all women who die in this way come from the world's poorest regions, with the world's highest population growth. Yet the causes are largely preventable. Low-cost, effective contraception used by women who do not want further children could, by itself, reduce maternal deaths dramatically.

Within the next half century humankind must, I am sure, complete the demographic transition to a world where the small family is the norm, in India as well as Italy. It will mean that women will have a choice about childbearing, and wanted children will survive to live fulfilling lives.

On this significant day, I humbly suggest that a sensitive dialogue should be opened between the Church and those who believe as I do that voluntary family planning is the best protection against abortion, as well as a major contributor to saving women's lives and a human right. Such a dialogue would, I believe, help women and men make good moral decisions, which benefit their children, their families and the world.

No reply was received.

Politics and ethics in family planning

This is a slightly shortened version of the paper: Politics and ethics in family planning, published in Senanayake, P. and Kleinman, R.L., eds. *Proceedings of the Meeting Challenges: Promoting Choices*, International Planned Parenthood Federation Family Planning Congress, New Delhi, Oct. 1992. Parthenon Publishing Group, p. 365-374.

The provision of family planning services is still a much felt need worldwide. The results of the World Fertility Survey conducted over the period 1977 1982 and those of the later Demographic and Health Surveys have confirmed that large numbers of women who want no more children or would wish to postpone the next birth by two or more years have no easy access to effective contraception. Jacobson has estimated the number of women in need at 300 million, which many consider an underestimate. In expanding family planning services to meet this increased demand, both qualitative and quantitative considerations should guide programme development. There are, however, major moral and ethical issues which have a strong influence on opinion, on the value of the services, and on the resources needed for their expansion. Many of those present think about some of these issues subconsciously all the time. But I believe it is time we consider them more overtly and make a serious effort to identify the ethical bases for our programmes and ideologies.

I should like to remind you of the fact that I am no ethicist - just a humble public health physician from Africa who has read a fair amount around the subject and who has been forced to think about ethics in health care a great deal because of the difficult and complex decisions I have been forced to make in the past. As background reading for our subject let me recommend two books with which I think all of us in the field of family planning should be familiar. One which was brought to my notice quite recently is The Cross of Unknowing - Dilemmas of a Catholic Doctor, by Joyce Poole. The other is the report of the conference on 'Ethics and human values in family planning', edited by Bankowski *et al.* This report is an excellent summary of the issues and debates as well as a pointer to what should be acceptable today.

Politics and family planning

Whether or not family planning is accepted and supported by a country is a political decision. It is politics at a national level that determines the extent to which it will be supported, whom it will be made available to, on what terms, and so on. Sometimes politics determines which of the technologies can be registered for use. Medical politics

rather than scientific necessity may assign a need for prescription which effectively shuts off the supply of some safe and effective contraceptive from a large proportion of a population. Roman Catholic Church politics rather than science or any serious theological concern forbids the use of all the better contraceptives. Global politics and bilateral political relationships play a role in decisions on official development assistance for population as much as for everything else, at times more so. I do not intend to dwell here on such issues, but would like to discuss the ethics and human values aspects of our work and how we may look at the many questions which we confront during the provision of services under diverse conditions.

Ethics and human values

Ethical and moral values are generally rooted in the social, economic, cultural and religious environments of societies. And like everything else, they may be subject to change. Thus there is no universal code of ethics. However, there are some common themes stretching across societies. These are usually based on how people should act one towards the other, rights to private and public property, the safety and well-being of the individual and the society as a whole, and at times even the requirements of individual and society gods. In spite of differences in nuances and interpretation there are in our field some principles worth considering as of fundamental and perhaps universal importance.

Three moral principles

Ruth Macklin has put forward three moral or ethical principles that we need to take into consideration when discussing the politics and ethics of family planning:

a: ***The principle of liberty***

This principle holds that the individual should be free to act as he or she chooses, so long as such action or behaviour does not interfere with the rights of others. I would like to submit that it is on this particular principle that our basic code of voluntarism in family planning should find its strength. The individual is free to practise or not to practise family planning and to select freely the method she or he would use.

b: ***The utilitarian principle***

Maintains that society's actions should seek to provide the greatest good for the greatest number of the population. Now, I believe that

this should be our basis for advocating family planning on a national scale, because we believe that family planning is a 'good'; it is for promoting health, it is good for the well-being of human beings, and it is good for the society if used properly to help balance society's resources with its population.

c: *The principle of justice*

The principle of justice or equity is the third principle. In any given society persons should have equal access to services that meet their basic needs. Now, equal in this respect, if translated literally, can create difficulties and confusion. I believe that the better translation for this is equity, because equity does not necessarily mean equalness. It has an implication of satisfying a need and the need may not necessarily be universal to the same extent.

According to Macklin, these principles can only be meaningfully applied if placed against a backdrop of the moral requirement of toleration. Toleration means respect for beliefs and practices of others different from our own; and I submit it is over this particular principle that family planning has had to meet its most overt challenges internationally today.

The right to family planning

We have several churches, including the Catholic Church, some fundamentalist religious groups and so-called advocates of the right to life, who seek to deny individuals the right to effective contraception. Even some advocates of women's rights are presently opposed either to scientific family planning totally, or to some of the methods used. Where such opposition derives from genuine concern over the rights of the user we should listen carefully. However, since we are now so convinced of the value of family planning to individuals and societies we should not flinch from advocating it as a right. Today I believe we derive the right to make family planning an international right and a global good, from a consensus that was reached in Teheran in 1968 but more forcefully expressed in Bucharest in 1974, where article 14(f) of the World Population Plan of Action stated that:

"All couples and individuals have the basic right to decide freely and

responsibly the number and spacing of their children and to have the information, education, and means to do so, the responsibility of couples and individuals in the exercise of this right takes in account the needs of their living and future children and their responsibilities towards the community."

This particular right was also stressed in Mexico City in 1984 and expanded to include requests to governments to see to it that governments provide the information and services for the people who want to have access to family planning. Once the world leaders accepted family planning, by international consensus, as a right, then I submit that it is unethical for countries to back off from what they have themselves accepted, and say they will not translate this into enjoyable rights for their citizens.

A right is not a right if it is not known. Therefore, if countries do not inform their citizens and they do not provide the services, or, if in providing the services they include so many restrictions that they nullify the intent of the international consensus, then I submit that they are not acting in an ethically correct way.

Incentives and dis-incentives

The ethics involved in incentives and disincentives will continue to exercise programme authorities for a long time, since it would be impossible to come to one set of conclusions to satisfy all situations. Generally, we may say that incentives calculated to make free and informed choice difficult for an individual should not be acceptable. Dis-incentives which discriminate against a social group are probably wrong, as are those that tend to be retroactive and penalize children already born. I am personally against all forms of monetary incentives to those who wish to practise family planning. Let them do this from conviction that they are doing something good for themselves, their children and their communities. A difficult question relates to those who would like to take up a method of family planning but are too poor to leave their work, home or family to go to obtain the method. Is a programme ethical in making the financial and other arrangements necessary for the individual to be able to get the method she or he has freely chosen? With a few provisos I would support such an approach.

Spousal consent

To what extent should special consent be considered when dealing with access to information and services? I think that special consent, where equality and good

communication exist between the spouses, is a good thing to seek; but to make special consent a pre-condition, and to make one spouse (generally the male) have veto power over whether or not an individual with their own personhood should have access to family planning information or services is, in my view, not correct. Naturally, we should seek to ensure that there is peace in family relations and act with due attention to family circumstances, but we should not support the maintenance of a slave relationship.

Counselling and society's responsibility

There is an ethical problem in the over-enthusiastic translation of the right to family planning that may amount to, or actually lead to, coercion. The reasoning goes something like this: "They say you should have family planning; therefore, whether you want it or not, we will give it to you". Or alternatively there is the "I know what is good for you" syndrome which is "You don't know too well what is good for you, I know, and since I have been charged to see to it that you have family planning, we will give it to you: and it is this method alone that we will give you".

An even worse reasoning is to force family planning or a particular method because it is good for some community or national ends. Now, this is where programmes could falter. They are so sure of their cause that the individual becomes a passive recipient. The programme would choose one method and say this method is the best method of family planning that we know at the present time and, without any real counselling at all, provide such a method. I believe that we have come a long way from such a position. Now we want to be sure than in our services, counselling takes precedence over everything else - that the freedom of choice of the individual is ensured. Good counselling ensures that the client is given enough information about family planning and the various methods available to suit the circumstances of the individual, their good points and their side-effects or difficulties. While the individual should have the fullest possible information this should not be couched in such terms as to frighten them away from making a free choice. The aim of counselling is to help the individual make a free and informed choice. Frightening the individual away could be as bad, ethically, as forcing a choice on her or him.

Society's versus individual's rights

There is social good and an individual good, and we in family planning meet with a great dilemma when we start looking at the possible conflicts that may arise. As mentioned above, society has a responsibility to provide family planning services to enable individuals

to make a free and informed choice. But does this mean society has no right to want to influence the choice one way or another? If society has the responsibility to satisfy the principles of justice and of equity in the supply of social services, then surely it should have a right to negotiate with the citizens the size of the demand and the rate at which it increases. I know countries that have actually got a social compact with their citizens. The political leadership has promised to provide free education and health services for the people, as well as job opportunities for all who qualify. When society makes that kind of contract, it should know in reasonable detail the current and projected size of the population with which it is dealing as well as its major dynamics. The family planning efforts to influence such variables may lead society into draconian measures, to try to restrict population growth, or migration of rural populations that has not been planned for. This may also lead societies to provide services that leave the individual with very little choice.

Harmonizing society's rights and responsibilities with those of the individual could be a serious ethical dilemma. The majority view, which I share, is that the individual should not be coerced to do anything in this field for the good of society. Intensive education to make the individual appreciate his or her social responsibility is the route to go.

After dealing with these general issues I should like to look at a few specific ethical conflicts which we confront in family planning. I will touch on quality of care, abortion, and one small aspect of the use of modern technology (amniocentesis and in vitro fertilisation).

Quality of care

While much has been written about quality of care, there is still a lot of misunderstanding about what constitutes good quality care. There are some who would only accept clinic services as capable of providing good quality and all others as second rate. But is this correct? Are services such as community-based distribution and social marketing ever likely to be of good quality? How ethical are they? There was a time when people felt that community-based distribution was probably an acceptable substitute for clinic services only where quantity services could not be ensured through clinics, but that it was not the best solution. I do not believe that people looked at the problem correctly. A quality concern which insists that only clinics with white walls, with people in white coats and with stethoscopes around their necks should be providing contraception, is being arbitrary and possibly discriminatory. Such a position does not necessarily guarantee quality, and it also leaves large numbers without any services at all.

262

Quality of care should start with the user. Where is the user located? What are the user's circumstances? What are the user's means of transport? How can that user be serviced best, and how will that user be made to feel most comfortable? These are the questions to ask of a service to ensure good quality care.

I would submit that the Colombian coffee worker, who receives her Pill supply from her colleague coffee worker who has been trained and who tells her what the likely side-effects are, and who tells her, "If you feel anything come to me and we will take you to A, B or C," is providing a better quality contraceptive for that particular woman than if that woman has been taken by bus to Bogota, seen a doctor for two minutes, got a prescription and gone into a drugstore to buy. So, we want to be sure when we are talking of quality care, that we do not set some arbitrary standards. We should always think in terms of the user.

Abortion

Abortion is still one of the major controversies in our field today. Unfortunately the politicisation of the issue in the USA, including the succour and protection given anti-abortionists by the Reagan and Bush administrations, ensures the continuation of violent confrontations and a blurring of the fundamental question. I do not hold that the early group of cells formed after fertilisation is a mere collection of cells, not worthy of any consideration; on the other hand I refuse to accept that the pregnant woman is no more than an animated incubator. The cells have got a potential, a potential for life. But a potential for life is not life, and we have got the rights of that potential to weigh against those of the one who is already alive - the mother to be. We should realize that if we do not look at abortion with humble understanding and an appreciation of the likely consequences, we will be mistaken.

In most developed countries safe abortions are available to women who choose them. In many developing countries that choice is denied.

Even in such circumstances the rich and the better educated classes get safe abortions. The poor, the illiterate and the very young often get unsafe care and even pay with their lives. There is no other condition in medicine where the legal denial of the use of a safe technology has such dire consequences for such a large number of people. I personally find no ethical justification for the criminalization of abortion and the removal of the freedom of choice from the woman involved. Our role as family planning associations is to use contraception to prevent abortions. But even our contraceptives

may fail. It is only in this field that we are being told that if our primary preventive measures fail, we should not go to the second level and try to do something for the person. I submit that the way to avoid an ethical conundrum is to get away from moral, religious and philosophical examination of the abortion issue and see it as an issue of a woman's choice and that of health. If we accept this approach our ethical duty is clear.

Amniocentesis and *in vitro* fertilization

There is concern about the use of amniocentesis for sex determination leading to a disproportionate and discriminatory abortion of female fetuses. While one can say this is unethical and should not be condoned at all, another question would be "Supposing a woman is pregnant with the fourth female child and she is to be thrown out of home on the birth of yet another girl what would you do?" My mind is not at all clear on this but it should be seriously discussed.

Abortion for sex selection is generally condemned, and rightly so if no sound reasons exist for it. But some very serious human problems may mitigate such a stand. Even though the family is changing in many ways, should science be used to accelerate the breakdown? Are we sure what such children will feel like when they grow up? We need to take time to study the implications and develop our own positions on them.

Conclusion

In sharing these thoughts with you I am not seeking to make you see things my way. It is my purpose to bring to your attention some of the major ethical issues that confront us. I have stated my own viewpoint rather forcefully, where I am sure I have a settled position. Many of the issues I mentioned and a lot more should be discussed at family planning association and regional meetings and if possible, national or regional position papers drawn up. Though a minefield, politics, ethics and human values in family planning is also a very fascinating field.

REFERENCES

Bankowski, Z., Barzelatto, J. and Capron, A.M. (eds.). (1989). *Ethics and Human Values in Family Planning.* CIOMS, Geneva.

Jacobson, J.L. (1992). *Improving Women's Reproductive Health: State of the World.* Worldwatch Institute, New York.

Macklin, R. (1989). Ethics and human values in family planning: perspectives of different cultural and religious settings. In Bankowski, Z., Barzelatto, J. and Capron, A.M. (eds.) *Ethics and Human Values in Family Planning.* CIOMS, Geneva.

Poole, J. (1989). *The Cross of Unknowing: Dilemmas of a Catholic Doctor.* Sheed and Ward, London.

United Nations. (1975). *Report of the United Nations World Population Conference, 1974, Bucharest.*

United Nations. (1984). *Report of the International Conference on Population, 1984, Mexico City.*

United Nations Population Award 1993 – Acceptance Speech
Adapted from a speech given at the United Nations, New York, 1993

There are many around the world with whom I have worked who have dedicated their lives to family planning in the fight against ongoing problems such as Kwashiorkor. It would be impossible for me to mention all my many mentors by name… In my current role as President of the International Planned Parenthood Federation I wish to acknowledge the work of my many colleagues, both volunteers and staff. Little by little we have worked side by side, setting our sights on a better life for humankind. It is a long-term mission of global dimensions, and not one that can be tackled alone.

And I salute the many millions of volunteers who share my concern for mother and child health, who respect that most basic of human rights – the ability to choose the size and timing of one's family – and witness for themselves the drastic improvements in the quality of life that family planning can bring.

But above all, perhaps the people who have most greatly shaped my career are the malnourished children themselves, among whom I have had the opportunity of working, and the parents of those children. The mothers, despite their lack of education and inability to grasp the concept of the diseases we were facing, nevertheless trusted in the future. I can recall the mothers who willingly helped in our various studies, mothers who were themselves so unsure of their hold on life that while they were laughing and joking they barely knew if they would survive to see the next rainy season. It is to these women, who represent the backbone of Africa, the courage of Africa and the hope of Africa, that I would like to dedicate this prize.

In the epitaph at the end of his *Elegy in a Country Churchyard*, Gray had this to say:
Here rests his head upon the lap of Earth,
A youth to fortune and to fame unknown.
Fair Science frowned not on his humble birth,
And Melancholy marked him for her own.

These word were written quite some time ago (in the 18th century in fact) to describe conditions faced in rustic England. But we know today that citizens of England are no longer deprived of education or access to science or her fruits; and if I could rewrite the famous quotation to describe Africa today, particularly in relation to our girls and womenfolk, I would say:

Fair Science frowns not on HER humble birth,
And Melancholy marks HER for her own.

The melancholy comes out of the drudgery of life, a drudgery with which girl babies are born and which they carry through with them until they go to their untimely graves through excessive childbearing or unregulated fertility, with little attention paid to their pressing health needs.

The drudgery and melancholy are directly related to the lack of access to general and science education which we know to be so closely linked with contraceptive prevalence and the ability to take care of oneself and one's children. In too many parts of Africa today the proportion of young girls who are exposed to even three or five years of education is quite small…

Let us work together to establish an "Education Peace Corps" which will bring that greatest of gifts – knowledge – to the women of the world, starting in Africa. Today in Africa, large numbers of high-school graduates are unemployed. In a few countries, there are even university graduates with no regular work to do. Is it beyond the capacities of our national, regional and continental political and other institutions to seek the financial and other support of friendly nations to help us harness this manpower for an assault on the curse of illiteracy? In my view, only a crash programme of gigantic proportions can get the job done in a reasonable time frame to help improve the lives of our women. Let us empower our girls through education, and transform their lives through insight, giving them the tools to embark on the path of life on a firm footing, in equal stride with their male peers.

In addition to their education, there is a need to look at the kinds of practices that interfere with the lives and livelihoods of girls and women in Africa and make life such a drudgery to them. Far too often we are allowed to hide behind anachronistic traditions and cultural practices, some of which are really morally indefensible, and do things to our women which should not be permitted. Female circumcision is one such example. There is no reason at the present time for any child to be coerced into marriage and to be forced to start having children, deprived of time to enjoy her childhood before she becomes a woman and a mother. This we do in the name of tradition and culture. Tradition and culture which so discriminate against some members of society cannot be accepted as a great help to the people at large.

Since 1987, we have been calling for more attention to the issues of safer

motherhood. I must say that despite five years of this constant call we cannot see any real breakthrough. Is it because this condition affects only women that progress has been so sluggish? This is a field in which we must really see the violence we are committing against our own people, our own kin, and address their needs as quickly as possible.

The technologies for tackling the issues of safer motherhood exist today in abundance. The delivery systems required to make these technologies effective have already been identified to very large extent. What we need now is the political will and the leadership that will bring the technologies to bear on the problem and bring relief to the people who need it so badly…

Finally, on the issue of safe motherhood, let me say once more that nothing has been found to be as effective as the ability of women to control their own fertility. Let us make it possible for all women the world over to have full control of their reproductive rights by providing them with the quality information and services to achieve that. And we must remember that the methods to control fertility, imperfect though they may be, are available. As we approach the 21st century, we must examine our consciences and make it our duty, our moral obligation, our ultimate goal to make these methods accessible to the women and the families who need them and are requesting them. This we must do with sensitivity and care, and in a way that accords with their own views and expectations.

ICPD Programme of Action – Its Relevance to the Africa Region

Statement to the Africa Regional Ministers Meeting, Dakar, Senegal June 2004 [Extracts]

Cairo went far beyond population and family planning concerns and developed the Programme of Action on a holistic platform which made the role and status of women central to human development needs generally and those related to sexuality and reproduction specifically.

Four essential points emerged from the ICPD processes to underpin the Programme of Action.

1. Population and development problems are not simply a relationship between numbers and development needs, such as schools, health care and low savings and investments – but also between numbers and development attainments – lifestyles and consumption patterns.

2. The need for poverty alleviation programmes between and within countries which is an essential plank to all efforts to lower fertility and human numbers.

3. Population problems cannot be tackled from a purely macro-numbers approach. Solutions must be found at the micro-level. So much of what is to be done depends on a proper understanding of people as individuals, families and communities, on the status and roles of women, their education economic pursuits, and the proper attention to their general health and reproductive health needs, in particular.

4. Population and development are issues of concern to many sectors. They should therefore be shared issues to be handled by many stakeholders, severally and in coalitions.

Based on these major principles a 20 year Programme of Action was developed which included the following actions by countries:

- ensure universal access to quality and affordable reproductive health services, including family planning and sexual health;
- enable couples to make real choices about family size through a series of social investments;
- improve rates of child survival. No country in the developing world has experienced a sustained reduction in family size without first

reducing infant and childhood mortality. Couples must feel confident that their children will survive before they are willing to have fewer children;

- expand educational opportunities, close the "gender gap" in education, and provide universal access to primary education. Educated women tend to want smaller families, and are better at looking after the children they do have;
- invest in women's development. When women can exercise their full legal and social rights, they often have both the desire and the ability to choose smaller families. Where women are valued as full human beings, there is less social preference for sons;
- expand opportunities for young women. In the year 2000 some 400 million adolescent girls stood on the brink of adulthood. If many choose to delay child-bearing, even for a few years, they will enhance their health, education and employment prospects.

... After ICPD many African leaders became more comfortable and courageous about speaking on family planning, sexuality and maternal health issues, some countries changed their policies and programmes ... Certainly in much of our region the political climate changed considerably. The shrill debate on family planning as population control came down by several decibels. The health and development rationale could win more hearts, and so did the attention to individual needs. Programmes got support by being more culturally sensitive and human focused rather than setting numerical targets ...

Through the efforts of the African Population Community, the ICPD message has also found acceptance in the African Union, and its major tenets have been accepted. Gender and women's rights, for instance, are recognized in the AU charter on human rights, and now in the NEPAD ...

In education, particularly of girls, many African countries have truly made advances. The gap between boys and girls at the primary level is narrowing. At the secondary level success is not so widespread. Since research shows that it is only after seven or more years of quality education that the health gains from education become obvious we still have a long way to go ...

Efforts at fighting gender-based violence are being intensified, not only through legislation, but also through advocacy and sensitization programmes and projects ...

Contraceptive prevalence rates are used to judge progress in family planning. The Dakar/Ngor Declaration envisaged the doubling of the regional contraceptive prevalence rate (CPR) from about 10 to about 20 per cent by the year 2000, and to 40 per cent by the year 2010. However, Africa is still doing rather badly except for a few countries in Southern Africa, all of which were doing fairly well before ICPD. South Africa has a rate of over 50 per cent, Kenya and Botswana over 30 per cent, Zimbabwe around per cent . In West Africa, the story is very different. The best is Ghana with 13 per cent contraceptive prevalence rate for modern methods ...

Africa has the worst maternal mortality figures in the world. Our women are dying from conditions no different from what kills women in other countries and regions. The knowledge to prevent or handle such problems is available at reasonable cost. And we ought to ask why we should let our women die in such numbers. Is it because they are women and therefore their lives are expendable in replenishing the African races? As policy makers we should feel diminished to learn that haemorrhage or severe bleeding around the time of birth or immediately thereafter, obstructed labour, post-partum infection due to abortion, spontaneous or induced are the major causes of the tragedy ...

An area of maternal death which creates great confusion and much debate is unsafe abortion... Whatever society or individuals feel, the facts are that unsafe abortion is a major, easily preventable, cause of maternal mortality. Ten to 50 per cent or more of maternal deaths are attributable to unsafe abortion in Africa. The average for the sub-continent is 13 per cent. With 12 per cent of the world's population we suffer 40 per cent of the world total of abortion deaths. And I personally do not believe we can make too much of a dent on maternal mortality if we did nothing about unsafe abortion ...

The HIV/AIDS pandemic has caused and continues to cause some of the biggest problems to socio-economic development in Africa. It is right that it should be singled out for emphasis. It is included in the ICPD goals. All reproductive health programmes could be made programmes for HIV too. Family planning education and counselling, the youth sexuality activities and the MCH services are all potential programmes to help with HIV/AIDS ...

Africa suffers from those effects of population on the environment which are mostly related to poverty and numbers. Deforestation is proceeding very rapidly in many countries as we destroy forests for farming. Many experts have been giving us warnings about the advance of the Sahara desert due to unsustainable water and land-

use ... But perhaps the most visible and pressing problems relate to urbanization. Accra, Lagos, Johannesburg, Nairobi and Dakar are examples of cities in distress. The rapidly increasing numbers of new immigrants, the establishment of shanty towns and the mounting heaps of refuse are a challenge to development.

Cutting down numbers will not make us rich overnight. But no major world region has grown rapidly out of poverty with population growth rates of 2 per cent per annum or more, as we have in much of Sub-Sahara Africa. With better technology we can manage some of these problems better. But we are too poor to buy so much technology. We must look at solutions from all angles. We must do something about our population growth rates. Whilst Cairo did not mention growth targets and the MDGs skipped them, we must look at them in relation to our development needs and work plans, particularly in the areas of education, employment and environmental conservation.

International commitments and guidance on unsafe abortion

Keynote speech: Action to reduce maternal mortality in Africa: a regional consultation on unsafe abortion (Extracts)

Addis Ababa, Ethiopia, February 2003

The World Health Organization, as the global leader in promoting and protecting the health of all people, clearly defined health over half a century ago. "Health is a state of complete physical, mental and social well-being and not merely the absence of disease or infirmity." These words are still instructive today as we look this week at the full range of approaches needed to prevent and address unsafe abortion in Africa. Ensuring good health is not just the responsibility of the health care system. It is the responsibility of communities, of individuals, of advocates, and of citizens. As we discuss and strategise, we should keep this concept in mind and look beyond the simple ways of solving this critical health problem through medical treatment.

Let's look first at the basis for our obligations to address this fundamental issue from all possible angles.

The Universal Declaration of Human Rights laid the groundwork in 1948 for the development of our existing human right system and led to the development of new standards and obligations for countries. In 1966, the International Covenant on Economic, Social and Cultural Rights articulated the right to health for the first time as "the right of everyone to the employment of the highest attainable standard of physical and mental health."

Convention on the Elimination of All Forms of Discrimination Against Women (CEDAW) came into force in the early 1980s and brought with it the legal duty for states to eliminate all forms of discrimination against women, including discrimination through denial of access to health services that only women need. By definition, then, these would include pregnancy, childbirth, and abortion-related care.

Over the past half century we as a global community have evolved our recognition of the importance for each individual person to make decisions about whether and when to have children, and to have the information and means to implement these decisions.

Ensuring that women go through pregnancy safely has long been a cause we've been in favour of. In 1948, Article 25 of the Universal Declaration of Human Rights stated that: "Motherhood and childhood are entitled to special care and assistance." Since then, many international conventions and conferences have reaffirmed governmental commitments to making motherhood safe.

But we seem to have forgotten a critical element of being pregnant, which is that often, pregnancy comes at the wrong time and is unwanted. We know that millions of unwanted pregnancies end each year in unsafe abortion, and yet, how many safe motherhood programmes have actively addressed unsafe abortion? How many women's lives could have been saved if safe motherhood programmes did not avoid addressing this issue?

WHO's Making Pregnancy Safer Initiative states that: "Access to safe abortion (where this is legal) and counselling to ensure informed decision making and consent by the woman, should be part of the services."

But it wasn't until 1994 at the International Conference on Population and Development, known as ICPD, held in Cairo, that the next leap forward occurred in terms of international support for addressing unsafe abortion. In Cairo, Governments agreed that abortion should be safe where legal and that women who suffered from unsafe abortion had a right to treatment for complications. This conference was a turning point for those committed to reproductive choice, rights and self-determination.

At the Fourth World Conference on Women, held in Beijing, China, in 1995, governments expanded on the Cairo commitments, stating that women should not be criminalized for having an abortion. These conferences were major breakthroughs in recognizing that unsafe abortion is a significant public health problem that requires immediate action.

Practical advice for health systems finally came in the 1999 five-year review of the Cairo agenda, adding recommendations that health systems "train and equip health service providers and take other measures to ensure that legal abortion is safe and accessible." This agreement obligates health systems to take action to ensure that legal abortion is not only safe, but accessible, and offers guidance for how we can accomplish this ideal.

These recommendations are critical for those of us seeking to reduce unsafe abortion, as women in Africa rarely have the right to make their own decisions about their health cares, and particularly regarding childbearing issues.

Recognition of the duty to provide safe legal abortion services is increasingly frequent and comes from many sources, including UN agencies, professional associations, and national bodies…

Let's turn our attention now from paper commitments to the realities of abortion in the world. While the last 20 years have seen a clear trend toward the removal of

legal barriers to abortion access, the right to choose abortion remains unavailable or under threat in many parts of the world.

In Africa, our women bear the brunt of these restrictive laws. Only South Africa and Tunisia permit abortion fully on request. The rest of our countries impose a variety of restrictions on when a woman can choose to terminate an unwanted pregnancy. Yet countries that have liberalized their laws and made safe abortion services accessible demonstrate significantly reduced maternal mortality rates.

In many traditional African cultures terminating unwanted pregnancies has long been an accepted practice. Anecdotal reports indicate many traditional communities regard Termination of Pregnancy as vital to maintaining societal order and harmony and had their own protocols for this.

In South Africa proponents of the Choice for Termination of Pregnancy Act highlighted traditional abortion practices to illustrate that terminating unwanted pregnancies was a familiar approach to fertility management in many traditional settings of that country.

But in the 19th century we adopted the European code as part of our colonial laws and have yet to get out from under the burden they impose on us.

What is the impact of these laws on our women?

- punishment – both women and doctors caring for them are considered criminals;
- poor women or those with least access to info and health care suffer most;
- inequitable access;
- lack of regulation means abortion remains secret, underground;
- providers can take advantage of women.

Is this what we want for African women and societies?

How many rights are violated daily to women denied access to safe legal abortion care?

- their right to health, and to health care – when a health care provider denies a woman legal services;
- the right to privacy and confidentiality, when a woman's need for abortion is not kept between the provider and the woman;
- the right to freedom from discrimination, when a woman is denied a legal service that only women need;

- the right to liberty and security of the person, when a woman is forced to seek unsafe services because the formal health system refuses to help her;
- the right to self-determination, when she is unable to make her own decisions about childbearing;
- the right to benefits of scientific progress, when health systems fail to introduce the safest and most appropriate abortion technologies, and
- the right to life, when we allow women to kill themselves through unsafe abortion.

Let us devote ourselves to finding the solutions, learning the skills, and building the networks that will allow us to move forward. Let us be willing no longer to allow our sisters to die neglected, alone, and needlessly. Let us go forth and ensure that African women no longer die from unsafe abortion.

Women's reproductive health and rights in Africa: biology and beyond
Plenary statement to the Amanitare Conference, Johannesburg SA. February 2003

I wish to express my gratitude for the honour done me, a male Public Health Physician, to be invited as a guest to your conference and to make a plenary presentation I also wish to thank the organisers and your executive members for choosing as theme for the occasion 'African Women's Reproductive Health and Rights Conference: Prosperity through Empowerment", a very important theme. I hope some of you here know and will recall that when the University of Ghana gave me the Aggrey/Fraser/Guggisberg memorial platform in 1994, I chose as my topic 'Adam and Eve and the Serpent' . I chose then to discuss extensively the Sexual and Reproductive Health needs of women within the holistic requirement for gender equity and rights. I feel doubly pleased therefore to be here and to take part in discussions which may help discuss operational implications of some of the recommendations made.

Women's health needs are now being given proper attention in many parts of the world; and we in Africa are being challenged to provide the maximum possible response with very limited resources. Throughout the period of this conference and the days after it will be appropriate for all participants to revisit some of the relevant international events of the past decade or so and reflect on how they impact on or inform our ongoing activities. I am referring here to the recommendations of the International Conference on Population and Development, Cairo 1994, and the Women's Conference, Beijing 1995 and the subsequent reviews of progress, as well as the various conferences on social, economic, and environmental issues held during the last decade and a half.

The rights and status of women were issues emphasised in one way or another by all of these conferences. Since these rights should really inform all programmes and activities aimed at improving women's health in general, and reproductive health in particular, let me remind you of these as distilled for the world by the International Planned Parenthood Federation during the time of my presidency of the Federation. These are: -

1   Right to life;
2   Right to physical integrity;
3   Right to equality in all forms;
4   Right to privacy;

5   Right to freedom of thought;

6   Right to information/education;

7   Right to choose whether to marry or not to marry;

8   Right to postpone childbearing;

9   Right to health care;

10   Right to enjoy the benefits of scientific progress;

11   Right to freedom of assembly – for example, women's right to meet and influence their future;

12   Right to be free from torture and ill treatment.

Reproductive health is an area of health in which nature itself can be accused of being sexist; of being truly biased against women and girls. Why else should the biological burdens in relation to reproduction and early nurture of the species lie so disproportionately on the female? Some religions, including the Judeo-Christian tradition, even add to the biological burdens by interpreting their dogma in ways which worsen the biological problems. And throughout the world anachronistic social cultural and legal provisions accentuate the biological iniquity.

Extreme poverty, lack of education and groaning disrespect of the basic human rights to shelter, food and water are factors producing unhealthy living conditions for many women. The historic-cultural and social bondage that restrict and diminish women's roles in general development and the lack of control over their own bodies are remote contributors to these health disparities. All these are demonstrated in severe measure in Sub-Sahara Africa.

Women have a Right to Life but do they? Every year some 585,000 women worldwide die in pregnancy and childbirth, about 1,600 pregnancy-related deaths per day. One woman dies every minute somewhere in the world because of a complication related to pregnancy or childbirth. 99% of these deaths occur in the developing countries. Africa, proportionately, has the worse figures, with an average maternal mortality ratio of about 500 per 100,000 live births. But this average hides a truly mind-boggling spread. There are still countries or areas within where the mortality ratio could be as high as 1,000 or even 1500 per 100,000 live births. When we consider the differences in the lifetime risk of maternal death we truly confront the disparity between advanced and developing countries. The average Africa risk is between 1 in 12 to 1 in 16. The average risk in Europe and much of North America is around 1 in 4,000.

In all parts of the world, the causes of maternal deaths are the same – haemorrhage, hypertensive disorders, prolonged and obstructed labour leading to rupture of the uterus, infections and complications of unsafe abortion. Women are not dying because of something physicians do not know or from causes they cannot prevent. Usually the non-medical, or beyond biological, issues make for the difficulties. It is quite common for women to watch their own blood draining out of them as they lose consciousness and bleed to death. Deaths occur in hospitals and clinics. They occur in homes, at market places and on the farms. Deaths occur because of delays in seeking help, getting to the place where help can be obtained, the help not being there, or not being properly trained, and the facility not being equipped or adequately supplied

Apart from death many women suffer serious ill health as a result of pregnancy and childbirth. It has been estimated that for every woman who dies 50 to 100 sustain serious medium or long-term illnesses. These include chronic pelvic pain, vaginal discharge, menstrual problems, problems with gait and walking, psychological problems, vesico-vaginal fistulæ and recto-vaginal fistulæ. This is both a travesty of justice and a tragedy.

In today's world violence is endemic and both men and women experience it in many forms. Considerable damage to health and well being results from it. But the nature and causes of the violence to which women are exposed are almost always different, and the impact on their lives is different. Most violence against women is domestic. Violence against women includes any hardship that physically or mentally affects a woman's body and endangers her life and that of her family and/or which deprives her access to basic services; such as education and health. Discriminatory denial, particularly denial of education and of access to cash income is a form of social violence against girls and women.

Women have a right to physical integrity. Any form of mutilation, especially female genital mutilation, infringes this right. They have the right to choose whether or not to marry. Forced marriage, particularly child marriage, denies this right. Violence against women exists in all societies and all social classes throughout the world. The dangers are greater in pregnancy where the mother and her child are placed in jeopardy. It is essential therefore that the diagnosis and approaches to management and elimination of violence against women be included in the training curriculum of every health worker, especially of obstetricians and gynæcologists. Every physician caring for women should be able to identify victims of domestic violence among his

or her patients, elicit comprehensive diagnosis, and know how to deal with this social evil. This would often require empathetic listening and questioning, since women seldom volunteer such information.

Abortions, spontaneous or induced are a major cause of maternal mortality. 4.2 million Unsafe abortions are performed in Africa resulting in 34,000 deaths, 40% of the world's abortion deaths. Complications of unsafe abortions performed by unskilled people in unsanitary conditions continue to kill our women. Practically no woman dies from unsafe abortion in those advanced countries with liberal abortion laws. The laws covering abortion are usually more liberal than many doctors realise. It will be good practice to get to know the laws and interpret them with compassion.

The tragedy resulting from unsafe abortion can be prevented through sex education, proper use of contraceptives and provision of safe abortion services, within the law, and competent post-abortion care.

Surveys demonstrate that contraceptive use in Africa is very low. In Ghana only 22 percent of married women are currently using a method; with 13% using a modern method.. Thirty two percent of men report current use of a method and, one in five reports the use of a modern method. Much of the male-female difference in current use is due to the higher reporting of condom use by men.

The female condom has been launched in many African countries. But uptake is still low. The female condom, more under the control of the woman than other methods, is effective and reliable. Apart from preventing unwanted pregnancy it prevents sexually transmitted diseases (STDs), including HIV/AIDS. The male condom is a very efficient method of pregnancy prevention and disease control too. But there is a need to tackle cultural obstacles, including lack of power, which make it difficult for women to negotiate its use.

Comprehensive, client oriented family planning will remove the need for induced abortion by preventing unwanted pregnancies. Women have the right to enjoy the benefits of scientific progress. They must have access to a wide range of contraceptives including emergency contraception.

Our populations continue to grow and so does the incidence of STIs and HIV/AIDS. Africa is the worst affected continent. The peak ages at which women are diagnosed as HIV infected is 25-29. It is 30-34 years for men. In many parts of Africa there are twice as many women infected as men. For the 15–19 year olds the girl-boy ratio could be even worse. The male female ratio in the more advanced countries is 6

men or more to 1 woman. The difference cannot be biological. For a condition without a cure or a vaccine, prevention and management require a thorough knowledge of everything contributing to its acquisition and spread. Social and cultural conditions, well described by many authors, account for most of the differences. I must admit though that here too the unfairness of biology has to be noted. From one act of intercourse with an infected partner the woman has a 50% chance of being infected, whilst the man's chance is 25%,

Adolescent childbearing is another problem area for reproductive health. Maternal mortality is high in adolescents and perinatal mortality is higher among children of adolescent mothers. There is about 30 percent risk of children born to adolescent mothers dying in infancy. Pregnancies among women aged 15-19 are common in Africa. Overall about 23 percent of such pregnancies end in an early loss – either spontaneous or induced abortion.

What I have been saying so far should help us conclude this discussion on the types of comprehensive approaches required for the maintenance and improvement of reproductive health and ensuring respect for reproductive rights of women. The whole of society must be involved. A life cycle approach needs to be developed. Comprehensive research and data gathering will help inform programmes and evaluate success. Among health workers, physicians, especially obstetricians and gynæcologists, have a leadership role, and they must be educated to play such a role.

Among the main challenges facing those advocating or providing general health care and particularly reproductive health care to women and girls today are:

- affirmation of women's right to be free from physical and psychological violence;
- applying new scientific advances which open the way to improve women's health;
- making sure the knowledge and care that is available to few reaches those who need it most, but do not get it – such as the rural poor;
- knowing the relevant laws that should govern the practice;
- sharing knowledge widely with the general practitioners and ordinary medical officers;
- redefining the role of obstetrics and gynaecology to doing more than delivering babies and fixing problems in the pelvis. This is not all that women want, important though it is. Women need a comprehensive

type of health service, which will look at them beyond carrying and delivering babies, beyond endocrine changes and cancers.

As advocates for women's reproductive health in the 21st century must set our sights very high. We must seek the improvement of women's health generally. We should seek the respect of the rights of all women. We should work for the social and economic empowerment of women. Obstetricians and gynæcologists, as specialist women's health physicians, should be leaders and act as social advocates for women. It is only in acting so comprehensively that the physician's true role of caring for the whole person can be realised. As leaders, the obstetricians and gynæcologists should work with general practitioners, midwives and other health workers. In all of this we must involve the people themselves – the women, their spouses, families, communities and even children – as a resource. Let us mobilise them, educate, train and empower them to help us help them. This way we can make community based Reproductive Health Care a reality and extend quality services far beyond what was thought possible.

Women's health in a multicultural world
Medical Women's International Association (MWIA) Conference Accra August 2007
Summary

Culture, in the form of long-held views, taboos and customs, lies behind the gender imbalance and the lower status given to women in practically all communities and nations, and is consequently of particular importance in the field of reproductive health. Internationally accepted human rights are frequently ignored, often in the name of culture or anachronistic laws and practices, and this is particularly so in Africa. While some traditions are beneficial, others are harmful or prejudicial.

Observers of maternal health and mortality in Africa have concluded that the major reason why African women are faring so badly is the lack of political will by African leaders and not the lack of knowledge, the lack of human resources or even the lack of financial resources. The subject is simply kept below the radar, as it were, because those most intimately concerned, the women themselves, are among the voiceless. There is a need for national women's organizations advocating gender equity to make sexual and reproductive health and rights a major focus of their work. A continent-wide federation should make this subject a priority campaign and get a mass movement employing all legitimate methods to make the continental and national leaders fulfill their promises to make life better for our women.

In April 2007, the African Union Conference of African Health Ministers meeting in Johannesburg South Africa adopted the Africa Health Strategy: 2007-2015, which significantly incorporated the African Charter's Protocol on the Rights of Women. This Protocol is ground breaking in a number of respects, not least in the sphere of reproductive rights, and abortion rights in particular: it is the first international human rights instrument to explicitly provide for abortion as a right in cases of rape and incest and for the mental and physical health of the pregnant woman.

Hopefully this milestone Strategy will lead to international recognition that, because family planning and reproductive health programmes are so important for health, demographic and general development reasons, it is essential that more, not fewer, resources be invested in this area. Many programmes are new and will need substantial funding as they expand. The numbers of women in the reproductive age groups are increasing, as are the proportions of those women who want to use

contraception: today there are nearly 1 billion women of reproductive age in the Third World (projected to rise to over 1.2 billion by 2010).

Finally, more needs to be done to change adverse cultural practices in Africa. Change of behaviour, individual or collective takes long. Confrontation usually is unhelpful. Greater emphasis should be given to girls' education and programmes to foster gender equity and equality, social and economic empowerment of women. There should be specific laws against female genital mutilation (FGM) and other forms of mutilation. But while legal change is useful, it is not always the first need, nor is it enough by itself. Safe abortion for example could be carried out within the existing laws in many African countries. Education, implementation and demonstration of need could be more useful approach.

The medical profession, in this and in other ways, needs to take its responsibilities more seriously. Doctors should have the courage to refuse to accept laws which infringe on human rights. They should use the public health justification for doing good – or at least doing no harm – more frequently than they sometimes do. As doctors, we should educate ourselves about the cultural and traditional environments, in which we operate, understand their interaction with our roles and make appropriate choices as to which are bad, which are neutral and which are good; with the community we should strive to advocate the good and eliminate the bad. In doing this we should have the humility of knowledge and the patience and empathy that in the end make our efforts acceptable.

selected references and further reading

Addae, S. (1996) *History of Western Medicine in Ghana, 1880-1960,* Durham Academic Press Ltd.

Ashitey, G. (2005) *A distinguished Advocate, Frederick T. Sai,* Compufin (Gh) Ltd.

Barnor, M.A. (2001) (Autobiography with Victor Osei Vieso), *A Socio-Medical Adventure in Ghana.* Universal Ghana Ltd.

Brachott, D. (1961), *The Health Services in Ghana: A 10 Year Programme,* Govt. Printing Dept. Accra.

Caldwell, J.C. and Sai, F.T. (2007) Family Planning in Ghana, in *The Global Family Planning Revolution, Three Decades of Population Policies and Programs,* Warren C. Robinson and John Ross (eds.), pp379-391, The World Bank.

Cook, R. and Senanayake, P. (1978) *The Human Problem of Abortion: Medical and Legal Dimensions.* IPPF, London.

Evans-Anfom, E. (2003) *To the Thirsty Land (Autobiography of a patriot),* Africa Christian Press Ghana.

Konotey-Ahulu, F. (1991) Kwashiorkor, Letter to *BMJ,* Vol. 302 pp180-181.

Government of Ghana. (1994) National Population Policy (Revised Edition), National Population Council.

IPPF. (1997) IPPF and its Future. Report of a study.

Lamptey. P. and Sai, F.T. (1985) Chapter 7, Integrated health/nutrition/population programmes in M. Biswas and P. Pinstrup-Andersen (eds.) *Nutrition and Development.* Oxford Medical Publications.

Mahler, H. (1987) Safe Motherhood Initiative. *The Lancet* Mar21:(8535)668-70.

Morrow, R.H., Sai, F.T. and Barker, L.F. (1971) Australian Antigen and hepatitis in Ghana: *BMJ,* vol.4, (5784) 389-391, 13th Nov.

Morrow, R.H., Sai, F.T., Edgcomb, J.H. and Smetana, H.F. (1969) Epidemiology of Viral Hepatitis in Accra, *Trans Roy. Soc. Trop. Med. & hygiene,* Vol.63, Issue 6, 755-767.

Morrow, R.H., Smetana, H.F.. Sai, F.T. and Edgcomb, J.H. (1968) Unusual features of Viral Hepatitis in Accra, Ghana, *An Int. Med.*, Vol.68, No.6, 1250-1264.

Platt, B.S. and Mayer, J. (1959) *Report of Joint FAO/WHO Mission to Ghana 27 Oct.-6 Dec. 1958*, FAO/59/5/3880, FAO, Rome.

Population Council. (1981) Family *Planning in the 1980s: Challenges and Opportunities.*

***Population Planning for National Progress and Prosperity.* (1969)** Quotes of Omaboe and content. (Omaboe: Preface) – Ghana National Population Policy, March.

Sadik, N. (ed.) **(2002)** *An agenda for people: the UNFPA through three decades*, New York University Press.

Sai, F.T. (1966) Making the Community Healthy, Ghana Academy Anniversary Conference, *Ghana Medical J*, Vol. 5 pp 148-155.

Sai, F.T. (1987) *Some Ethical Issues in Family Planning*, Occasional Essays, No.1, IPPF.

Sai, F.T. (1977) *Population and National Development (the dilemma of developing countries)*, Occasional Essays, No.2, IPPF.

Sai, F.T. (1977) *Food Population and Politics*, Occasional Essays, No.3, IPPF.

Sai, F.T. (1977) *Defining Family Health Needs, Standards of Care and Priorities with Particular Reference to Family Planning*, Occasional Essays, No.4, IPPF.

Sai, F.T. (1995) Putting People First, *International Series on Population Issues*, The John D and Catherine T. MacArthur Foundation, Lagos.

Sai, F.T. (1995) *Adam and Eve and the Serpent*, Aggrey/Fraser/Guggisberg Memorial Lectures, University of Ghana Press.

Sai, F.T. (2002) *Fred Sai Speaks out*, IPPF, revised edition.

Sai, F.T. (2005) *A Critical Look at the Health System in Ghana: What Place Ethical Issues?* Anniversary lecture Ghana College of Physicians and Surgeons, December.

Sai, F.T. (2007) *Why Should Africa's Woman Continue Crying for Life?* Second annual Ransome-Kuti Memorial Lecture, Abuja, Nigeria, May.

Sai, F.T. (2010) Chapter 39, Women's Health in a Multicultural World: Challenges and Progress in Africa, in P. Murthy and C. Lanford Smith (eds.), *Women's Global Health and Human Rights*, Jones and Bartlett Publishers.

Sai, F.T. (2010) Chapter 16, Population Growth, Reproductive Health, and the Future of Africa, in L. Mazur (ed.) *A Pivotal Moment: Population, Justice and the Environmental Challenge*, Island Press.

F.T. Sai, P.L.H. Davey, P. Whitby, (1962) A national Food and Nutrition Survey Project. *Postgrad Med J,* 38(436) 112-120, February.

Sai, F.T. and Measham, D.M. (1992) Safe motherhood initiative: Getting our priorities straight. *Lancet,* 339(8791): 478-480, 22 February.

Sai, F.T. , Shirname, T.G. and Manni, M. (1961) *Report to the Government of the Somali Republic on Survey of Food Shortages,* ETAP Report No.1471, FAO, Rome.

Wadia, A.B. (2001) *The Light is Ours (Memoirs and Movements),* IPPF.

Suitters, B. (1973) *Be brave and angry: Chronicles of the International Planned Parenthood Federatio*n, IPPF London.

UNFPA. (1994) Programme of Action: International Conference on Population and Development (ICPD) Cairo.

UNFPA. (1999) Key Actions for the Further Implementation of the Programme of Action of ICPD. Adopted by the 21st special session of the General Assembly New York.

timeline

1936-1939	Osu Presbyterian Senior boys school (Salem).
1940-1943	Achimota College: Secondary School Ending with Cambridge School Certificate.
1944-1946	Achimota College: Intermediate or pre-university; ending with London Intermediate BSc.
1947-1953	University College and U.C. Hospital, London ending with Bsc. in Physiology (1950) and MB, BS (1953).
1954, Jan-Jun	House Appointment in Poole, Dorset, UK.
1954 August	Returning to Ghana, House Appointment Korle Bu, Accra, Ghana.
1955-1956	Medical Officer Korle Bu and later Kumasi,
1956-1957	London School of Tropical Medicine and Hygiene for DTM&H and studies in Nutrition.
1957, Mar.	Ghana's Independence
1957-1958	Medical Officer in Charge of Human Nutrition based in Accra. Platt/Mayer Study (Oct-Dec. 1968)
1959-1960	Edinburgh Postgraduate Medical Studies for MRCP then Harvard for MPH.
Late 1960	Appointment as Physician, Specialist Human Nutrition.
1961-1962	Assistant Director of Medical Services, equivalent to Deputy DG today.
1963-1966	FAO Regional Nutrition Adviser February.
1966	The overthrow of the Nkrumah Government.
1966-1972	Professor of Preventive and Social Medicine,
1966	Start of Danfa as Rural Area for Field Training and Research (Involvement of UCLA for "the Danfa Project", 1970).
1967	Launching of the Planned Parenthood Association of Ghana (PPAG).

1969	Launching of National Population Policy.
1971-1972	Director of Medical Services and still Professor in charge of the Department.
1972-1978	Assistant Secretary General IPPF, resident in London.
1974	Population Congress, Bucharest, Romania.
1978-1982	UN University, Adviser to Secretary General of IPPF.
1982-1984	Freelance consultant.
1984	Mexico City Population Conference.
1985 -1990	Senior Population Advisor, World Bank.
1986, May	All Africa Parliamentarians Conference on Population and Development, Harare, Zimbabwe.
1987	Safe Motherhood Conference, Nairobi, Kenya.
1989-1995	President, International Planned Parenthood Federation (IPPF)
1993	Receives UN Population Award
1994	International Conference on Population and Development (ICPD) Cairo, Egypt.
2001-2008	External Director Bank of Ghana, Presidential Adviser Ghana AIDS Commission.

index

The index does not cover the foreword and preface. Page numbers in **bold** refer to illustrations